The Bible, as this book demonstrates, plays a key role in nearly all D. H. Lawrence's work. It supplies not only the inspiration but on occasion the target for his parody. Wright establishes that Lawrence was familiar with the modernist critique of the Bible by higher critics and by anthropologists of religion. He also argues, however, that Lawrence's playful reworking of the Bible, like that of Nietzsche, anticipates postmodernism.

After considering the extraordinary range of Lawrence's reading and the intertexts between the Bible and his own writing, Wright engages in a theoretically informed but clear exploration of the textual dynamics of Lawrence's writing. His writing is seen to reveal a prolonged struggle to read the Bible in a much broader spirit than that encouraged by orthodox Christianity. Wright's study sheds light not only on Lawrence's work but on the Bible and on the creative process itself.

TERRY R. WRIGHT is Professor of English Literature at the University of Newcastle. His publications include *The Religion of Humanity* (Cambridge, 1986), *Theology and Literature* (1988), *Hardy and the Erotic* (1989) and *George Eliot's 'Middlemarch'* (1991). He is also one of the European Editors of the *Journal of Literature and Theology*.

D. H. LAWRENCE AND THE BIBLE

T. R. WRIGHT

CAMBRIDGE
UNIVERSITY PRESS

PUBLISHED BY THE PRESS SYNDICATE OF THE UNIVERSITY OF CAMBRIDGE
The Pitt Building, Trumpington Street, Cambridge, United Kingdom

CAMBRIDGE UNIVERSITY PRESS
The Edinburgh Building, Cambridge CB2 2RU, UK
40 West 20th Street, New York, NY 10011–4211, USA
10 Stamford Road, Oakleigh, VIC 3166, Australia
Ruiz de Alarcón 13, 28014 Madrid, Spain
Dock House, The Waterfront, Cape Town 8001, South Africa

http://www.cambridge.org

First published 2000
Reprinted 2001

Printed in Great Britain at the University Press, Cambridge

Typeset in Baskerville 11/12.5pt   CE

A catalogue record for this book is available from the British Library

ISBN 0 521 78189 2 hardback

Contents

Abbreviations

All references to Lawrence's work, unless otherwise stated, are to the Cambridge Edition of the Letters and Works of D. H. Lawrence, published by Cambridge University Press, using the following abbreviations of their titles:

A	*Apocalypse and the Writings on Revelation*, ed. Mara Kalnins, 1980.
AR	*Aaron's Rod*, ed. Mara Kalnins, 1988.
BB	*The Boy in the Bush*, ed. Paul Eggert, 1990.
CP	*The Complete Poems of D. H. Lawrence*, ed. Vivian de Sola Pinto and Warren Roberts, 2 vols, London: Heinemann, 1962.
EC	*The Escaped Cock*, ed. Gerald M.Lacy, Santa Barbara: Black Sparrow Press, 1978.
EE	*England, My England and Other Stories*, ed. Bruce Steele, 1990.
EP	*Sketches of Etruscan Places and Other Italian Essays*, ed. Simonetta de Filippis, 1992.
Fant	*Fantasia of the Unconscious and Psychoanalysis and the Unconscious*, Harmondsworth: Penguin, 1971.
FLC	*The First Lady Chatterley*, Harmondsworth: Penguin, 1973.
Fox	*The Fox / The Captain's Doll / The Ladybird*, ed. Dieter Mehl, 1992.
JTLJ	*John Thomas and Lady Jane*, Harmondsworth: Penguin, 1973.
K	*Kangaroo*, ed. Bruce Steele, 1994.
LAH	*Love Among the Haystacks and Other Stories*, ed. John Worthen, 1987.
LCL	*Lady Chatterley's Lover*, ed. Michael Squires, 1993.
Letters	*The Letters of D. H. Lawrence*, ed. James Boulton and others, 7 vols, 1979–93.

LG   *The Lost Girl*, ed. John Worthen, 1981.
MEHa   *Movements in European History*, ed. James T. Boulton, Oxford
        University Press, 1971.
MEHb   *Movements in European History*, ed. Philip Crumpton, 1989.
MM   *Mornings in Mexico and Etruscan Places*, Harmondsworth:
        Penguin, 1960.
MN   *Mr Noon*, ed. Lindeth Vasey, 1984.
Phoenix *Phoenix, The Posthumous Papers of D. H. Lawrence*, ed. Edward
        McDonald, London: Heinemann, 1936.
Phoenix II Uncollected, Unpublished and Other Prose Works, ed. Warren
        Roberts and Harry T. Moore, London: Heinemann, 1968.
Plays   *The Plays*, ed. Hans-Wilhelm Schwarze and John Worthen,
        1999.
PM   'Paul Morel', the manuscript of the second version of the
        novel at the Humanities Research Center at Austin, Texas.
PO   *The Prussian Officer and Other Stories*, ed. John Worthen, 1983.
PS   *The Plumed Serpent*, ed. L. D. Clark, 1987.
Q   *Quetzalcoatl: The Early Version of 'The Plumed Serpent'*, ed.
        Louis L. Martz, Redding Ridge, CT: Black Swan Books,
        1995.
R   *The Rainbow*, ed. Mark Kinkead-Weekes, 1989.
Ref   *Reflections on the Death of a Porcupine and Other Essays*, ed.
        Michael Herbert, 1988.
SCAL   *Studies in Classic American Literature*, Harmondsworth:
        Penguin, 1971.
SL   *Sons and Lovers*, ed. Helen Baron and Carl Baron, 1992.
SLC   *Selected Literary Criticism*, ed. Anthony Beal, London:
        Heinemann, 1967.
SM   *The Symbolic Meaning: The Uncollected Versions of 'Studies in
        Classic American Literature'*, ed. Armin Arnold, Arundel:
        Centaur Press, 1962.
SS   *Sea and Sardinia*, ed. Mara Kalnins, 1997.
StM   *St Mawr and Other Stories*, ed. Brian Finney, 1983.
STH   *Study of Thomas Hardy and Other Essays*, ed. Bruce Steele,
        1985.
T   *The Trespasser*, ed. Elizabeth Mansfield, 1981.
TI   *Twilight in Italy and Other Essays*, ed. Paul Eggert, 1994.
WL   *Women in Love*, ed. David Farmer, Lindeth Vasey and John
        Worthen, 1987.
WP   *The White Peacock*, ed. Andrew Robertson, 1983.

WRA   *The Woman Who Rode Away and Other Stories*, ed. Dieter Mehl
        and Christa Jansohn, 1995.

All biblical quotations, unless otherwise stated, are taken from the
Authorized or King James Version, with standard abbreviations of
individual books. Abbreviations of the titles of other works by
Friedrich Nietzsche and Helena Blavatsky will be found in the
references at the end of the book.

Acknowledgements

I am grateful to both the Leave Committee and the Research Committee of the University of Newcastle upon Tyne for combining to give me a year's sabbatical from February 1995, followed by a further semester's leave in 1998. The Small Grants Research Fund also helped me to complete the project, supporting additional visits to the British Library in 1998. I am also grateful for the help and advice of colleagues in the Department of English Literary and Linguistic Studies, in particular John Batchelor and John Saunders, whose books I often borrowed, and librarians in the Robinson Library, in particular Jessica Plane, who helped to obtain some of the more obscure material. I should also thank the staff of other libraries on whom I have relied for help: the Harry Ransom Humanities Research Center, the University of Austin at Texas, who gave permission to quote from the manuscript of 'Paul Morel', the British Library in London and at Boston Spa, the Bodleian Library in Oxford, the Durham University Library, the Central Library and the Literary and Philosophical Society of Newcastle upon Tyne. The anonymous readers at Cambridge University Press contributed significantly to the improvement of the manuscript while Ray Ryan, my editor, showed great patience in persevering to the end, whose arrival he must often have doubted. Gerald Pollinger of Laurence Pollinger Limited and the Estate of Frieda Lawrence Ravagli, holders of the Lawrence copyright, kindly gave permission for me to quote from published and unpublished work and to reproduce a copy of the watercolour, 'Throwing Back the Apple'.

Closer to home, I would like also to acknowledge the patience of my family, my children Andrew and Catherine and my wife Gabriele, who put up with such a huge demand on my time. Finally I would like to pay tribute to my father, who died in June 1999. It was in his somewhat battered Penguin edition that I first encountered Lawrence's works. He would not have liked this book that much, I fear, never having understood my fascination with the Bible or with theories of intertextuality. But it is largely to him that I owe my enthusiasm not just for Lawrence but for literature in general. May he rest in peace.

CHAPTER I

'The Work of Creation': Lawrence and the Bible

In one of his *Last Poems*, 'The Work of Creation', Lawrence makes the familiar Romantic comparison between the divine creation of the world and the artistic process of writing. 'Even an artist', he claims, knows that the 'mystery of creation' is not a conscious or controlled process, the deliberate realisation of a carefully planned intention:

> he could never have *thought* it before it happened.
> A strange ache possessed him, and he entered the struggle,
> and out of the struggle with his material, in the spell of the urge
> his work took place, it came to pass . . .   (*CP* 690)

The poem characteristically reverts to the somewhat archaic biblical phrase, 'it came to pass', from the King James or Authorized Version, where it occurs more than thirty times (Cruden 1954: 99), to introduce the idea that even God 'knows nothing before-hand' but acts spontaneously: 'His urge takes shape in the flesh, and lo! / it is creation'. 'Lo', of course, has an equally biblical ring, which is again appropriate, for much of the material with which Lawrence's own writing struggles is biblical. It is a commonplace of modern literary criticism that all writing is intertextual, that every text involves the 'absorption and transformation of another text' or texts (Newman 1995: 2). It is equally a commonplace of Lawrence criticism, of course, that the Bible is the text which his own work most obviously and most often reworks. His writing, at all stages of his career, contains frequent references to biblical characters and symbols while, even when not invoking any particular passage from the Bible, his language is permeated by the rhythms of the Authorized Version. The aim of this book is to explore this truism more carefully, to pay close attention to the details of this 'struggle' of creation, to see what 'comes to pass' in Lawrence's work as a result of this creative and critical struggle.

There is a broader concern here too, for this intertextual wrestling, as I hope to demonstrate, amounts to a powerful, wide-ranging and sustained critique of the Bible in the light of modernity, the application of the most 'enlightened' thought to the foundational text of western civilisation. Lawrence, I will argue, anticipates many of the problems facing all of us belated postmoderns as we enter the new millennium, in particular in the west, as we are forced to address the complexity of our relationship to the Judaeo-Christian tradition. However much we may struggle against it, we define ourselves, we understand ourselves, whether in acceptance or rejection (or somewhere in the spectrum between these two poles) in terms of its language and mentality. One of the discomforting aspects of reading Lawrence is that he reminds us of this. Even if we lack his detailed familiarity with every part of the Bible, we are forced by his constant reference to it to reassess our own attitude to it. We are forced to reread it as well as him. Lawrence's 'decidedly radical stance' both towards what he saw as 'a limiting Christian orthodoxy' and towards scientific modernity, 'the secularist and rationalist ideologies of bourgeois society', offers a challenge to all of us. For he pressed the truth 'that God finally transcends language . . . to an unacceptable extreme' while still managing 'to communicate a richer sense of God than almost any other twentieth-century author' (Eagleton 1973: 87, 100).

Lawrence's relationship to modernity in the sense of 'progress' and technology, of course, was as ambivalent and problematic as his attitude to the Bible. In some respects, he can more accurately be described as a precursor of postmodernism than as a modernist. His playful reworking of biblical material, redeploying fragments of the crumbling Judaeo-Christian tradition in his own creative writing, can be read as a form of postmodern bricolage, building provisional beliefs with the otherwise discredited tools that lie to hand. His deconstruction of the western metaphysical tradition, as I hope to show, anticipates (in a less technical, more accessible way) the work of such postmodern theorists as Derrida. His reading of Nietzsche, chronicled in chapter 4, provides perhaps the most significant bridge to Derrida. He was familiar, however, as I show in chapter 3, not only with the results of higher criticism and the pioneers of religious anthropology such as Frazer, but also with less 'scientific' religious writers such as Madame Blavatsky and other theosophical revampers of rabbinic and kabbalistic traditions. His own reworking of the Bible accordingly combines a thorough-going 'scientific' critique characteristic of modernity with a bold freedom of interpretation more often associated with postmodernity.

The Bible, of course, in Northrop Frye's phrase, itself borrowed from Blake, is *The Great Code* of western civilisation, the prime source of literary meaning, the model from which much other writing proceeds (Frye 1982). As David Lyle Jeffrey says in the preface to his *Dictionary of Biblical Tradition in English Literature*, it has been 'foundational for Western literature', in particular English literature from the earliest reworkings in Anglo-Saxon of the books of Genesis and Exodus through the mystery plays to Milton and the Romantics. It continues, of course, to feed much of the literature of the modern period (Jeffrey 1992: xiii). Lawrence is clearly a part of this broad tradition and it is in this sense that the Bible can be said to be a major component in the genesis of his fiction, a stimulus to his imagination, what Bloom calls a precursor-text or poetic father which his own writing attempts to emulate. His work can even be seen as a Derridean supplement to the Bible, both adding to and attempting to supplant the original. Bloom and Derrida's theories of intertextuality, as I will explain in the following chapter, along with those of Bakhtin, provide a particularly appropriate framework within which to place him, recognising as they do the creative rivalry involved in all literary influence, the tensions set up within the text by competing and often conflicting citations.

This is how Lawrence will be found to struggle with his material, wrestling with the Bible, as Jacob with the angel, to use one of Bloom's favourite analogies, often transforming it into something almost unrecognisably different. But with Lawrence, as with the Bible as he read (and rewrote) it, nothing is fixed. As he wrote in the introduction to the American edition of his *New Poems* of 1920, he wanted 'nothing fixed, set, static' (*Phoenix* 219). Or as he wrote in relation to 'Art and Morality' in 1925, characteristically subverting a biblical image of permanence and stability, 'We move and the rock of ages moves . . . Each thing, living or unliving, streams in its own odd, intertwining flux, and nothing, not even man nor the God of man, nor anything that man has thought or felt or known, is fixed and abiding' (525). Even the Bible, in other words, has to be rewritten, to be understood differently, in each generation, a view to

be found in the rabbis responsible for creative midrashic interpretation of the early centuries of the Christian era as well as in their
postmodern descendants such as Bloom and Derrida.

What Lawrence found most objectionable about his upbringing,
as he complained in *Apocalypse*, was the uncritical way he had been
taught to read the Bible:

From earliest years right into manhood, like any other nonconformist child
I had the Bible poured every day into my helpless consciousness, till there
came almost a saturation point. Long before one could think or even
vaguely understand, this Bible language, these 'portions' of the Bible were
douched over the mind and consciousness till they became soaked in, they
became an influence which affected all the processes of emotion and
thought. So that today, although I have 'forgotten' my Bible, I need only
begin to read a chapter to realise that I 'know' it with an almost nauseating
fixity. And I must confess, my first reaction is one of dislike, repulsion, and
even resentment. My very instincts *resent* the Bible. (*A* 59)

The fact that 'the interpretation was fixed', Lawrence insists, led to
all interest being lost. For 'a book lives as long as it is unfathomed.
Once it is fathomed, it dies at once . . . A book lives only while it has
power to move us, and move us *differently*; so long as we find it *different*
every time we read it', discovering new levels of meaning on each
occasion. 'The Bible,' he concludes, 'is a book that has been
temporarily killed for us, or for some of us, by having its meaning
temporarily fixed' (59–60).

An earlier draft of *Apocalypse*, published as an Appendix to the
Cambridge edition, develops this point, that it is not the Bible that is
dead but we who have failed to recognise its vitality, 'years of narrow
monotheism' having contributed to a widespread misreading:

We have taken the Bible out of its setting, cut it off from the contact with
history and the living races it plays amongst, and set it in unreal isolation,
as an absolute. We have been wrong. We have taken the Old Testament at
its own value of a One God of a Chosen People cursing and annihilating
everybody else . . . (158)

The nonconformist tradition in particular, according to Lawrence,
inherited from Judaism a narrow model of being the 'chosen people,
. . . the elect, or the "saved"' (63). I will return in chapter 13 to a
more detailed consideration of *Apocalypse* as illustrative of the way in
which Lawrence had learnt by the end of his life to read the Bible
differently, to appreciate its own complex intertextuality, its tendency
to rework earlier material within its pages as well as material from

other religions. The point to emphasise now is that, however narrowly he may have been taught to read the Bible, he did as a child imbibe a deep and thorough knowledge of it along with powerful if ambivalent feelings towards it.

Literary critics such as Hartman and Bloom employ both the biblical metaphor of wrestling with the angel and an Oedipal model of ambivalence and rivalry for the process by which a writer struggles creatively with his or her precursors. Lawrence also wrote of the process of writing as one in which he had to 'wrestle' with his 'Angel' (*Letters* II 669). He was well aware of the importance of the Bible to his work, even poking fun at his own pretensions to rewrite it. 'I do think it is wonderful,' says the drunken Halliday in *Women in Love*, reading out one of Birkin's more pompous, almost Pauline letters in a clerical voice. 'It almost supersedes the Bible' (*WL* 382–3). 'Almost supersedes' here, like the supplement of which Derrida writes, is ambiguous. Halliday implies that Birkin tries to replace the Bible but fails while Lawrence, I suggest, is nudging his readers (albeit ironically and with a certain endearing self-deprecation) towards a recognition of the deeply religious mission on which both Birkin and he are engaged. In a similar way, readers of the *Daily Express* in 1929 may initially have registered some surprise at the lengthy quotation there of his defence of his paintings in which he cites the Song of Solomon as an example of a great poem whose 'loveliness' was 'all interwoven with sex appeal' (Nehls 1959: 374). It is not only the recognition of eroticism in the sacred text which is important here but the implicit bracketing of his own work with the Scriptures.

A number of critics, from Richard Aldington onwards, have found Lawrence's continued use of biblical symbols and images objectionable, considering 'how far he had . . . gone in repudiating Christian ethics and beliefs' (Aldington 1950: 129). As a character in Compton Mackenzie's *West Wind of Love* complains of Rayner, the thinly disguised Lawrence-figure in that novel, it appears somewhat strange to base his own writing on the Bible when he claims to have 'exhausted the Christian faith,' refusing to accept its doctrine and regarding its moral teaching as 'impotent' (Nehls 1958: 27). It is, of course, the case that he stretches the meanings of many biblical terms, going well beyond what could be regarded as 'orthodox'. But then, as he will be found frequently to argue, even the most basic religious words cannot be tied to a 'signified' or 'mental concept' that is in any sense adequate. He continually agonised over words such as 'God', at one point, when revising his *Collected Poems*, carefully removing all uses of the term (Ellis 1998: 384). His play *David* also finds an astonishing array of alternative terms for the unpronounceable sacred name. Having declared only a few years earlier that he found God 'an exhausted concept', he surprised Earl Brewster in his last few months by announcing not only that he did not 'any longer object to the word God' but that he intended to find Him (Brewster 1934: 224). Anyone looking for systematic theology in Lawrence will be disappointed; he didn't think systematically, regarding all such attempts to 'capture' the 'truth' about 'God' as seriously misguided. One of the ways in which he anticipated postmodernism was in placing scare quotes around such problematic words; another was his recognition of the way this particular word functions as a 'glyph', derived from the Greek for carving, an act of linguistic sculpture whose representation of ultimate reality is necessarily approximate, dependent upon the limitations of its medium (*Ref.* 187). Lawrence clearly appreciated the fact that the Bible made no systematic theological claims, embodying its religious insights in a range of self-conscious literary forms: story, fable, myth, epic, history, poetry, letter and vision.

Lawrence's love of the Bible found expression throughout his life in his letters and in records of his conversation, which are full of references to all parts of the Bible, from the Book of Genesis to the Apocalypse. My chronological analysis of his writing will draw attention to the extent to which it can be seen to reflect the structure of the Bible itself, beginning with creation and ending with apocalypse. The early chapters of Genesis are perhaps the most dominant not only in his writing but in other forms of art. Like Will Brangwen, for example, he planned a wood carving of the 'Temptation of Eve, with painted apples on a painted tree, and Eve with rabbits at her feet, and a squirrel looking at her, russet, out of the apple tree', about which he wrote to Lady Ottoline Morrell in 1916 (*Letters* II 597–8). He also painted Adam and Eve on the door of the Del Monte ranch (Luhan 1932: 174). Dorothy Brett describes a plasticine version of the Garden of Eden for which she was allowed to make the trees and apples and John Middleton Murry the snake. Lawrence, however, insisted on having responsibility for Adam and Eve, producing an Adam which scandalised his co-workers, who forced him to 'snip off his indecency, and then mourn him for his loss' (Nehls 1958: II 311–12). On another occasion, Brewster recalls Lawrence pouncing upon a marble statue of Eve and subjecting it to a mud-bath on the grounds that she looked 'too demure after her fall' (Brewster 1934: 277). It is characteristic of Lawrence, on the last two of these occasions, that he should insist on drawing attention to aspects of the biblical story of creation, in particular its celebration of the flesh, overlooked or bowdlerised by conventional Christian reading.

Lawrence's critique of conventional Christianity and its moralistic reading of the Hebrew Bible (misreading, as he would have it, since it failed to appreciate the celebration of the flesh which pervades Genesis) also dominates his many retellings of the supposed 'Fall' of man. Frieda and he, expelled from conventional respectable society in 1912, will be seen to have enjoyed playing Adam and Eve around the world, searching for a route back to paradise, a theme which runs all the way through Lawrence's writing from his early novels and poems to *Lady Chatterley's Lover*. Frieda, of course, brought her own expectations to the role of Eve, having heard (probably from her earlier lover Otto Gross) of the fall into bourgeois domesticity and the need to recover paradise through polymorphous perversity (Green 1974: 44–5). *Not I, But the Wind* admits how fanatically she believed 'that if only sex were "free" the world would straightway turn into a paradise' (Jackson 1994: 103) while her fictional account of her relationship with Gross has the central autobiographical figure give a 'quite different' version of the story:

The Lord can't have been such a bad psychologist as not to have known that Eve would want the apple the minute it was forbidden. He really wanted Adam and Eve to eat it. And when they had eaten it, they weren't ashamed of their nakedness at all. 'Look, Adam. There is a pool down by those willows and we will have a swim, and then we'll dry ourselves in the sun. Hurrah! I shall have a small Adam, and you will make him a cradle out of the willows, and then you'll work to get us something to eat while I sing to the baby.' (212–13)

Frieda could here be imitating her husband (there are, as we shall see, passages in *Studies of Classic American Literature* quite similar to this). The point to emphasise, however, is the freedom and exuberance with which both of them responded to the original biblical text.

That exuberance emerges also in an episode described in H.D.'s novel *Bid Me to Live*, in which the Lawrence character Rico arranges a charade based upon the opening chapters of Genesis. Rafe and

Bella (Richard Aldington and his then mistress Arabella) are cast as
Adam and Eve with Vane (the adulterous Cecil Gray) playing the
angel preventing their return, brandishing an umbrella in place of a
flaming sword. Julia (H.D. herself), having been given the role of the
apple-tree, is instructed by Rico (Lawrence) on her dance while Elsa
(Frieda) is told to 'growl and writhe' as the serpent. 'Serpents don't
growl', she objects before 'she obligingly plumped herself flat on the
floor and wriggled on the blue carpet'. Lawrence inevitably casts
himself as 'Gawd-a'-mighty', taking up 'a Jehovah-like pose by the
fire-place' and chanting from an imaginary scroll before he is
interrupted by the others and reprimanded for departing too far
from the original (H.D. 1984: 111–12). This, of course, is an objection
to which much of his reworking of the Bible is open; he both
challenges his readers to question their own interpretation of the
sacred text and risks their rebellion against his own.

Biblical charades, it is well documented, were one of Lawrence's
favourite pastimes. Jessie Chambers' younger brother David recalled
how Lawrence played the part of Pharaoh at Haggs Bank 'with the
milksile on his head for crown, and hardened his heart ineluctably
against the pleas of Moses and the children of Israel', while David
Garnett remembered Frieda and Lawrence performing Judith and
Holofernes at Mayrhofen in 1912 (Nehls 1957: 47–8 and 177).
Another of Lawrence's favourite roles, repeated for Brewster as well
as for the Chambers family, was that of St Peter on Judgement Day,
filtered through the mind of a revivalist preacher (Nehls 1959: 131
and 603). A similar scene, of course, is enacted by Paul Morel in *Sons
and Lovers* while in *Women in Love* Gudrun and Ursula are made to
perform a balletic version of Ruth. It is evident from these accounts
how Lawrence appreciated the drama of the Bible, responding
imaginatively and with a splendid sense of humour to some of its
more outrageous episodes.

Lawrence's sense of humour, emphasised by Brenda Maddox in
her portrait of him (Maddox 1994), is less evident in his letters,
where, as Cynthia Asquish recalled, he was 'more of a Jeremiah . . .
than in his talk' (Nehls 1957: 440). Mark Rampion, the Lawrence-
figure in Aldous Huxley's novel *Point Counter Point*, styles himself 'a
Jeremiah pervert', lambasting his society for its many failings
(Huxley 1933: 564). This prophetic role was one in which many of his
contemporaries cast him. Bertrand Russell, for example, both
deplored his religiosity and acknowledged his 'amazing powers of

discernment. He is like Ezekiel or some other Old Testament prophet' (Kinkead-Weekes 1996: 190). John Middleton Murry ended some verses sent to Lady Ottoline Morrell addressing Lawrence directly as 'My mouse-haired, intolerant prophet' (822). This identification with the prophets may have been encouraged by the beard, grown during illness in October 1914.

Christ, it has to be said, was Lawrence's favourite role, especially in the war-years, when the metaphor of crucifixion became irresistible. 'The War finished me,' he wrote to Cynthia Asquith, 'it was the spear through the side of all sorrows and hopes'. He proceeds to describe his soul as lying 'in the tomb – not dead but with the flat stone over it' before claiming to have 'risen' full of hope and a 'new shoot of life' (*Letters* II 268). Lawrence's identification with Christ in the years of the war could take on absurd proportions, as on his visit to Augustus John in 1917, when, having muttered, 'Mortuus est. Mortuus est', he repeated the lugubrious refrain, much to the painter's puzzled amusement, 'Let the DEAD PAINT THE DEAD!' (Nehls 1957: 44). His identification with Jesus, like Nietzsche's, has been called 'the bond of one tablet-breaker with another'. Nietzsche and Lawrence can be said paradoxically to imitate Christ most when they rebel against Christianity, the conventional religion of their own time (Goodheart 1963: 2). Neither of them could ever forgive Jesus for being first with the good news. In addition, they held him personally responsible for the fear of sexuality inherent in Christianity. The Lawrencian Mark Rampion in Aldous Huxley's *Point Counter Point* identifies Christ's 'disease' as 'hatred of sex' (Huxley 1933: 161–6) although when Cecil Gray accused him of 'playing Jesus Christ to a regiment of Mary Magdalenes' Lawrence claimed that 'the pure understanding between the Magdalen and Jesus went deeper than the understanding between the disciples and Jesus' (*Letters* III 176 and 179–80). He was, of course, to write a novella, *The Escaped Cock*, on the subject of Jesus learning the significance of sexuality only after his resurrection. This and other late narratives of the Risen Lord will be the subject of chapter 12.

Examples of Lawrence being cast by others in the role of Christ include the famous 'Last Supper', the dinner at the Café Royal when Lawrence returned to England in 1923. Middleton Murry's version of the story has Lawrence putting his arms around him (Murry) and saying 'Do not betray me!' while Catherine Carswell expanded the narrative even further (in her later gospel), giving herself the put-down line to Murry, 'it wasn't a woman who betrayed Jesus with a kiss' (Ellis 1998: 150–1). None of those who knew and wrote about Lawrence, it seems, could resist the comparison: Mollie Skinner, Willard Johnson and even the boys in the streets of Oaxaca (30, 114, 635). Brett risked his wrath by painting him on the cross, a painting which she initially destroyed but went on to compose again, after her model was safely dead (291, 670). In Brett's painting *Biblical Scene*, Lawrence appears more modestly as a John the Baptist, while she also used him as a model for Joseph and for one of the wise men when he visited them in Ravallo in 1927 (Cushman 1992: 67). Near the end of his life, Earl Brewster could not help comparing Lawrence's emaciated figure with 'one of the haggard, medieval, carved figures of the crucified Jesus'. These comparisons, as Ellis complains, 'followed Lawrence for much of his adult life' (528) not simply, I would suggest, because he wore a beard but because people sensed in him an intensity of religious passion which marked him out as different. Enemies like Clifford Bax would grumble about his being 'a pseudo-Messiah' wanting financial support 'to write his gospels' (Nehls 1957: I 440), a comparison which betrays a certain ignorance about their authorship. But there was a sense in which Lawrence was quite accurately perceived by his contemporaries as the author of a supplementary sacred text, a revised Bible of his own.

The final biblical role model to which Lawrence can be said to have aspired is that of visionary writer of apocalypse. It is hardly surprising that the First World War should have appeared to him (as to many others) to mark the end of civilisation. His letters of 1915 are full of references to an apocalyptic struggle with evil, 'a great struggle with the Powers of Darkness' (*Letters* II 315). It seemed as though 'the whole thing were coming to an end – the whole of England, of the Christian era' (II 433). Other letters of this period also refer to the imminent end of the world, whether through another flood, fire and brimstone, or bombs (II 330, 338; III 20). On moving to Zennor in February 1916 he wrote more positively of 'a new heaven and a new earth' (II 556), a hope transferred to the United States in a letter of January 1917 (III 80). Even in the 1920s, as we shall see, Lawrence continued to clothe his hopes in the renewal of the world in the language of the Book of Revelation, the book of the Bible on which he chose to base his own posthumously published *Apocalypse*.

It is abundantly clear, even from this brief sketch, not only that Lawrence was saturated with the Bible but that he continued throughout his life to reproduce its images. My study of his writing, while tracing his career chronologically, will also retain some of the biblical structure outlined above, moving from Genesis through Exodus and the prophetic books to the gospels and ending with the Book of Revelation. After considering (in chapter 3) the role of biblical criticism in his break with Christianity and (in chapter 4) the impact of his reading of Nietzsche and other Romantic writers, I begin my analysis of Lawrence's writing (in chapter 5) with his fascination with Genesis, with creation, visions of paradise and the 'fall' into consciousness as evinced in his early work from *The White Peacock* to the collection of poems *Look! We Have Come Through!* in which he and Frieda are clearly presented as revisionist types of Adam and Eve. The following chapter (6) is devoted to *The Rainbow* as a 'counter-Bible', a book that advertises itself as a reworking of the biblical original, re-marking the biblical account of the covenant between God and his people symbolised by the sign given by God to Noah. Chapter 7 explores the prose writing of the years before and immediately after the war, from 'The Crown' to the early versions of what became *Studies in Classic American Literature*, which provide clear evidence of his interest in theosophical theories about the Bible. Chapter 8 considers the novels of this period, from *Women in Love* to *The Lost Girl* and *Mr Noon*, as an attempt to reconcile the Book of Genesis with the Gospel of John, to marry the opposites which they are seen to represent: beginning and end, flesh and word, female and male.

The structure of the Bible, it will already be apparent, cannot be imposed arbitrarily on the chronological development of Lawrence's work although the Book of Exodus succeeded Genesis for a while in Lawrence's favour, featuring prominently not only in *Aaron's Rod* but also in the Australian novels, *Kangaroo* and *The Boy in the Bush*, which are the subject of chapter 9. Chapter 10 considers the way in which his poetry, essays and short stories of the 1920s deconstruct the 'Logos', that essential term of dogmatic metaphysics, so dominant in the development of early Christian theology. Chapter 11 focuses on the prophetic elements to be found in both his Mexican novel *The Plumed Serpent* (and its predecessor *Quetzalcoatl*) and in his play *David*. These texts celebrate what I label 'red mythology', a mode of religious understanding which avoids what Derrida called 'white mythology', that logocentric metaphysics blind to its own limitations, its own figurative and metaphorical dimensions. Chapter 12, as I have said, will consider Lawrence's retelling of the resurrection, not only in *The Escaped Cock*, but in all three versions of *Lady Chatterley's Lover*. Chapter 13 focuses on Lawrence's teasing out of the conflicting strands of power and love in the Book of Revelation. *Apocalypse*, I will argue, in this respect anticipates deconstructive modes of reading, drawing both on orthodox biblical criticism and a more active Nietzschean critique of early Christianity. The final chapter looks at the *Last Poems*, in which Lawrence, faced with his imminent death, confronts what Christian tradition calls the four last things: death, judgement, heaven and hell. I should stress once again that Lawrence's writing refuses to fit neatly into any schema, biblical or otherwise. By focusing separately and in detail on each text I hope to do justice to the complexity of the writing and its exuberant excess of meaning, which constantly exceeds and resists the interpretative structure I am imposing upon it. I hope it will become apparent in the course of my analysis not only how important the Bible is to Lawrence's work but how his writing can be read fruitfully as an interpretation of the Bible, a midrashic commentary and creative exegesis of it.

Similar claims have been made before, of course, the most fully sustained being Virginia Hyde's study in *The Risen Adam* (1992) of what her subtitle labels *D. H. Lawrence's Revisionist Typology*. Hyde is particularly illuminating on the graphic iconographical tradition with which Lawrence was familiar in painting, ecclesiastical architecture, stained-glass windows and sculpture (her dissertation was in fact entitled 'D. H. Lawrence's Debt to Medieval and Renaissance Graphic Arts'). The graphic art on which she is perhaps least convincing, however, is writing. What I hope to achieve in this study, which should therefore complement hers, is a greater sense of the textual dynamics involved in Lawrence's struggle with his material, a closer analysis of what 'comes to pass' in the text as a result of this intertextual conflict. I also devote more space to the mediating intertexts between Lawrence and the Bible, exploring the importance of Renan and Nietzsche, Frazer and Blavatsky, to name some of the better-known figures whose impact on Lawrence has not been fully appreciated. Much of what Lawrence makes of the Bible, I will argue, only makes sense in the context of this reading. To read Lawrence in an intelligent and informed way, as I hope to demonstrate, is to be brought into contact with a whole tradition of grappling with the Bible, a dazzling and at times disturbing process. This requires a reasonably sophisticated model of intertextuality of the kind I will now outline.

CHAPTER 2

Biblical intertextuality: Bakhtin, Bloom and Derrida

Intertextuality, as M. H. Abrams explains, is a somewhat loose term, covering a multitude of possible scenarios, signalling 'the multiple ways in which any one literary text echoes, or is inseparably linked to, other texts, whether by open or covert citations and *allusions*' or 'simply by participation in a common stock of literary and linguistic procedures and conventions' (Abrams 1988: 247; cf. Fewell 1992: 21–4). Such theories of intertextuality, it should be noted, are less interested in the 'control' of meaning, in authorial intention or even 'correct' interpretation than in the creative process set in motion by a citation, the possibilities of meaning generated by the juxtaposition of conflicting material. The structuralist Michael Riffaterre, for example, distinguishes between *'obligatory* intertextuality', which demands that a reader take account of the text referred to, and 'aleatory' intertextuality, 'which allows the reader to read a text through the prism of all and any familiar texts' (Still and Worthen 1990: 26). Poststructuralist exponents of the term such as Roland Barthes and Julia Kristeva deliberately employ it to subvert the 'humanist' understanding of language as a vehicle for communication, the former parading an 'anti-theological' agenda which delights in hijacking the intended meaning of any word, but particularly *the* Word (18).

It is not necessary to share this agenda, of course, to find this more recent understanding of intertextuality useful in opening up the text, allowing for a fuller recognition of the dynamics of textuality, the range of meanings to be found sometimes in conflict within any single text. Three theorists of intertextuality whose work I believe to be of particular relevance to the relationship between Lawrence and the Bible, Mikhail Bakhtin, Harold Bloom and Jacques Derrida, share a fascination with religion in general and the Bible in particular. Bakhtin was not only a literary critic but 'a religious philosopher in the orthodox tradition' (Clark and Holquist 1984: ix), sharing the Russian Orthodox belief in the holiness of matter, the corporeality of Christ, and the corresponding significance of the flesh (84–7). He was also 'part of a much wider movement in modern thought to sustain the conceptual power of almost two millennia of Christian thought while still taking into account the challenge posed to traditional theology by post-Enlightenment developments' (82). Bloom and Derrida are also part of this wider wrestling with religious tradition in a postmodern age, albeit from a Jewish perspective. Bloom, of course, has become famous (or perhaps infamous) for championing the power of the canon, both sacred and secular, against the 'rabblement' of anti-humanist critics among whom he now includes his former colleague Derrida. While recognising the differences between all three of these critics, differences which will emerge as I expound their ideas, each of them brings key elements to an understanding of intertextuality between literature and the Bible which help to explain what happens in Lawrence.

Bakhtinian theory has previously been used by Lawrence critics mainly with reference to the charge of monologism, that claim to be the 'ultimate word', that deafness to the voice of the other, which Bakhtin brought against Tolstoy in contrast with Dostoyevsky. Lawrence, incidentally, also complained of Tolstoy's idealism, his refusal to accept 'the relatedness and interrelatedness of all things' (*STH* 185). Bakhtin, it has been suggested, can help us to recognise the complexity of the dialogue which takes place in Lawrence, the play of languages to be found in his work (Peters 1996: 205–8; Hyde 1991; Fleishman 1985: 175). David Lodge specifically compares him with Dostoevsky as a producer of 'a kind of philosophical adventure story whose chief characters are questing, with religious fervour, for some new, ultimately satisfying way of life', a quest that borrows from a range of religious sources of which the Bible is perhaps the most important (Lodge 1990: 62, 66). But the Bible itself is only one of the many voices to be found in the text, its meaning often undergoing interrogation from a variety of sources.

For Bakhtin, as for Lawrence, the question of how to read the Bible is a key issue. Whenever Bakhtin discusses words the theological dimension of the Word is never far away (Clark and Holquist 1984: 82). Shklovsky's paper on 'The Resurrection of the Word', delivered at St Petersburg in December 1913 (the year before

Bakhtin transferred there from Odessa), had argued that Futurist poetry 'had emancipated words from their traditional significance and made it possible to perceive them afresh' (Clark and Holquist 1984: 28). Bakhtin, by contrast, denies that words can escape so easily from their original historical contexts. *The Dialogical Imagination* insists that language is not 'neutral' but carries with it the ideological baggage acquired in historical use. Every word 'tastes of the context and contexts in which it has lived its socially charged life' (Bakhtin 1981: 293). To transfer a word from one context to another, therefore, to borrow someone else's words, sets up a tension between the original context and the one into which they are transplanted. There are certain forms of discourse, however, such as epic poetry and the Bible, which are particularly resistant to appropriation, demanding a pious and uncritical attitude, seeing themselves as 'sacred and sacrosanct'. At one point Bakhtin recognises 'a whole spectrum of possible relationships toward this word . . . beginning at one pole with the pious and inert quotation that is isolated and set off like an icon, and ending at the other pole with the most ambiguous, disrespectful, parodic-travestying use of a quotation' (69). Later in the book, however, he closes down these options, insisting that the Bible is 'the word of the fathers' (342), monological, authoritarian and consequently semantically 'static and dead', coming to us 'fully complete' with an authorised 'single meaning', demanding not a 'free appropriation and assimilation' but 'unconditional allegiance' (343). He accordingly dismisses its role in the novel as 'insignificant'. When it is quoted in a novel, as the gospels are towards the end of Tolstoy's *Resurrection*, it remains 'a dead quotation, something that falls out of the artistic context' (344) in contrast with 'internally persuasive discourse', which is open to the other and can be 'affirmed through assimilation, tightly interwoven with 'one's own word" (345–6). *The Dialogical Imagination* ends with a celebration of this 'process of re-accentuation' which is of such 'great and seminal importance for the history of literature' (422) even if the Bible, as Bakhtin continued to argue in later essays, remains incapable of such dynamic interaction because it necessarily 'retards and freezes thought', removing itself from dialogue and displaying an 'extremely limited ability to combine in general and especially with profane – not sacred – words' (Bakhtin 1986: 132–3).

Bakhtin, I would suggest, often overstates the polarity between 'authoritative' and 'internally persuasive discourse' at the expense of his earlier more fruitful model of a 'spectrum of possible relationships towards the Bible'. He also, as Harold Fisch has argued, overlooks the sheer range of discourse to be found in the Bible, taking the 'naive confessional' form of the Psalms as characteristic of all biblical writing, a judgement unfair to the Psalms themselves, let alone other biblical texts (Fisch 1988: 131–2). Fisch also claims that Bakhtin overemphasised the 'parodic-travestying use' of the Bible in medieval literature at the expense of its serious, typological resonance while totally ignoring 'the powerful *formative* presence of the Bible in the tradition of the English novel from Bunyan to Dickens and beyond' (133). It is precisely its revolutionary mixture of styles, its heteroglossia in Bakhtinian terms, which Auerbach, in *Mimesis* and elsewhere, saw as characterising biblical as opposed to classical style. Like Fisch, I would argue that Bakhtinian categories remain of use to the study of the Bible, and of biblical intertextuality in the novel, *in spite* of his own failure to see the Bible as other than authoritative. A Bakhtinian understanding of intertextuality, in other words, alert to the tensions between different discourses in a text, can contribute to an understanding of the textual dynamics of a writer such as Lawrence, who is heavily reliant upon the language of the Bible and eager to appropriate it for his own purposes.

Another theorist who can shed light on Lawrence's use of the Bible is Harold Bloom, who wrote a lively defence of Lawrence's poetry against the New Critical (and Christian) orthodoxy of R. P. Blackmur as early as 1959. Bloom's theoretical project, advanced in a number of books from the 1970s, involves a general de-idealisation of poetic influence in terms of family romance. *The Anxiety of Influence* (1973) portrays the relationship of poets to their precursors as one of struggle, the 'ephebe' or youthful aspirant wrestling to avoid submission to the poetic father, the poet who first awakened creativity. After spelling out a variety of ways in which poets attempt to escape the control of their precursors, whether by completion, repetition or swerving (Bloom's own terms, it must be admitted, derived from Alexandrian gnostics, are somewhat arcane), he announces a number of principles of 'Antithetical Criticism' of which the most important is his belief that the 'meaning of a poem can only be another poem' which is necessarily 'a misinterpretation of a parent poem' (Bloom 1973: 94–5). He deliberately overstates the case in order to make his general point that all writing is a form of reading and vice versa; in his view the most powerful readings are creative and the most interesting criticism therefore is to be found among the poets.

Bloom proceeded to develop this general theory of poetic influence with detailed reference to Jewish revisionism, for which Lurianic kabbalism provides the clearest model. He explains that kabbala literally means 'tradition', that which has been received or handed down. Such handing down within the Jewish tradition includes active interpretation and development as in midrash, whether by exegesis or by narrative augmentation. Bloom, however, brings to the midrashic and kabbalistic concept of revision ideas drawn from Kierkegaard and Nietzsche, creating a model of relating creatively to tradition which goes well beyond the weak reading permitted by orthodoxy. Lawrence's own enthusiasm for Nietzsche, to be explored in chapter 4, and his interest in rabbinic literature, possibly initiated by his uncle Fritz Krenkow, an Arabic scholar whose extensive library was the subject of an enthusiastic letter of 1908 (*Letters* I 77), makes Bloom's model particularly appropriate for considering the relationship of his own writing to the Judaeo-Christian tradition. The point is that a 'strong' response to the Bible, for Bloom, must be a creative one, not passively submitting to an orthodox reading but struggling, in the way Lawrence does, against the power of the original. It should not come as a surprise that Bloom finds room for several of Lawrence's works in his list of major works that comprise *The Western Canon* (1994), that secular rival to the sacred text.

A third theorist who can contribute to an understanding of the complex intertextuality between Lawrence and the Bible is Jacques Derrida, a former colleague of Bloom's at Yale whose work provides another example of what Susan Handelman has called 'the return of the Rabbinic repressed' in modern literary theory (Handelman 1982: 166). Deconstruction, of course, is itself a sophisticated theory of intertextuality, concerned with understanding (and to some extent dismantling) a tradition using terms and methods derived from that tradition. Just as in postmodern architecture, according to Lyotard, there is an abundance of repetition and quotation from earlier traditions, whether 'ironically, cynically, or naively' (Docherty 1993: 48), so Lawrence can be seen to have transplanted or 'grafted' passages from the Bible into his work, generating surprising new meanings in the process.

As with Bakhtin, there are, as Gerald Doherty has remarked, a number of similarities between Lawrence and Derrida: 'Both assume that the way we think about reality and the way we construct it is warped by confinement within enclosed and enclosing conceptual sets' (Doherty 1987: 477). Both have Nietzsche as 'a strong precursor', both 'have a potent sense of living at the end of an epoch, in a condition of ongoing crisis which their writings probe and precipitate'. Both detect 'apocalyptic fissures or cracks in the metaphysical heavens' and both work 'unremittingly to overturn those metaphysical oppositions which have structured Western modes of perception' (478). Both 'regraft new senses on to old names' in a manner which disrupts and subverts traditional modes of thinking, releasing 'a radically new kind of writing' (478). There are, of course, differences. Lawrence was not involved in Heideggerian or post-Saussurean discussions of referentiality, tending if anything to celebrate that sense of 'self-presence' and communion with the 'reality' of which Derrida is so sceptical. One cannot transform Lawrence into a fully-fledged 'Derridean *avant la lettre*' (484). One can, however, apply Derridean terms to Lawrence in the knowledge that they are not entirely inappropriate.

For Derrida, of course, everything is textually mediated. As Vincent Leitch explains, intertextuality replaces tradition (Leitch 1983: 122). 'Différance' (the deferral and displacement of meaning through repetition with small changes) continually generates new meaning, whether in the kabbala or in a novel such as *Numbers*, by Philippe Sollers, whose spaces operate as 'a kind of cabal or cabala in which the blanks will never be anything but provisionally filled in', demanding fresh interpretation with each reading (Derrida 1981: 344–5). Derrida's own writing often demonstrate the new meanings which can be generated by the juxtaposition of texts. 'Living On: Border lines', for example, has a continuous footnote, rather like a Talmudic commentary, supplementing the main text. The very word supplement, like the concepts of the graft and the re-mark, illustrates Derrida's concern with citation and repetition (with difference) as a mode of generating meaning, both adding to and replacing the original. The graft in writing, a quotation introduced within a text, operates as in horticulture to stimulate new meaning. A mark or a sign, as Derrida shows, can never be completely reproduced *without* difference since it always occurs in new contexts with different intertexts. Hence the notion of the re-mark, which exemplifies what it represents, that repetition with difference characteristic of all signifying systems and all traditions. However hard institutions may try to control and regulate meaning, to delimit 'proper' interpretation, all linguistic signs will open themselves to fresh meanings as they collide with different intertexts. Lawrence's work can thus be called re-markable in this sense (as well as the more conventional one), citing the Bible in juxtaposition with such critical and creative readers of it as Nietzsche to produce a dazzlingly polysemic play of meanings.

Derrida illustrates this kind of creative intertextuality with reference to the Bible in *The Gift of Death*, which comes close to producing a postmodern form of midrash in its commentary upon Kierkegaard's own commentary upon the Akedah in *Fear and Trembling*. His relationship to Judaism, his own religious tradition, particularly clear in the 'Circumfession' he attaches as a running footnote to Geoffrey Bennington's book *Jacques Derrida*, is complex and problematic. He reads it in ways which run counter to the conventions of normative Judaism. Harold Bloom is similarly 'beyond the pale' of Jewish orthodoxy, while Bakhtin's relationship to the Russian Orthodox Church, as we have seen, was similarly ambivalent. This, I suggest, makes their theories particularly appropriate for that most dissident of dissenters, Lawrence, struggling to clarify his relationship with the Judaeo-Christian tradition in general and the Bible in particular. There is a peculiar blend of continuity and discontinuity in these theorists' readings of their respective traditions, a necessary ambivalence which is part of the postmodern condition, entailing both a modernist critique of the normative canon *and* a reassertion or rereading of that tradition retaining at least some of its component elements, which provides a particularly appropriate framework within which to explore Lawrence's similarly critical and creative reworking of the Bible.

CHAPTER 3

Higher criticism: Lawrence's break with Christianity

The exploration of intertextuality, it should be recognised, is not just a matter of high-powered theory but of detailed research, a kind of grafting not always associated with followers of Derrida, in order to discover which texts in particular contributed to Lawrence's understanding of the Bible. His familiarity with higher criticism, for example, requires more attention than it has so far received. Higher or historical criticism, as William Robertson Smith explained in a passage of his 1881 series of lectures on *The Old Testament in the Jewish Church* cited in the *Oxford English Dictionary* in its definition of the term, addressed itself to 'questions affecting the composition, the editing, and the collection of the sacred books' as opposed to the literal 'verbal criticism which preceded it' (*OED* 1961: II 1180). Smith's belief that the new scholarship enhanced faith by setting it upon a surer intellectual foundation was somewhat tested by the heresy trials to which he was subjected (Clements 1983: 2) and by his ejection from his professorial post at the Free Presbyterian College in Aberdeen but his 1889 *Religion of the Semites* quickly became 'the standard history of religious development in the Old Testament' (Chadwick 1970: II 58). It is regularly cited in books Lawrence read in the years which saw him finally break with Christianity in part at least over the limits placed upon 'orthodox' reading of the Bible. The purpose of this chapter is to explore this early reading on his part, demonstrating the extent to which his familiarity with the latest developments in biblical criticism contributed both to his break with orthodox Christianity and to his subsequent attitude towards the Bible.

The Congregationalism in which Lawrence was brought up, it needs to be stressed, would not have involved any 'slap-bang bibliolatry' (Aldington 1950: 37). By the late nineteenth century the Congregationalists had added intellectual independence to the

political liberalism of the Independents from whom they were
descended. Many of their leading clergy had quickly accepted the
principles of the higher criticism (Chadwick 1970: II 105). Not all of
them would have been as liberal theologically as R. J. Campbell,
author of a book entitled *The New Theology* which Lawrence discussed
with his own minister Robert Reid (McGuffie 1985: 31–4). But they
(and Reid in particular) were aware of developments in biblical
criticism. The Congregationalists at Eastwood, as Jessie Chambers
recalled, could also boast not only of a stone-clad spire superior to
the 'barn-like' Primitive Methodist chapel but of a range of 'improving' activities, including regular lectures, lantern shows and even a
Literary Society, which played an important part in Lawrence's
development (Worthen 1991: 64–8). Lawrence's own account of the
role of 'Hymns in a Man's Life', written in 1928, when he claims to
have 'got over the Christian dogma' by the age of sixteen, acknowledges that he was glad to have been 'brought up a Protestant', and a
Congregationalist in particular, because of 'the direct knowledge of
the Bible' that it gave him. He was certainly relieved not to have
been a Primitive Methodist, for 'they were always having "revivals"
and being "saved", and I always had a horror of being "saved"'
(*Phoenix* II 597–600).

The preaching at Eastwood Congregational Chapel, while
Lawrence worshipped there, seems to have been decidedly liberal.
Charles Butler, minister from 1874 to 1890, abandoned Congregationalism for the even more liberal Unitarians, while his successor,
John Loosemore, a 'charming young Welshman', offended
Lawrence's mother by expounding the early chapters of Genesis
about the Garden of Eden as 'a beautiful fairy-tale' (Chambers 1980:
16–17). Robert Reid, who succeeded Loosemore in 1896 (and
tutored Lawrence in Latin) used, according to Jessie Chambers, to
give 'lectures' rather than' sermons' (83). Margaret Masson has
called his preaching 'oddly nebulous', even 'pretentious' (Masson
1990: 58–9), but the newspaper reports of his sermons in the years
that Lawrence attended Eastwood Congregational Chapel on which
she draws for her assessment of 'D. H. Lawrence's Congregational
Inheritance' confirm that he encouraged a relatively sophisticated
level of debate about religion in general and the interpretation of the
Bible in particular.

The three sermons on 'Religion and Science' which Reid delivered
in December 1907 can be read as a direct response to questions raised

by Lawrence in a letter to his minister that year. They attempt a reconciliation between these two embattled areas by focusing on the apparent conflict between the theory of evolution and the accounts of creation in Genesis. The first explains that the 'main idea of Genesis was to give man a knowledge of God, not an exact description of the creation'. The second argues that 'the beautiful story of Adam and Eve' records the origins of man's moral sense. Later theological elaboration of the doctrine of the Fall, Reid insists, should not be allowed totally to override the biblical account, in which Adam is not 'described as perfect' but portrayed along with Eve as a child learning from experience, which is 'exactly what science taught with regard to primitive man' (Masson 1988: 71–2). The third and final sermon in this series characterises as 'a common mistake' the tendency ' to regard the Bible as literally the words of God' when it is rather a record of the 'gradual growth of understanding of God's attributes' (74). The Bible, in other words, should be read intelligently in the light of science, from which it has nothing to fear.

There were, of course, some limits placed upon this intellectual freedom. Jessie Chambers recalls Lawrence at the age of sixteen perplexed by 'what passed as religious life among us' (Chambers 1980: 48) and at twenty-one, in his first year at College, resenting 'the tone of authority adopted by the conventionally religious people, including his mother':

He used to complain that in chapel one had to sit still and seem to agree with all that the minister said. He would have liked to be at liberty to stand up and challenge his statements. It was a matter of grief to him too that whoever opposed the orthodox teaching was cast out of the church, which claimed to have a monopoly of the right way of living. (84)

Even in his early student days, however, according to Jessie Chambers, he was sufficiently open to the idea of becoming a minister himself to flick open the Bible at random in the hope of receiving supernatural guidance on the subject (85). Her brother David recalls a particular moment of rebellion at the age of twenty-two on a summer evening on the way back from chapel when 'he began to inveigh against the Chapel and all it stood for and especially against the minister, the Reverend Robert Reid, . . . a fierce, uncontrollable tirade, an outpouring of long pent-up rage', which was also, of course, a rebellion against his mother, who had first 'fastened the Chapel bonds around him' (Chambers 1972: 15).

Lawrence's letters to the Reverend Robert Reid, only quite 'recently discovered' and made available to critics (*Letters* I 3), help to chart the intellectual side of this long-brewing rebellion. A letter of October 1907 lists some of the authors who had 'seriously modified my religious beliefs': Darwin, Spencer, Renan, J. M. Robertson, Blatchford and Vivian (I 36–7). The impact of the first two will be discussed in the following chapter and I will turn to the third, Renan, in a moment, considering his *Life of Jesus* in particular. It is impossible to identify which of the many works of James Robertson, historian of Christianity, humanism and freethought, he read. But it is clear that Robert Blatchford's *God and My Neighbour*, Philip Vivian's *The Churches and Modern Thought*, and a book mentioned later in the letter, R. J. Campbell's *The New Theology*, deserve more attention than they have previously received. All of them focus on biblical criticism, confirming Lawrence's awareness of recent developments in the subject. His letters to Reid deny having much sympathy with any of these works, calling Campbell's position 'untenable, indeed almost incomprehensible to an ordinary mind that cannot sustain a rationalist attitude in a nebulous atmosphere of religious yearning' (I 37). But, as Duncan McGuffie argues, Lawrence is overstating his objections to Campbell, whom he labels 'practically an agnostic', aware of Reid's own distrust of the New Theology (McGuffie 1985: 34). Jessie Chambers recalls that Campbell's book fed directly into their discarding of 'such things as the Virgin Birth, the Atonement, and the Miracles . . . as irrelevant to the real matter of religion' (Chambers 1980: 82), a claim confirmed by Lawrence's letter to Reid, which presses the minister to say whether or not the Churches were with Campbell on these three issues, on 'the Divinity of Jesus' and on 'such questions as Evolution, with that the Origin of Sin, and as Heaven and Hell' (*Letters* I 37).

The New Theology, a label others had given to the views Campbell held, claims to object not so much to the 'venerable creeds' themselves as their 'ordinary interpretation', attempting 'a restatement of the essential truth of the Christian religion in terms of the modern mind' (Campbell 1907: 3–4). The problem, for Campbell, was that Christianity had 'become associated in the popular mind with forms of statement which thoughtful men find it impossible to accept' (8). God, for example, was understood anthropomorphically as 'a finite being, stationed somewhere above and beyond the universe' (18). The Bible was read as an 'infallible book' (177), to be relied upon as if 'written by the finger of God Himself, and let down from heaven'. Such literalism led quickly to disbelief when inconsistencies were discovered in its pages. But the Bible for Campbell was merely 'a collection of books' which had 'come to be reverenced, not because of any supernormal attestations of its authority, but because we have found it helps us more than any other book' (182). Nor, according to Campbell, had God 'stopped speaking to men' thousands of years ago: 'We are writing a Bible with our own lives to-day . . . for the same eternal Spirit of Truth' which had taught 'the Elijahs, Isaiahs, and Pauls of history, is with us to-day as He was with them' (184–5).

This is the positive teaching in Campbell; its negative side too entails a more critical reading of the Bible. Doctrines such as the Fall, he insisted, the belief that 'Man was originally innocent and pure . . . but by an act of disobedience to a Divine command . . . dragged down the whole creation and blighted posterity', were based upon a misreading of the Book of Genesis, 'a composite, primitive story . . . in existence as oral tradition long before it became literature' whose 'narrative says nothing about the ruined creation or the curse upon posterity' (54–5). Campbell is equally critical of traditional teaching on the incarnation; for him Jesus is 'divine' because uniquely possessed by love. 'If there be one thing which becomes indisputable from the reading of the gospel narratives,' Campbell argues, 'it is that Jesus possessed a true human consciousness, limited like our own, and, like our own, subject to the ordinary ills of life' (78). The 'dogma of the Deity of Jesus', he claims, was 'a comparatively late development in Christianity' whose results had been unfortunate (79–80). The doctrine of the Virgin Birth, absent in Mark and Paul but built into the 'very beautiful' infancy narratives of Matthew and Luke through the mistaken pressing of Old Testament prophecies 'into the service of Christian dogma', is seen to belong 'to the poetry of religion, not to history' (98–101). Campbell devotes three chapters to his least favourite Christian doctrine, the Atonement, which preserved far too much of ancient and barbaric sacrifice for his taste. The point, which Lawrence cannot have missed, even from what he calls a 'glance' through the book (*Letters* I 37), is that many of the traditional doctrines of Christianity were built upon interpretations of biblical texts which were, at the very least, debatable.

A further letter from Lawrence to Robert Reid of December 1907 discusses Blatchford's outspoken attack on Christianity in *God and My Neighbour* in similarly disparaging terms as those used of Campbell. Again, however, it is clear that Lawrence is being very careful not to offend his minister, very conscious of Reid's own views when he writes, 'As you say, violent, blatant writers against Christianity do not affect me – I could not read *God and My Neighbour* with patience.' He denies having been influenced by the book: 'I care not for Blatchford or anybody. I do not wage war against Christianity – I do not hate it – but these questions will not be answered' (1 39, 41). As John Worthen has noted, however, Lawrence's letter employs arguments taken directly from Blatchford (Worthen 1991: 176), for instance that the suffering, squalor and depravity of the slums is 'not compatible with the idea of an *Omnipotent*, pitying Divine' (*Letters* 1 40). Blatchford, in a chapter entitled 'What I Can and Cannot Believe', had dwelt on the same difficulty: 'I cannot discern the hand of a loving Father in the slums' (Blatchford 1904: 10). Blatchford announces at the outset of his book, 'I am a Socialist', committed to following Christ in deeds rather than words (x). He ends the book appealing again to the Epistle of James, on 'pure religion' as 'visiting the fatherless and widows in their affliction' (James 1: 27), helping to relieve poverty (Blatchford 1904: 194). Lawrence, adopting some of Blatchford's own rather self-important rhetoric, tells his minister that 'true Socialism is religion; that honest, fervent politics are religion; that whatever a man will labour for earnestly and in some measure unselfishly is religion' (*Letters* 1 40). He clearly took rather more from Blatchford than he was prepared to tell Reid.

The main focus of Blatchford's book is the Bible, against which he unleashes a peculiar mixture of crude and sophisticated arguments, drawing upon respected biblical scholars to reach less respectable conclusions. His main complaint is that the Bible is historically inaccurate; it contains errors of fact, inconsistencies and morally dubious elements which cannot be regarded as divinely 'inspired'. He accepts that the author of the Book of Genesis 'was a man of literary genius' (Blatchford 1904: 27) and that there are other parts of the Bible that are equally impressive as literature but sees most of the book as characterised by 'a jumble of ancient myths, allegories, and mysteries drawn from many sources . . . adapted, altered, and edited so many times that in many instances their original or inner meaning has become obscure' (36). Among Blatchford's many and lengthy quotations are several from J. M. Robertson's *Christianity and*

Mythology including a reference to the Bible as 'a medley of early metaphysics and early fable' (37). This may account for the reference to Robertson in Lawrence's letter; certainly, many of the authors Blatchford recommends feature among Lawrence's early reading: not just Robertson but also Renan, Huxley, Spencer, Haeckel and Frazer. He may even have been following Blatchford's recommendations, although he may have turned to these writers independently, recognising their relevance to any critical study of religion.

The most interesting passages in Blatchford's book, it is fair to say, are the quotations, often from liberal theologians such as Dean Farrar (whom, as we shall see, Lawrence would also have encountered in his beloved *International Library of Famous Literature*). Farrar is cited welcoming the way 'the Higher Criticism has slowly and surely made its victorious progress' (38) while the Revd. T. Rhondda Williams is quoted describing the 'theology of the Jahwist' as 'very childish and elementary' and explaining the documentary hypothesis, first propounded by German biblical scholars such as Wellhausen and Gunkel, that the Pentateuch could be divided into different strands, the earliest of which was labelled J (for the Jahwist, so called because of the name this part of the text uses for God). Williams explains that the Yahwist (as he is normally anglicised), whose account of creation begins at Genesis 2: 4,

thinks of God very much as in human form, holding intercourse with men almost as one of themselves . . . Jahweh *moulds* dust into human form, and *breathes* into it; *plants* a garden, and puts the man in it. Jahweh comes to the man in his sleep, and takes part of his body to make a woman, and so skilfully, apparently, that the man never wakes under the operation. Jahweh *walks* in the garden like a man in the cool of the day. He even *makes coats* for Adam and Eve.

The Yahwist, unlike many modern readers, has 'no difficulty in thinking of God in this way' (48), Williams explains, arguing for a more historical rather than a literal reading of the Bible along with a more sophisticated theology. Blatchford himself misses the point, lampooning the portrait of God in the Bible as 'fickle, jealous, dishonourable, immoral, vindictive, barbarous, and cruel' (47). 'The historical books of the Old Testament,' he continues, 'are largely pernicious, and often obscene' (67). He concedes that the Bible has its literary moments, 'in Job (which is not Jewish), in Ecclesiastes (which is pagan), in the Song of Solomon (which is an erotic love song)' and in some of the prophets (70). But he concludes that it is not 'a fit book to place in the hands of children' (72).

Much of this, of course, is standard freethinking polemic, as is the attack on the historicity of the gospels which follows. Blatchford has no time for miracles, especially for the Resurrection. What evidence is there, he asks, in a suggestion possibly responsible for the opening of *The Escaped Cock* (along with other literary analogues to be discussed in chapter 12), 'that Christ did not recover from a swoon' rather than die and return to life (95)? Again, Blatchford cites a number of respectable biblical scholars on the 'unhistorical' nature of much of the gospels in order to conclude that the religion he had been 'taught as a boy in Church of England and Congregationalist Sunday Schools' can no longer be credited. Like Campbell, he finds traditional doctrines such as the Fall unacceptable: 'God is all-powerful. He could have made Adam strong enough to resist Eve. He could have made Adam strong enough to resist the Serpent. He need not have made the Serpent at all' (134). Unlike Campbell, his solution is to not to modernise or modify that religion but altogether to reject it.

It is easy to see why Lawrence should tell Reid that he was unable to read Blatchford 'with patience'. The anti-Christian polemics are crude; but he would have gained some insight into developments in biblical criticism if only from the citations from more respectable writers. His letter to Reid of 3 December 1907 continues with quite a long discussion of his own religious temperament, which he labels 'emotional, perhaps mystical' before recording the frustrations incurred while waiting for a Pauline-style conversion that never came and in which he has now ceased to believe. On the contrary, he explains, it now seems to him that

a man gradually formulates his religion, be it what it may. A man has no religion who has not slowly and painfully gathered one together, adding to it, shaping it; and one's religion is never complete and final, it seems, but must always be undergoing modification. (*Letters* I 40)

Lawrence goes on to explain that he cannot believe in the divinity of Jesus or in 'a *personal* God', given the amount of suffering and disorder in life. He can, however, accept what he calls 'a Cosmic God', unknowable and inscrutable, no longer a source of personal comfort or consolation (I 40–1).

Another of the books cited in Lawrence's letter to Reid is Philip

Vivian's study of *The Churches and Modern Thought*. Vivian (whose real name was Harry Vivian M. Phelips) devotes a lengthy chapter to 'The Destructive Character of Modern Biblical Criticism'. The problem, according to Vivian, is that the 'ordinary man is highly ignorant of the "Higher Criticism"' (Vivian 1906: 88), unaware, for example, that 'Jonah is a Jewish Midrash, or tradition, like the histories of Tobit and Susanna' (95), that the gospel accounts of the crucifixion contains 'truth mixed with doubtful legend' (97) or that the apocalypse is 'an admixture of Jewish with Christian ideas and speculations' (104). Lawrence, of course, was going to go much further into these arguments about the Book of Revelation in his own *Apocalypse*. He was also to investigate some of the other religions discussed by Vivian in his chapter on comparative religion. Vivian notes some of the similarities between Aztec religion and Christianity, for instance that 'the "Saviour" Quetzalcoatl was born of a pure virgin who was called the "Queen of Heaven"' (144). Vivian was by no means the only source for Lawrence's knowledge of Quetzalcoatl, as we shall see in chapter 11. Vivian himself quotes Robertson's study of *Pagan Christs* along with *The Golden Bough*, both of which contain detailed descriptions of Aztec sacrifices. The point, anyway, is not to establish the exact 'source' for Lawrence's interest in the Aztecs but to recognise the extent to which even a book such as Vivian's contributed to his changing attitudes towards the Bible.

These are just some of the books that we know Lawrence read in the period which saw him abandon his long-held faith in Christianity. He never, of course, abandoned his love for the Bible. When Reid left Eastwood in March 1911, Lawrence wrote to thank him for all his help, acknowledging how often he turned 'back to the Bible' ashamed of his 'old insolence': 'If only we were allowed to look at Scripture in the light of our own experience, instead of having to see it displayed in a kind of theatre, false-real, and never developing, we should save such a lot of mistakes' (*Letters* I 244). It was the attempt to fix its meaning within narrow doctrinal limits that he resented. Other letters of this period reveal both how far and how quickly he travelled from orthodox Christianity and how much he continued to think in its terms. His correspondence with Blanche Jennings, for example, a freethinking socialist and suffragette with whom he could be more irreverent than with Reid, shows him in 1908 laughing at the kind of 'prayings and slobber' he associated with parsons (I 51). The 'secret of religion', he tells her, is a regression to childhood dependence, 'grown-ups' turning to Jesus for comfort as children with toothache to their mother (I 62). It was in his first year at college, he explains, that he lost his own 'rather deep religious faith' along with his 'idealism' (I 72). This did not prevent him reprimanding her in characteristically biblical terms in December of that year for being so severe towards Christianity: 'You women, when you turn, are like Lot's wife, pillars of salt, immutable.' He no longer believes in 'a Personal God', he confesses, 'but the sound of Christianity does not rile me' as it does her (I 98–9).

Lawrence's abandonment of belief in a personal God finds fuller expression in a sympathetic letter of April 1911 to his sister Ada, who was undergoing her own crisis of faith. There is, he argues, no need to feel stuck with traditional Jewish or Christian concepts of God:

Jehovah is the Jew's idea of God – not ours. Christ was infinitely good, but mortal as we. There still remains a God, but not a personal God: a vast, shimmering impulse which wavers onwards towards some end, I don't know what . . . When we die . . . we fall back into the big, shimmering sea of unorganised life which we call God . . . It is a fine thing to establish one's own religion in one's own heart, not to be dependent on tradition and second hand ideals. (I 255–6)

The view that religious belief and biblical interpretation should never remain fixed or static but should continue to evolve was to remain with him for the rest of his life. But he retained from Eastwood Chapel not only an 'unconscious submersion in the language and imagery of the Bible . . . a consciousness . . . truly soaked in the Bible' but a lasting commitment to a religious way of life (Worthen 1991: 67–8). It was also entirely within the spirit of late-nineteenth-century Congregationalism that he should have sought to enrich his understanding of religion in general and his reading of the Bible in particular with reference to the widest possible range of thinkers.

One of the earliest sources for the broadening of Lawrence's understanding of the Bible in his teens was the twenty-volume *International Library of Famous Literature*, edited by Richard Garnett, which was bought by his brother Ernest soon after its publication in 1899 and bequeathed to the household on his death two years later. Jessie Chambers records that this was 'one of the most treasured possessions of the Lawrence household . . . regarded with a reverence amounting to awe', the medium for many of Lawrence's 'literary acquaintances' (Chambers 1980: 92). Worthen accepts that

'Lawrence doubtless read widely in them' but plays down their importance partly because of the necessarily brief nature of the extracts and partly because of their omission of key figures in Lawrence's intellectual development such as Nietzsche (Worthen 1991: 111). But they have much to say on the Bible. The first volume, for example, which contains fragments of ancient religious literature from a variety of traditions, explains in its introductory essay on 'The Use and Value of Anthologies' that 'The Bible and the Talmud, the Vedas, the Mahabarata [*sic*]' and other ancient texts 'are not the works of one man but of many men. They are full of fragments of older writings, frequently recognisable as such' (Garnett 1899: I xviii). Its very first extract is taken from 'The Chaldean Account of Genesis' with an explanatory note celebrating this Assyrian legend as 'one of the oldest in the world', itself compiled from 'pre-existent materials, already sufficiently venerable to have acquired a sacred character' (1). This opening volume also contains several examples of recent reworking of biblical texts: Charlotte Yonge's 'The Cup of Water' (dramatising David's thirst while being persecuted by Saul), Charles Mackay's narrative poem 'Tubal Cain', George Croly's poetic retelling of the Book of Exodus, 'The Seventh Plague of Egypt' and Mrs Alexander's poem 'The Burial of Moses'. Later volumes include an extract from Henry Sienkiewicz's historical novel *Quo Vadis* (vol. III) and Robert Buchanan's 'Ballad of Judas Iscariot' (vol. V). It seems unlikely that the young Lawrence would have failed to notice these examples of biblical material or of its later literary reworking.

The later volumes of the *International Library* also include some biblical criticism. Volume VII begins with an essay by Dean Farrar on 'The Literature of Religious Criticism', containing a strong defence of liberal theology. Farrar expresses a clear preference for the honest agnosticism of the ancient rabbis over 'the utterly false, meaningless, and fanatical dogma' of literal inspiration, the belief that every letter of the Bible 'came direct from God' (VII xvii). He charts the development of critical reading of the Bible in the modern period from Erasmus onwards, citing Luther calling the Book of Revelation 'an insoluble enigma' and the French Oratorian, Richard Simon, whose *Critical History of the Old Testament* first remarked on the 'difference between the Jehovistic and Elohistic documents in Genesis' (xviii). Further developments in higher criticism in both Germany and Britain, Farrar acknowledges, mean that 'it is now regarded as a matter of established fact, among all serious and competent scholars, that the Pentateuch is composed of composite documents' (xix). As well as providing a summary of recent developments in biblical criticism, Farrar's essay gives a clear explanation of midrash or *Haggada*. After clarifying the difference between the two main schools of Jewish commentary, *Halacha*, the 'minute exposition of . . . the written and oral law' and '*Haggada*, which dealt more with moral and religious teaching, and gave play to the imagination', Farrar continues,

> there is nothing whatever derogatory to the sacred majesty of the Bible in the beliefs [*sic*] that divine truths should have been sometimes conveyed in the form of allegory or Parable. Our Lord's parables convey the divinest lessons which God has ever communicated to man; yet they are confessedly '*Parables*' – i.e. they are truths conveyed by imaginary stories. (xx–xxi)

Farrar proceeds to quote Coleridge on the need to be alert to ancient eastern hyperbole, to take 'talking snakes' as a clear indication of allegory (xxi). To read the Bible intelligently, he argues, requires sophisticated skills such as genre recognition, enabling us to see Haggadic elements in the Book of Jonah and to recognise the last sixteen verses of St Mark's Gospel as 'a later and dubious appendix to that Gospel' (xxiii). Farrar draws the line at the two most notorious Lives of Jesus of the century, by Strauss and Renan respectively. While acknowledging the literary and scholarly qualities of Renan's work, he rejects his accounting for the resurrection by the 'power of love' alone (xxvii) not to mention his accusing Christ of deceit over miracles (xxix).

The penultimate volume of the *International Library* includes a chapter from Renan's *Life of Jesus*, which is one of the books Jessie Chambers describes reading with Lawrence around 1906. She reports that he was in some respects disappointed, feeling that it presented 'Jesus according to the likeness of Ernest Renan' (Chambers 1980: 112). He cannot, however, have failed to pick up from Renan a recognition of the imaginative nature of ancient eastern religious texts, in particular the gospels. Renan's apparent denigration of 'eastern' standards of historical accuracy opens him to accusations of 'orientalism', of a patronising attitude to the east, and there certainly are passages in the *Life of Jesus* which play up the contrast between 'the deeply earnest races of the West', with their commitment to honesty, and 'the Oriental', for whom 'literal truth has little value' and who thinks nothing of embellishing a sacred text with what 'we should term a fraud' (Renan 1927: 147). But the primary target of Renan's criticism is the inappropriate mode of reading the Bible characteristic of literalism, which brings modern western assumptions to ancient eastern texts.

Renan (like Lawrence, as we shall see) values the specificity of the synoptics much more highly than the abstractions of John's Gospel, finding 'the spirit of Jesus' much better represented in their 'profoundly Hebraistic idiom' than in the Johannine discourses, with their 'desire to prove a thesis', their 'obscure Gnosticism' and 'distorted metaphysics' (15). It does not bother Renan that some of these details in the synoptics 'are not true to the letter' since they capture 'the very spirit of Jesus', like an imaginatively restored vase in which some of the pieces may not be original (25, 29). The impression produced by the whole story is what counts. His own portrait of Jesus, as many critics have recognised, is an extremely romantic one, presenting the young lover of nature, of flowers and of children as happiest at the very outset of his career, gallivanting with friends among the Galilean hills, before becoming embroiled in the religious and political controversies of his time. For Renan it is axiomatic that miracles do not happen, that modern science will always in principle be able to explain them. He depicts Jesus as allowing his disciples to believe him capable of miracles, external signs of power whose temptation he had earlier resisted. He insists that there was no 'theology or creed' in the early days of Christianity. Only later in the development of Christian theology were concepts such as that of the Holy Spirit or Paraclete developed, the latter being a Greek word which 'it is very doubtful whether Jesus used'. Renan, like Derrida after him, is very alert to the imposition of Greek metaphysical concepts on to Jewish metaphors. He presents the development of the Lord's Supper from an act of memorial to a metaphysical sacrament as another example of the way in which Jesus' vivid metaphorical language was 'afterwards taken in a very literal sense' (171).

It is clear that the young Lawrence would have found his distaste for literal reading of the Bible reinforced by Renan. His reported disappointment with the *Life of Jesus* should not be allowed to obscure its significance to his religious development and to his understanding of the Bible. Renan's sophisticated awareness of the complexity of historical criticism, the difficulty of getting back to the 'original Jesus' behind the layers of interpretive faith and the literary complexity of the gospel narratives, would all have played a part in liberating Lawrence from literal acceptance of every detail in the gospels to a broader appreciation of their continuing literary power. Given Lawrence's own rewriting of the gospels later in his career, in particular in *The Escaped Cock*, it is important to recognise the model Renan provided for such an imaginative exercise. Had he needed any encouragement to rewrite the Bible, he would certainly have found it in Renan.

Finally, it is worth mentioning another figure who would have provided a model for the imaginative but unorthodox appropriation of the Bible, Edward Carpenter. Lawrence himself is curiously silent about Carpenter, but Jessie Chambers claimed that he had read all of Carpenter's works (Delavenay 1971: 170). William Hopkin, a key figure in Eastwood intellectual life, records attempting unsuccessfully to persuade a reluctant Lawrence to meet him (Cobau 1976: 128). But Emile Delavenay demonstrates the detailed similarities in their thinking as they made the transition from Christian orthodoxy to a broader, eclectic religious faith drawn from eastern mysticism, theosophy and a range of radical philosophies. This may have been simply a matter of sharing the late-Victorian 'mental atmosphere' associated with early Fabianism, the Fellowship of the New Life and journals such as *The New Age*, which both of them read. But it is worth briefly considering some of Carpenter's ideas in the context of Lawrence's understanding of the Bible.

Carpenter gives a particular twist to the doctrine of the Fall. A section of *Civilization, Its Cause and Cure* (1889) entitled 'The Fall and the Return to Paradise' argues that the purpose of the fall is the development of human self-consciousness. Civilisation, as in other romantic accounts of human history, is blamed for 'the abandonment of the primitive life and the growth of the sense of shame (as in the myth of Adam and Eve). From this follows *the disownment of the sacredness of sex*', which ceases to be 'a part of religious worship' (cit. Delavenay 1971: 63). The recovery of paradise, the return to Eden, involves escaping the sense of guilt about sex, casting off clothing altogether and returning to a state of unity with nature. *Love's Coming of Age* (1896), Carpenter's best-known casting-off of Victorian sexual inhibitions, celebrates the joys of outdoor sex in a way that seems to have left its mark on Lawrence's fiction, continuing the motif of a return to Eden, a paradise characterised by 'free woman' and 'free love' (cit. Delavenay 105). Carpenter, according to Delavenay, anticipates and provides a model for Lawrence's own attempt 'to rejuvenate and interpret anew Christian and Jewish religious concepts' even if Lawrence goes further than Carpenter in the way in which 'he tears at the law, and deifies the Flesh at the expense of the Word' (116–17).

Carpenter can also be seen to have anticipated Lawrence's use of biblical language to give richness and depth to ideas which were his own. Delavenay claims that *The Art of Creation* (1904) anticipates a whole cluster of images which recur in *The Rainbow*: 'rainbows, arcs, circles and auras abound in his prose, symbolizing as in Christian iconography, integration, unity, as opposed to the disintegration and dissociation of thought' (128). 'Transfiguration' is another traditional religious image which both writers employ to indicate the achievement of the highest states of consciousness (155). *Angels' Wings: A Series of Essays on Art and Its Relation to Life* (1898) contains a chapter on 'Tradition, Convention and the Gods' which could be taken as a blueprint for Lawrence's career, explaining the way in which writers should use traditional religious symbols thrown up by 'the Collective Consciousness of the race' but develop and transform them in the process, evolving new ways of feeling and thinking about religion (178–9). The point is not, of course, to attempt a precise calculation of Lawrence's 'debt' to Carpenter but to draw attention to the possible role even of such unorthodox biblical criticism in his rejection of orthodox Christianity.

CHAPTER 4

Poetic fathers: Nietzsche and the Romantic Tradition

Biblical criticism, as we have seen, provided one strand of Lawrence's break with conventional Christianity but there were, of course, many other 'poetic fathers', to use Harold Bloom's term for those precursors who help to shape a poet's writing both by direct 'influence' and by providing a model for imitation and rivalry. This chapter will consider some of these fathers, the most important of whom, in my view, was Nietzsche. It was Nietzsche, I would suggest, who provided Lawrence with the prime example of a critique of Christianity which was also creative, going beyond Christianity by means of the tradition, employing the Bible against itself. Nietzsche's work, like Lawrence's, finds expression in a range of writing difficult to categorise, combining elements of philosophy, literary criticism, religious prophecy and biblical parody. As with all influence, it is difficult to prove or to quantify, although there are sufficient specific references to Nietzsche in Lawrence to warrant careful study.

First, however, it is important to acknowledge the sheer range of Lawrence's reading. It would be impossible to provide a comprehensive account of this either in his two years at University College Nottingham (1906–8) or in his years of teaching at Croydon (1908–12). He was, as Worthen says, 'wonderfully self-educated' with a wide range of literary and philosophical interests (Worthen 1991: 345–6). Lawrence himself gives a number of autobiographical sketches of this reading in his early fiction, for instance in 'A Modern Lover', written in 1909–10, in which Cyril Mersham looks back on his intellectual development, smiling 'as he traced the graph onwards, plotting the points with Carlyle and Ruskin, Schopenhauer and Darwin and Huxley', passing through a range of French and Russian novelists to end with Nietzsche and William James (*LAH* 33). *Sons and Lovers* tells a similar tale of religious emancipation through identifiable phases of interest in individual writers. Miriam becomes 'the threshing floor' on which Paul Morel 'threshed out all his beliefs', whether it is Spencer (*SL* 251) or when, a little later in the novel, he passes through 'the Renan *Vie de Jésus* stage' (267).

Jessie Chambers, as we have seen, provides her own account of this process in *D. H. Lawrence: A Personal Record*. It was during his years at university, according to her, that Lawrence encountered the challenge to traditional religious thought posed by contemporary science (Chambers 1980: 84–5). A further wave of 'materialistic philosophy came in full blast' with books by Huxley, Darwin and Haeckel, closely followed by Spencer, Mill and William James. At 'a time of spiritual fog,' Jessie explains, 'he tried to fill up a spiritual vacuum by swallowing materialism at a gulp' (112–13). Not all the thinkers named here, of course, were materialists and, if Lawrence can be said to have 'swallowed' them, he was soon to digest them and develop in his own profoundly religious way. Nevertheless, Huxley, Darwin and Spencer all presented him with a world of conflict rather than benevolent design, a world in which species battled for survival and in which ethics were introduced as man's attempt to resist the cosmic process. *Man's Place in Nature*, the title of a book by Huxley which Jessie mentions they had read, is one of interdependence in a vast natural cycle of growth, decay and eventual disappearance in which all animals and plants are involved (Ebbatson 1987: 92). The *First Principles* of this universe, as described by Herbert Spencer, are of perpetual change, the evolution and dissolution of ever-changing forms of life, the first cause of which was unknowable. 'The Unknowable' is the title of the first part of *First Principles*, which begins with a chapter on 'Religion and Science' attempting to reconcile the two. 'Religion,' Spencer argues, 'everywhere present as a warp running through the weft of human history, expresses some eternal fact', while Science too sees itself as 'an organized body of truths, ever growing, and ever being purified from errors'. Each side, according to Spencer, should recognise the validity of the other (Spencer 1911: 1 15). Forms of religion, however, must adapt, like all other organisms, in order to represent as honestly as possible the 'fundamental verity' underlying the variant forms (90). Spencer anticipates Lawrence in using a range of capitalised terms in order to refer to the Absolute, the Unknowable, the Inscrutable Power and so on, although he operates on a much more abstract level of discourse than Lawrence was ever to feel happy with.

Another materialist account of religion which Lawrence encountered in his college years was Ernst Haeckel's *The Riddle of the
Universe*. Haeckel recognised 'one sole substance in the universe',
variously referred to as 'God and Nature' or 'body and spirit' but the
two sides of these binary oppositions were actually inseparable
(Haeckel 1929: 11, 16). Haeckel's, according to Ebbatson, was a
version of pantheism adapted for a scientific age, insisting on a
broader religious reverence for nature than that provided by Christianity. Haeckel insisted on worshipping in 'the temple of nature'
rather than 'the gloom of the cloister'; he needed 'no special church,
no narrow, enclosed portion of space' (Ebbatson 1987: 96–7).The
monism of Spencer and Haeckel, as Worthen has argued, provided
Lawrence with an important ground on which to abandon orthodox
doctrines for a broader religious position. It was, however, as
Lawrence told his botany teacher at Nottingham, only a temporary
resting place before pragmatism and on the way to pluralism
(Worthen 1991: 179–80; *Letters* I 147).

It was William James' *Pragmatism*, published in 1907, which
highlighted some of the limitations of this monistic materialism while
offering a compromise between the only alternatives contemporary
philosophy appeared to offer: tough-minded, irreligious empiricism
on the one hand and tender-minded, religious idealism on the other.
James, according to Montgomery, exposed the limitations of Haeckel
and Spencer in particular, the former with his 'ether-god' and the
latter with his 'hurdy-gurdy monotony' and altogether 'wooden'
system (Montgomery 1994: 27–30). James' version of pragmatism, by
focusing upon the practical consequences of belief, avoided endless
metaphysical disputes, allowing philosophical agnosticism to accom-
pany continuing religious commitment. It is clear from Lawrence's
letters of 1908 that he shared William James' suspicion of monism,
whether of the Buddhist or scientific variety, echoing his mockery of
its appeal to rest in 'the everlasting arms' of a vaguely defined God
(Worthen 1991: 538). It was William James' exposition of *The Varieties
of Religious Experience* (1902) and *A Pluralistic Universe* (1909), Black
argues, which enabled Lawrence to find a middle path between the
narrowly orthodox Christianity in which he had been brought up
and the materialistic scientific philosophies which claimed to replace
it. He was to remain 'religious and theist' throughout his career,
striving continually to 'reformulate religious belief, starting from the
sense of God' (Black 1991: 448).

This kind of reformulation of traditional religious belief had, of course, been taking place for some time. M. H. Abrams famously employed Carlyle's term, *Natural Supernaturalism*, for a range of Romantic writers who aimed not so much at 'the deletion of religious ideas' but rather at their assimilation and reinterpretation, their 'displacement from a supernatural to a natural frame of reference' (Abrams 1971: 12–13). Abrams brackets in this broad tradition independent artists such as Blake, for whom the Bible was 'the Great Code of Art', certainly the primary source for much of his own writing, and a range of German thinkers from Schiller, who developed some of his leading ideas in the form of a commentary on the Pentateuch, to Fichte, Schelling, Hegel and Novalis, all of whom attempted to 'translate religious doctrine into their conceptual philosophy' (33). These German philosophers, of course, exerted great influence upon English writers such as Coleridge and Carlyle, the latter of whom had been the object of an intense period of study by Lawrence in the spring of 1906 (Chambers 1980: 101–2; *Letters* I 49).

This kind of intellectual genealogy, of course, is endless. Carlyle in turn, as Barry Qualls shows in *The Secular Pilgrims of Victorian Fiction*, provided the inspiration for a number of Victorian novelists, in particular Charlotte Brontë, Charles Dickens and George Eliot, to write what he calls 'biblical romances' or 'secular scriptures' reinscribing traditional Christian values in decidedly this-worldly settings (Qualls 1982: xi). Nor was Carlyle the only Victorian sage to present himself as re-writing the Bible in terms credible to 'modern man'. Anne Fernihough, in discussing Lawrence's 'Victorian Predecessors', compares Carlyle's 'lugubrious parody of Genesis, in which the fire-throated machines rise into day' in *Chartism*, with a passage from Ruskin invoking 'the "breath of life" of Genesis' in order to celebrate the natural qualities of iron (Fernihough 1993: 133–4). The two writers use the biblical original very differently in order to make diametrically opposed points. But they both turn to the Bible for moral authority while demonstrating the need to re-interpret it for their own age. Lawrence, an avid reader of both these writers, would have found in them, as in the German Romantic thinkers, a model for the kind of creative reading and rewriting of the Bible which he himself was to perform.

It is important also to notice that this strand of Romantic thought, retrieving religious belief from the wreckage of dogma and relocating it in the natural world, passed from Carlyle to American transcendentalists such as Emerson, whom Lawrence was also busy reading in 1905–6 (Schneider 1986: 47). Abrams writes of 'the persistence, from Emerson and Thoreau . . . of the ideal of the child's innocent eye which . . . transforms the old world into a new Eden', presenting the American as 'a new Adam, emancipated from the burden of history and the corruptions of the Old World' in a 'pristine garden-like Eden' (Abrams 1971: 411–2). This attempted recovery of paradise, as we shall see, will dominate Lawrence's *Studies in Classic American Literature*. He would also have found in Emerson an open appreciation of the Bible as a work of literature to be criticised like any other product of the imagination. It was in the 'Divinity School Address' of 1838 that Emerson spelt out most clearly his relation to the biblical tradition, complaining of the irrelevance of official church dogmas, which had been built upon a misreading of Jesus's tropes and had become 'wholly insulated from anything now extant in the life or business of the people' (Emerson 1994: 1041). Emerson attacks the 'stationariness of religion; the assumption that the age of inspiration is past, that the Bible is closed' (1042). He concludes the address by calling for a new scripture, a new religious literature which will develop the stagnant orthodox tradition in ways that speak to 'modern' needs, a call which Lawrence clearly heard (whether directly from Emerson or not) and to which his own writing can be seen as a response.

Lawrence would have encountered a similar message in Whitman whose later prefaces present his own work as an alternative 'set of holy scriptures', the effusions of a modern prophet (Schneidau 1983: 19). Lawrence, as we shall see, could be quite critical of Whitman, especially in *Studies in Classic American Literature*, but his own free verse was deeply indebted to Whitman both in form and content. This whole strand of Romanticism, running from Blake through Carlyle to the American transcendentalists, can be seen to have drawn deeply upon the Bible, interpreted freely and creatively as a record of inner spiritual experience rather than objective metaphysical 'facts'. It also provided Lawrence with a number of 'poetic fathers', a range of models for the creative reworking of Scripture.

The most dramatic philosophical impact upon Lawrence's intellectual development in these years, however, encouraging him to adopt a boldly independent position critical of orthodox Christianity, came from Schopenhauer and Nietzsche. Jessie Chambers certainly believed that Lawrence was 'profoundly influenced by Schopenhauer'

(Chambers 1980: 106) although John Worthen argues, on the contrary, that Lawrence merely '*used* Schopenhauer: adapted what he read to what he wanted to find', in particular a good reason for failing to love Jessie Chambers (Worthen 1991: 174). There were two essays by Schopenhauer in the *International Library*, the first of which, 'Thinking for Oneself', casts its argument in provocative biblical terms, attacking reading as 'a mere surrogate for original thought' and thus 'a sin against the Holy Ghost' (Garnett 1899: XVI 7530). Reading, he argues, creates 'a Babylonian confusion of tongues in the head' (7532), a critique continued in the second essay, 'On Reading and Books'. Possibly as a result of reading these essays, Jessie Chambers recalls Lawrence persuading one of her brothers to give her a copy of Mrs Rudolf Dircks' translation of Schopenhauer's *Selected Essays* for her birthday in 1906. She also remembers him reading to them aloud the particular essay on 'The Metaphysics of Love', an essay he annotated carefully in the margins (Chambers 1980: 111). This essay, however, has more to say about desire as the vehicle for the perpetuation of the species than about religious belief. What it does say about this, that the 'will to live' of the species is 'the only immortal part' of a man, is questioned by Lawrence in the margins of his copy (Nehls 1957: 66–70).

More relevant to Lawrence's religious development is Schopenhauer's essay 'On Religion', collected in Dircks' volume from *Parerga and Paralipomena*. This begins as a dialogue between Philalethes (literally lover of truth) and Demopheles (lover of the people), who upbraids his friend for being 'sarcastic and even openly derisive about religion' (Schopenhauer 1974: 324). Demopheles defends religion as 'the only way to proclaim and make plain the high significance of life' in a way that the masses can understand. It is 'an allegorical way of expressing the truth', which may seem 'preposterous, burlesque, and apparently absurd' to the cultured but which brings home to ordinary people 'the lofty meaning of existence' (325). Philalethes is unhappy with this, pointing to the dark side of religion: inquisitions, persecution and intolerance. In an argument that would have had some resonance for Lawrence (and which, as we have seen, he was to reproduce in *Apocalypse*) he complains that its 'precepts and dogmas are inculcated so earnestly, deeply, and firmly at the earliest age' that 'they remain indelibly impressed', paralysing their victims' 'capacity for original thought and unbiased judgment' (326). He is particularly aggrieved that such dubious dogmas are forced upon children with the help of threats of eternal punishment (329). Demopheles argues that such threats are needed to 'restrain the rabble', that allegories, myths and parables serve a useful social purpose, only for Philalethes to give the counter-instance of Greece, an ordered civilised society that 'had no sacred records and no dogma' (330–1). He also objects on principle to 'truth appearing in the guise of falsehood' (333–4). The argument continues with Demopheles stressing the gap between the educated and the masses and Philalethes looking forward to a time when 'mankind bids farewell to religion', like a child moving on from a nurse to a private tutor (347). He finds the Old Testament particularly unedifying, celebrating as it does 'the infamous black-guardism of the patriarchal Jacob' and the violence of 'the murderer Moses' (357).

This dialogue is the only portion of Schopenhauer's essay 'On Religion' reprinted in Mrs Dircks' *Selected Essays*, the only part we can safely assume that Lawrence read. In *Parerga and Paralipomena* the essay breaks out of dialogue into more conventional discursive mode, complaining of the treatment of the animals in Genesis, handed over by the Creator 'so that man may *rule* over them and thus may do what he likes with them' (370). A section on 'Theism' attacks orthodox theology as a linguistic form of idolatry while another on 'The Old and New Testaments' continues his critique of the former, referring to 'the revolting and iniquitous example of Abraham' expelling Hagar and Ishmael (379).

Schopenhauer, it has been claimed, lies behind more general attitudes towards religion to be found both in Nietzsche and Lawrence (Janaway 1994: 101). Other aspects of Schopenhauer's thought which Lawrence would have found congenial include the 'better consciousness' of artists and saints, the superiority of imaginative over conceptual thought, the centrality of sex to human existence and the significance of the *Wille zum Leben*, that un-conscious force which he saw as responsible for all human drives and emotions. But the most significant legacy of Lawrence's encounter with Schopenhauer, according to Montgomery, was an increased scepticism about the value of western metaphysical thought. The point about the contrast between Will and Idea in Schopenhauer, as between Flesh and Word in Lawrence, is that the former element in both oppositions refuses to fit into the neat categories of the latter (Montgomery 1994: 44). The Will, in the terminology of Lawrence's

1908 paper to the Eastwood Debating Society on 'Art and the Individual', may be 'the germ of the God-Idea' but Lawrence follows Schopenhauer in deploring the way in which, in western metaphysics, 'as the plant develops from the germ, it is twisted and clipped into some fantastic Jehovah-shape' (*STH* 128). Ideas of God, in other words, impose an arbitrary and artificial control over the inchoate reality Schopenhauer calls the Will.

Lawrence appears to have found in Schopenhauer's Will a more fluid, less rigid model of 'the ultimate, eternal, indestructible, force' behind all phenomena than the orthodox Christian concept of God (Schneider 1986: 49). The Will, as Schopenhauer conceived it, has been described as

the ground of all being. It is a formless, non-rational, endlessly creative energy, a plenitude which, in constantly striving to realise itself, gives rise to the various and changing world we inhabit. Because it is not a rational, self-consistent or even intelligent force, but a sort of blind, incessant striving, the world the Will brings into being is far from being an orderly or harmonious one – it is characterised instead by pain and struggle and waste. (Milton 1987: 6)

Colin Milton argues that Schopenhauer's concept had a particular appeal to those like Lawrence still reeling from the discoveries of nineteenth-century science: 'reality conceived in this way seemed a more plausible creative principle than the traditional Christian conception of a creating Godhead' (6). Certainly, the dark god of whom Lawrence writes, far removed from the benevolent father of Christian orthodoxy, appears to have at least some of the characteristics of Schopenhauer's Will.

By 1912, according to Brunsdale, Lawrence had rejected the pessimistic tendencies in Schopenhauer for a more 'positive conception of conflict' as a necessary stage 'in the development of a religious sense' which he found in the work of Nietzsche (Brunsdale 1978: 125). He would also have found in Nietzsche a critique of Christianity going beyond Schopenhauer's 'historical refutation' to a fiercer 'genealogical' attack in terms of its underlying psychological motivation as an embodiment of the principle of *ressentiment* or revenge, a principle deeply hostile to life (Salaquarda 1996: 90–1). It seems to have been in the winter of 1908–9, when he moved to Croydon, that Lawrence first discovered Nietzsche. It was then, Jessie Chambers somewhat ruefully records, that 'I began to hear about the "Will to Power"' (Chambers 1980: 120), a phrase that recurs throughout Lawrence's work. Manuscripts of 1910, however, still struggle to spell his name correctly (Worthen 1991: 210). As with so much of Lawrence's reading, it is difficult to establish precisely either which books he read or how thoroughly he read them. Burwell lists under his reading of September 1909 the generous selection to be found in the Croydon Central Library of the eighteen volumes which comprised the Levy translation of *The Complete Works of Friedrich Nietzsche*, published from 1909 to 1913 (Sagar 1970: 69). He certainly read *The Will to Power* in 1909 (72) while letters of 1915 and 1916 respectively refer to *The Gay Science* and *Thus Spoke Zarathustra* (77, 84). He even toyed with the Nietzschean titles 'Morgenrot' (deliberately and perhaps jokingly anglicised, suggesting a mind not too easily swayed by foreign ideas?) and 'The Gay Science' for *The Study of Thomas Hardy* (*Letters* II 295; *STH* 3). One of his early poems, as we shall see, plays with another Nietzschean title, *Beyond Good and Evil* (*CP* 242–3) while other Nietzschean references will be found scattered through his works. None of this, of course, provides proof of careful detailed reading but it does justify a more thorough consideration of what Nietzsche made of the Bible (in both senses, what he thought of it and what he did with it in his own writing). As Colin Milton argues in his study of *Nietzsche and Lawrence*, the importance lies not in 'particular detached borrowings' as of general ideas which 'determine the large-scale patterns and structures of Lawrence's writing' (Milton 1987: 18). One major element of this, to which Milton gives surprisingly little attention, was the way it led Lawrence to reassess the whole Judaeo-Christian tradition, to rewrite the Bible, the main precursor-text for both of them.

Nietzsche, of course, was at the height of his influence in Britain between the turn of the century and the outbreak of the First World War, a period which has been labelled 'the Nietzschean decade' (Bridgwater 1972: 13). Lawrence's friend Edward Garnett in *The Outlook* in 1899 found in Nietzsche 'the most brilliant psychological analysis' of Christianity ever produced (15) while A. R. Orage sang his praises in the *New Age*, a periodical which Lawrence seems to have begun reading around 1908 (Worthen 1991: 541). Between May 1907 and the end of 1913, David Thatcher records, Nietzsche's views were constantly trumpeted in the *New Age* (Thatcher 1970: 235). In what amounted to a concerted campaign to make Nietzsche better known in Britain, Orage not only produced books about Nietzsche and condensations of his thought, such as *Nietzsche in Outline and*

Aphorism (1907), but appears to have 'used the *New Age* to prepare public opinion' for the Oscar Levy translation. Even 'leading literary organs, like the *English Review*, [in which Lawrence published his first short stories] followed the lead of the *New Age* by taking Nietzsche seriously' (42).

Lawrence went out of his way in a 1913 review of 'Georgian Poetry' to mention Nietzsche's 'demolishing . . . the Christian religion as it stood' (*Phoenix* 304) but the last three words of this quotation are of great importance: Nietzsche provided a model for the rejection of conventional Christianity, with its fear of the body and slave morality, but his whole opus, Hollingdale argues in the introduction to *Thus Spoke Zarathustra*, can be seen as a reformulation, a remoulding of Christianity in non-metaphysical terms (*TSZ* 28–9). His critique of Christianity is paradoxically embodied in a style full of 'biblical motifs, phrases, quotations, and allusions (Salaquarda 1996: 94). In Bloom's terms it is certainly a 'strong' reading, a violent misprision or swerving away from the original, but a consistent and powerful one whose appeal to the young Lawrence it is easy to imagine. There is also, as Kingsley Widmer has noted, a similarity of style between these two writers whose 'obsessively energetic flow . . . rarely found a consistent form'. Both were 'poet-polemicists, iconoclastic myth-makers, visionaries full of anti-moral moralizings,' who sometimes 'wrote brilliantly' and at other times reverted to 'a fractured and murky rhetoric of rage' (Meyers 1985: 129).

Nietzsche had himself escaped from a Lutheran background as constricting as Lawrence's own (his father and both grandfathers had been ministers). Walter Kaufmann likens him to one of 'the ancient prophets', an Amos or an Isaiah, in his contempt for the comforts of modernity and in his awareness of 'the agony, the suffering, and the misery of a godless world' (Kaufmann 1968: 96–8). His early work transforms Schopenhauer's pessimism about the uncontrollable Will into a joyful affirmation of the human capacity to understand, accept and transform both the world and themselves (Montgomery 1994: 84). *The Birth of Tragedy*, for example, celebrates the Hellenic capacity to accept the suffering of the world by making it into art. This opening work maintains a 'discreet and hostile silence' towards Christianity although it finds 'nothing . . . more opposed to the purely aesthetic and justification of the world as taught in this book than Christian doctrine, which is *only* moral' and 'relegates art, *all* art, to the realm of *falsehood*' (*BT* 8). *The Birth of*

Tragedy, which is famous for its contrast between Apollonian consciousness, that intellectual approach to existence which 'attempts through the imposition of images and rational forms to separate man from nature and control it', and the Dionysian celebration of unity with nature and of emotional excess (Goodheart 1963: 71–3), ends with a paean to art, especially music and tragic myth, in which 'dissonance and the terrible image of the world charmingly fade away'. It is artistic myth rather than dogmatic religion which expresses 'the Dionysiac capacity of a people' (*BT* 116).

The decade from 1878 to 1888, brought Nietzsche's most outspoken critique of conventional Christianity. *Human, All Too Human* (1878) begins both the onslaught on Christianity and the aphoristic style for which Nietzsche is famous. Nietzsche announces in the preface that he writes 'as an enemy and challenger of God' (*HA* 4). He also describes what he calls the 'decisive event' in the ripening of the 'free spirit' which is the '*great separation*' from the religious tradition in which he or she was brought up. Nietzsche captures the initially painful nature of this separation in terms which appear particularly appropriate to Lawrence's own experience: it often 'comes suddenly, like the shock of an earthquake', leaving 'the young soul . . . devastated, torn loose, torn out', full of powerful but ambivalent feelings, 'a hatred of love' which leads to 'a desecratory reaching and glancing *backward*, to where it had until then worshipped and loved' (6). In a characteristic biblical image, however, he proceeds to describe how such free spirits pass 'from the desert of these experimental years' to 'that *mature* freedom of the spirit' that enables them to 'live *experimentally*' and to the full (7). No longer burdened by conventional morality, in particular the Ten Commandments, 'the free spirit *knows* which "thou shalt" he has obeyed, and also what he now *can* do, what he only now is *permitted* to do' (10). Many of Lawrence's characters, as we shall see, achieve a similar sense of liberation by casting off these tablets of stone.

Human, All Too Human also clarifies how much further Nietzsche was prepared to go than Schopenhauer, whom he accuses of retaining a 'medieval Christian world view' (31). For Nietzsche it is not enough to offer philosophy as a substitute for religion, meeting metaphysical needs created by Christianity: 'these needs themselves can be *weakened* and *rooted out*', especially those involving 'anguish, the sighing about inner depravity, concern about salvation' (32).

Again, in direct repudiation of Schopenhauer's Kantian distinction between the noumenal and the phenomenal world, the 'thing-in-itself' and how it appears, Nietzsche argues that it 'is not the world as a thing in itself, but the world as idea (as error) that is so rich in meaning, deep, wonderful, pregnant with happiness and unhappiness'. He calls for a *'logical denial of the world'*, a re-creation which is also artistic recreation. Who, he asks, apart from theologians, cares if 'the world is a botched job'? And 'who worries about theologians these days (except the theologians)?' (33–4).

Section Three of *Human, All Too Human* addresses itself to 'Religious Life', whose origin Nietzsche attributes to ignorance of natural laws, which leads primitive people to see 'all nature' as 'the sum of the actions of conscious and intentioned beings' (81). Christianity, for Nietzsche, is primitive in this respect. He marvels at the fact that he is still woken on Sunday mornings by bells tolling for 'a Jew, crucified two thousand years ago, who said he was the son of God' (84). Nietzsche's hatred of conventional bourgeois protestantism emerges all too clearly in such passages. But he also displays an appreciation of the beauty embodied in the 'Catholic Church, and before it all ancient worship', the resonance of a 'church reverberating with deep sounds', the invocations of priests and 'the atmosphere of the architecture', the whole 'inner world of sublime, tender, intuitive, deeply contrite, blissfully hopeful moods . . . begotten in man primarily through worship'. These feelings, he believes, can be maintained 'without any conceptual content' in music and art (89–90). He proceeds to pour scorn on Jesus's asceticism and to attack him for having 'furthered men's stupidity' by taking 'the side of the intellectually weak'. The German Reformation completed this process, continuing the 'energetic protest of backward minds' against the advances in culture made by the Italian Renaissance (146–7), a broad conception of history which will be found to inform to inform Lawrence's *Twilight in Italy* (another title with Nietzschean connotations).

In *Daybreak* (1881) Nietzsche launches a savage attack on that reverence for tradition, 'the hegemony of custom' which prevents people escaping from conventional morality (*D* 10–11). Religion, according to Nietzsche, derives from fear and impotence, world-weariness and self-hatred, while Christianity is the invention of St Paul; without him, Nietzsche insists, 'we would hardly have heard of a little Jewish sect whose master died on the cross' (39). This 'tormented, very pitiable, very unpleasant man', unable to live up to the moral standards required by the law, found relief in hailing Christ as its destroyer, his 'moral despair . . . blown away . . . on the Cross'. Others followed him in enjoying liberation from sin through Christ's grace. Christianity was thus able to appeal to the poor and downtrodden, avenging themselves on the powerful 'by imagining the sudden destruction of the world to be near at hand', an argument Lawrence was to reproduce almost verbatim both in *Movements in European History* and in *Apocalypse*.

Daybreak goes on to find in Christianity 'something Oriental and something feminine' (as opposed to 'European' and 'noble'), objecting in particular to its '*diabolising* of Eros', which only succeeded in giving love the attraction of sin (45). Nietzsche pokes fun at Lenten preachers glorifying 'the torments of the 'closet', (47–8). What he most resents, however, is 'how the Bible is pummelled and punched' by Protestant preachers, who impart 'the *art of reading badly*'. The Christian appropriation of the Hebrew Bible, 'the attempt to pull the Old Testament from under the feet of the Jews' and read it typologically, every mention of a piece of wood being taken as 'a prophetic allusion to the wood of the Cross' comes in for savage satire (49–50). It is the opening book of *Daybreak* which contains the most outspoken attacks on Christianity, but there are also some astonishing passages in Book II, notably the paragraph '*On the knowledge acquired through suffering*', which speculates that on the cross Christ himself may have experienced the 'supreme sobering-up through pain', coming to realise, like the man in *The Escaped Cock*, how mistaken he had been (69–70).

The Gay Science (1882), the title of which Lawrence toyed with for what eventually became the *Study of Thomas Hardy* (*STH* 3), draws attention to its 'light-hearted defiance of convention' and its 'poetic' style, referring to the *gai saber* of troubadours in southern Europe as opposed to northern teutonic gravity (*GS* 4–6). Nietzsche portrays himself as burrowing like a proto-deconstructive 'worm' into such theological concepts as sin, repentance, grace and sanctification (178), bringing out the tensions and contradictions to be found within them. It is in *The Gay Science*, of course, that the madman makes his first appearance in the marketplace announcing the death of God to the utter incomprehension of his listeners. Even in doing so, however, the madman adopts the apocalyptic language of Christ himself, describing the churches in the terms Christ applied to the pharisees, as 'the tombs and sepulchers of God' (181–2). It is not, in Kaufmann's words, 'a dogmatic statement about a supernatural reality' so much as 'a declaration of what he takes to be a historical fact' (1968: 100). Nietzsche himself glosses the phrase 'God is dead' later in the book as the view that 'the Christian god has become unbelievable' (*GS* 279).

In *The Gay Science* Nietzsche deliberately taunts conventional Christians by mocking their most cherished beliefs. Prayer, for example, 'has been invented for those people who really never have thoughts of their own' (184). Sin is 'a Jewish invention' appropriated by Christianity, which aimed 'to "Judaize" the world'. The Christian concept of God himself is that of 'a powerful, overpowering being who enjoys revenge', an 'honor-craving Oriental in heaven' (187–8), while Christ was only possible

in a Jewish landscape . . . one over which the gloomy and sublime thunder cloud of the wrathful Jehovah was brooding continually . . . Only here could Jesus dream of his rainbow and his ladder to heaven on which God descended to man. Everywhere else good weather and sunshine were considered the rule and everyday occurrences. (189)

When the biblical images of Noah's rainbow and Jacob's ladder appear in *The Rainbow*, we should recognise (after Bakhtin) that they carry with them not only their original biblical gravity but an element of Nietzschean playfulness (as well as Lawrence's own re-accenting).

The Will to Power, another of Nietzsche's books that we know Lawrence read, comprises notes made between 1883 and 1888. Only posthumously edited and published, it begins with an outline for the whole book, registering the irony of Christianity dying 'at the hands of its own morality', 'the sense of truthfulness' which it had developed being turned against its own 'interpretations of the world and of history' (*WP* 7). Its 'Critique of Religion' begins with a similar account of the genesis of religions as given in *Human, All Too Human*: external entities are credited with being the causes of internal human feelings such as hope, resignation or repose. The inexplicable '*feeling of power*' experienced in a heightened state of consciousness is thus attributed to a higher being, a divinity, while feelings of weakness remain the property of man (85–7). The 'Critique of Religion' continues with an attack on the 'posturing and posing' of priests, their claim to exclusive possession of truth and their 'extreme fear of sensuality' (88), which leads to the attempted 'castration' of others (90–1). Nietzsche distinguishes between what he calls 'an *affirmative* Semitic religion, the product of a *ruling* class', to be found in 'the older parts of the Old Testament', and 'a *negative* Semitic religion, the product of an *oppressed* class', exemplified in the New Testament (93). These two kinds of power will reappear in Lawrence's *Apocalypse* along with Nietzsche's argument that Christianity embodies its own lust for power, a desire for revenge, on the part of 'the weak and ill-constituted', 'the morally obsessed', the weary and self-hating (95–6).

A section of *The Will to Power* entitled 'History of Christianity', contrasts genuine Christianity, the original teaching of Jesus, with Christian theology as it later developed, blaming St Paul for reversing the teaching of Jesus, turning 'a Buddhistic peace movement . . . into a pagan mystery doctrine' with its own blood-drinking ritual and constructing a theology from an 'appalling mishmash of Greek philosophy and Judaism' (100–2). Jesus, the original historical figure, thus became a mere 'motif' in a show for which Paul 'wrote the music' (108). Nietzsche has little but scorn for the 'bad manners' he finds throughout the New Testament. 'How one reacts to the New Testament,' he claims, 'is a test of whether one has any *classical taste* in one's bones', a taste which should ensure that 'one withdraws one's hand as if to avoid being soiled' by its abominable superstition. Jesus, according to Nietzsche, paid for 'having directed himself to the lowest class of Jewish society and intelligence' by being reconceived by them 'in the spirit they understood' as a 'personal redeemer' in a 'salvation story'. The New Testament is the product of 'people of the basest origin . . . raised away from even the *smell* of culture' (116–17). In spite of all this, Nietzsche still displays a hankering for the 'real' Christianity of Jesus himself. 'Christianity,' he claims, 'is still possible at any time' without being 'tied to any of the impudent dogmas that have adorned themselves with its name', doctrines such as that of 'a personal God', immortality, sin and redemption, the whole metaphysical superstructure of 'faith'. Christianity, he insists, 'is a *way of life*, not a system of beliefs. It tells us how to act, not what we ought to believe' (124–5). He continues, however, to deplore 'this systematized disfiguring and castration of life' (143), along with 'the lunatic exposition of the Bible as is still cultivated by the church' (139). His 'Critique of Morality' is similarly radical in its rejection of the herd's will to power over the strong and independent (160–1), 'the *emasculation* of a man's character' by the 'extirpation' of the passions and the belief that 'only the castrated man is a good man' (207). This, I will argue in chapter 12, is a view which informs Lawrence's writing both in *The Escaped Cock* and in *Lady Chatterley's Lover.*

That Nietzsche is opposed to Christianity rather than religion becomes even more apparent in *Thus Spoke Zarathustra*, written between 1883 and 1885, a book which was a favourite with Frieda as well as with D. H. Lawrence (Byrne 1995: 59). As with many of the mouthpieces of Lawrence's views, the device of a prophetic figure from whom the author can occasionally distance himself, a familiar convention of Romantic irony, allows Nietzsche to make his Zarathustra, based, of course, upon the founder of Zoroastrianism, play often blasphemously with biblical material. Zarathustra's account of the madman who announces the death of God, for example, involves even even more biblical parody than is in *The Gay Science.* The onlookers mock the madman in the manner of Elijah taunting the prophets of Baal: 'Has he gone on a voyage? or emigrated?' they laugh, while the madman asks, in the language of Psalm 51, 'who will wipe this blood off us? With what water could we purify ourselves? What festivals of atonement . . . shall we need to invent?' (*TSZ* 14). Other biblical elements include an Adam complaining about the theft of his rib (143), a parable of the gods laughing themselves to death when one of their number announces, 'There is one God! You shall have no other gods before me!' (201) and a mock-apocalypse entitled 'the Seven Seals (or: The Song of Yes and Amen)' (244). A section 'Of the Compassionate' suggests Man's 'original sin' is to 'have enjoyed himself too little' (112) while Zarathustra in the Prologue produces an alternative set of beatitudes: 'I love the great despisers . . . I love him who lives for knowledge . . . I love him whose soul is lavish . . . I love him who is of a free spirit and a free heart' (44–5). He also has a section 'Of Love of One's Neighbour' suggesting that this commandment of Jesus' often masks excessive love or hatred of oneself; better, in his view, to love 'the most distant', 'the man of the future', the Superman (86–8). Another section, 'Of Old and New Law-Tables', dramatically casts its rejection of the Ten Commandments in the manner of Jesus' preaching, rejecting the old law for the new before urging his followers to 'shatter the old law-tables' (219).

Perhaps Zarathustra's most fruitful suggestion, however, from Lawrence's point of view, is that had Jesus lived longer, remaining in

the desert 'far from the good and just . . . he would have learned to
live and learned to love the earth – and laughter as well' (98), which
again appears to point towards Lawrence's imaginative retelling of
the resurrection in *The Escaped Cock*. Colin Milton notices the
similarity between the symbolism of Zarathustra, who cherishes
what he calls 'my animals' (52–3), a serpent coiled around an eagle's
neck, and the symbolism of the new religion preached in *The Plumed
Serpent*. Less persuasively perhaps, he also identifies the 'three strange
angels' admitted at the end of 'The Song of a Man Who Has Come
Through' with the 'three evil things' celebrated by Zarathustra:
'*Sensual pleasure, lust for power, selfishness*' (Milton 1987: 230, 170–2). It is
certainly characteristic of both Nietzsche and Lawrence, however,
that these temptations come in the form of 'a round apple . . . a ripe,
golden apple with a soft, cool, velvety skin', which it would be sinful
not to eat (*TSZ* 206). Zarathustra also makes much of the rainbow
both as a biblical symbol of recovery after storms and as a bridge to
the Superman (78).

Beyond Good and Evil (1886) also devotes an entire section to 'The
Religious Nature', presenting Christianity as 'a protracted suicide of
reason . . . a sacrifice . . . of all freedom, all pride, all self-confidence
of the spirit', a form of 'enslavement and self-mockery, self-
mutilation' (*BGE* 57). Nietzsche again expresses his preference for
the Old over the New Testament, praising the former for its grand-
ness of style. A 'taste for the Old Testament' is seen by Nietzsche as
an Arnoldian 'touchstone' separating the literary sheep from the
philistine goats:

To have glued this New Testament, a species of rococo taste in every
respect, on to the Old Testament to form a *single* book, as 'bible', as 'the
book of books': that is perhaps the greatest piece of temerity and 'sin
against the spirit' that literary Europe has on its conscience. (61–2)

Later in *Beyond Good and Evil*, Nietzsche acknowledges the achievement of Christianity in having preserved the Bible by instilling into
the masses such reverence for it. He proceeds to explain that
'Modern philosophy . . . is, covertly or openly, *anti-Christian*' but 'by
no means anti-religious' (62). *On the Genealogy of Morals* (1887) also
develops the contrast between the Old and New Testaments, the
former presenting 'great men, a heroic landscape, and . . . the *strong
heart*' while the latter chronicles 'only the petty business of sects',
displaying a 'worrying and pawing intrusiveness towards God'.

Nietzsche is particularly dismissive of 'that most desolate of all the written outbursts', the Apocalypse (*OGM* 121–2), the subject of Lawrence's most extended biblical commentary.

Nietzsche's two books of 1888, *Twilight of the Idols* and *The Anti-Christ*, embody his final onslaught on Christianity. They are, of course, anti-Christian rather than anti-Christ, distinguishing between the admirable if misguidedly otherworldly figure who died on the cross and the mischievous followers who invented the religion that bears his name. It is Christianity which is held responsible for the '*anti-natural* castration of a God into a God of the merely good'. Again, Nietzsche displays a preference for the God of the Old Testament, who represented 'everything aggressive and thirsting for power' over the Christian God of the sick and weak (*TI* 138–9).The Bible itself is seen in this respect to document the 'falsification' of the concept of God, the reduction of Yahweh from a symbol of power into a principle opposed to life (149). Nietzsche presents an entertaining reworking of the opening chapters of Genesis in which God 'promenades in his garden: but he is bored'. So he invents man to entertain him: 'But behold, man too is bored.' So God, whose 'sympathy with the only kind of distress found in every Paradise knows no bounds', creates the animals, only to discover that this is his '*first* blunder'. Man doesn't find the animals entertaining (and certainly doesn't want to be one) so he dominates them. Whereupon God makes woman, his '*second* blunder'. She, like a true serpent, hankers after knowledge, allowing science into the world. And since 'science makes *equal to God*', this makes man a rival. So man has to be expelled from Paradise and prevented from thinking, to which end God 'invents distress, death, the danger to life in pregnancy, every kind of misery, age, toil, above all *sickness*' (with which Nietzsche, at this stage of his life, was by all too familiar). Thus the 'beginning of the Bible', according to Nietzsche, 'contains the *entire* psychology of the priest', the hatred of independent thought, the inducement of guilt and the consequent need for punishment and forgiveness (176–7). It is a powerful vision of the origins of religion as recounted, albeit unwittingly, in the opening book of the Bible, one which may well have served as a model for the many similarly subversive reworkings of Genesis to be found in Lawrence.

That Lawrence saw himself in some ways continuing the Nietzschean tradition of irreverent and critical but nevertheless prophetic writing is evidenced by the Nietzschean titles we have seen him considering for what became the *Study of Thomas Hardy*. Nietzschean arguments, as we shall see, are probably most powerfully present and most openly acknowledged in *Apocalypse*, with its careful teasing out of the strands of love and power in the Book of Revelation. But Nietzsche also features strongly in the reading of Lawrence's characters: in *The Trespasser* Helena even takes him on holiday to the Isle of Wight (*T* 66), although in the prologue to her original 'Freshwater Diary' Helen Corke had made her heroine Sieglinde, noticing a volume of Nietzsche next to a teddy bear on top of the piano, advise her lover *not* to bring it with him as 'much too heavy for the holidays' (Atkins 1992: 19). Other Lawrence characters are more critical of Nietzsche: Birkin in the 'Prologue' to *Women in Love* is presented as a 'youth of twenty-one, holding forth against Nietzsche' (*WL* 491), while Ursula in the same novel attacks Gerald Crich's 'lust for bullying – a real Wille zur Macht' (548). Lawrence himself in his *Study of Thomas Hardy* calls the 'Wille zur Macht . . . a spurious feeling', picking up, as Ursula does, some of the misogyny in Nietzsche (*STH* 104). Rawdon Lilly too distances himself from the German philosopher, insisting that the 'love-urge' must be replaced by a 'power-urge. The will-to-power – but *not* in Nietzsche's sense' (*AR* 297, my italics). Richard Somers in *Kangaroo* acknowledges his debt more openly, referring explicitly to *Thus Spoke Zarathustra* (*K* 161 and 387). The point, however, is not so much to identify particular Nietzschean references in Lawrence as to indicate that there are sufficient traces in the texts to support the view that Nietzsche, more than any other single figure, has the strongest claim to be recognised as Lawrence's poetic father, his most powerful precursor in the creative rewriting of the Bible.

It should also be recognised that Lawrence read many of Nietzsche's disciples, such as the Ukrainian Leo Shestov, the German Houston Chamberlain and the Austrian Otto Weininger. Lawrence even collaborated with his Jewish friend S. S. Koteliansky on a translation into English of a volume of Shestov whose literal title 'Apotheosis of Groundlessness' he wisely insisted on renaming *All Things Are Possible* (Kinkead-Weekes 1996: 512–13). Lawrence's foreword to the translation, originally published in 1920 and later reprinted in *Phoenix* (215–18), summarises Shestov's teaching as a belief that 'Each being is . . . a Godhead, a fountain from the unknown', a belief which Shestov himself refrains from stating for fear that it will trap his Nietzschean 'free spirit' (Shestov 1920: 11).

Shestov himself insists that we can 'know nothing of the ultimate realities of our existence' and that the 'business of philosophy is to teach men to live in uncertainty', 'not to reassure people but to upset them' (24), principles that Lawrence himself took to heart. Privately, in a letter to Koteliansky, he confessed that he found Shestov's 'many-wordedness . . . cloying, wearying,' along with his continual 'tilting' at Kantian metaphysics. But he liked his ' "flying in the face of Reason", like a cross hen' (*Letters* III 387).

Shestov, like Nietzsche, draws frequently on the Bible, as in a passage expounding his belief that 'modern educated man' is no nearer to answers to 'ultimate questions' than he was in the beginning. It was Adam and Eve's desire 'to know' which caused them to take the apple while 'Nobody has ever been able to understand why God preferred Abel's sacrifice to that of Cain' (68–9). Shestov indulges in a number of extravagant Nietzschean outbursts against conventional religion and philosophy, supporting Protestantism in its rebellion against the tendency of medieval Catholicism 'to maim and mutilate a man *ad maiorem gloriam Dei*' (205). He also, like Bakhtin, celebrates Dostoevsky's exposure of the Church's tendency to repress the uncomfortable teaching of Christ (116–17). Lawrence would go on to write the preface to Koteliansky's translation of *The Grand Inquisitor* (1930), the section of *The Brothers Karamazov* in which Jesus learns how unpalatable his teaching has become (*Phoenix* 283–91). Again, the point worth emphasising here is the extent to which both Shestov and Lawrence could be said to have learnt from Nietzsche the potential of biblical narrative to be retold against the grain of its original authorial intention.

Houston Stewart Chamberlain and Otto Weininger have become infamous because of their proto-Nazi racial theories, but Schneider sees Chamberlain behind the *Study of Thomas Hardy*'s contrast between 'Law' and 'Love', the latter represented by Jesus, celebrated as an individualist and rebel, no longer a slave but a Nietzschean master (Schneider 1986: 160–1). Weininger too, consistently dismissive of the Jewish race as 'negative' in religious matters, meanly monotheistic in contrast with the 'superabundant religious richness' of the Aryan race, may well have contributed to the portrait in that book of the jealous single God of the Old Testament as a 'female conception' in contrast to the 'masculine principle, the generative element' to be found in Christianity (Delavenay 1972: 311). Again, however, the point is not to measure 'influence' but to recognise that

Lawrence was part of a widespread Nietzschean movement in European thought to repudiate certain elements in its Judaeo-Christian roots.

The overall effect of Lawrence's reading of Nietzsche and of his disciples can only have been to increase, at least for a time, his hostility towards Christianity. John Jones, in whose house Lawrence lodged throughout his time at Croydon, recalls how 'very bitter' Lawrence was about religion, a subject on which they 'used to argue a lot' (Nehls 1957: 83). Bertrand Russell recalls similarly fierce disagreements in 1915, when Lawrence had 'developed the whole philosophy of fascism before the politicians had thought of it', claiming that such thinking 'led straight to Auschwitz' (Kinkead-Weekes 1996: 810). In an extraordinary letter of October 1908, about the time when Jessie Chambers claimed he first encountered Nietzsche, Lawrence paraded his lack of any vestiges of Christian sympathy with the weak and degenerate, sardonically proposing to 'build a lethal chamber' into which he would usher 'all the sick, the halt, and the maimed' to the sound of a military band playing the 'Hallelujah Chorus' (*Letters* I 81). It would be unfair, of course, to take this outburst as a serious suggestion but it is worth noticing the vehemence with which Lawrence at this stage of his career repudiates the familiar images of the Bible. The reference to 'the maimed, and the halt', for instance, comes from Luke 14: 21 while not only the Hallelujah Chorus but the gentle leading suggest Isaiah (40: 11). Like Nietzsche, in other words, Lawrence displays a terrifying tendency to turn the Bible against itself, to repudiate the Judaeo-Christian tradition in its own phrases, contributing to the tension which pervades all of his writing. What Lawrence, like Nietzsche, seems to be struggling with more than anything else is the Bible and with that the whole of the religious tradition in which he had been brought up. This, as we shall now see, is apparent even in his early work.

CHAPTER 5

Pre-war poetry and fiction: Adam and Eve come through

Lawrence's writing up to the First World War includes a large amount of poetry, a number of short stories and three novels, which I will consider in that order, focusing upon a major concern in all three genres with the biblical account of Adam and Eve. Their temptation by the serpent, eating of the forbidden fruit and subsequent banishment raises for Lawrence fundamental questions about Judaeo-Christian morality, especially its privileging of the spirit over the body, a binary opposition not evident in the earliest strands of the biblical narrative. The word 'flesh', for example, appears as something to celebrate more than a dozen times in Genesis, three times at the end of chapter two, when Adam celebrates Eve as 'flesh of my flesh', a partner with whom he can become 'one flesh', living together as man and wife, 'naked' and not 'ashamed' (Gen. 2: 23–5). Lawrence's early work, I want to claim, attempts to recover from Genesis a celebration of the flesh, too readily subordinated to the spirit or word in the Christian tradition. Adam and Eve become for him the biblical types for most of the lovers in the writing of this period, most notably in his poetic account of the way he and Frieda had 'come through' their various difficulties.

The opening chapters of Genesis, as Lawrence could have read in Blatchford's *God and My Neighbour* (1904) or heard from his minister Reid, present very different accounts of creation. Elohim, the God of the opening chapter, taken by scholars to be the work of the Priestly Writer, is solemn and majestic, very much transcendent, in complete control of the whole process of creation, which is orderly and systematic (Habel 1971: 27). He tells his creatures, including man, 'Be fruitful, and multiply' (Gen. 1: 22, 27), although He displays little interest in the manner in which they should do so, in 'flesh' as such. Yahweh, on the other hand, the God of chapters two and three (the different name helping to identify this earlier strand of the text), is much more down to earth, the product of an earlier, more anthropo-morphic theology. He moulds man out of clay, breathes life into his nostrils, plants him a garden, models animals to keep him company and brings forth Eve from Adam's rib. It is Yahweh who forbids Adam and Eve on pain of death to eat of the fruit of the tree of the knowledge of good and evil (2: 16–17), and when they do so (Eve having been persuaded by the serpent that they will not die but become 'as gods, knowing good and evil'), curses all three of them (3: 14–17). Nevertheless, He also shows them a certain pity, making them coats to cover their nakedness (3: 21), while His motives for expelling them actually bear out what the serpent said (as well as the name of the tree); He expresses concern that 'the man is become as one of us, to know good and evil' and decides to banish him from Eden 'lest he put forth his hand and take also of the tree of life, and eat, and live for ever' (3: 23–4). These ambiguities in the biblical narrative have not been ironed out by centuries of orthodox Christian interpretation, which from the fourth century has been dominated by Augustine's notion of original sin, laying the blame for all subsequent human weakness, especially the temptations of the flesh, upon Adam and Eve. There is little in Genesis itself, however, to suggest that sexuality is evil in itself; on the contrary, as we have seen, prelapsarian Adam and Eve are presented at the end of chapter 2 as 'naked' and 'not ashamed'. Lawrence is therefore able to claim that his reading of Genesis, attempting to recover the glory of the flesh, is truer to the original than subsequent Christian interpretations.

Lawrence's fascination with Adam and Eve went beyond the account in Genesis itself. At the end of 1908, he sent Jessie Chambers a copy of Charles Doughty's long poem, *Adam Cast Forth* (a self-consciously midrashic development of the biblical narrative and its pseudepigraphal offspring which features significantly in *The Trespasser*) with instructions to note the passage 'where Eve, after long separation, finds Adam', who 'tells her to bind herself to him with the vine strands, lest they be separated again by the Wind of God' (*Letters* I 95). This, of course, is a complex manner of saying that he misses her, which would only make sense to a couple already conditioned to perceiving themselves as characters from the Bible. But it was not only to Jessie Chambers that Lawrence described his own life in terms of biblical events or characters, especially those of Genesis; he called Louie Burrows 'strong and rosy as the gates of

Eden' (I 195) and likened an unidentified but presumably married woman, who 'plucked me', to 'Potiphar's wife', the attempted seducer of Joseph in Genesis 39: 12 (I 208). It was a habit of mind which never left him, whether in his correspondence or in his creative writing, symptomatic of his saturation in the Bible.

Some of Lawrence's earliest poetry celebrates the prelapsarian Adam and Eve in the Garden of Eden. 'Renascence', for example, first published in *Love Poems* in 1913 but existing in an earlier draft entitled 'Renaissance', which Worthen dates 'by January 1909' (Worthen 1991: 480), presents Jessie Chambers as Eve with Haggs Farm as paradise. Both poems describe a range of animals and birds to be found on the farm, which is 'wider than paradise' before turning in the final two stanzas to Eve herself, from whom the persona of the poem (Lawrence playing the part of Adam) has learnt to borrow their instinctive wisdom. The earlier version ends by celebrating Eve's kisses as teaching more than her words; the second acknowledges the whole valley 'fleshed like me' (*CP* 38). Both emphasise the importance of the 'flesh' and of 'animal' instincts as central to Lawrence's concerns (and to his reading of Genesis) although his Eve would become less conventional once Frieda assumed the role.

Another poem which first appeared in *Love Poems*, 'Michael Angelo', describes 'The Creation of Adam' as mediated by that painter in the Sistine Chapel, with additional intertextual allusions to Blake. It begins with a series of questions addressed to Adam as generic man:

> Who shook thy roundness in his finger's cup?
> Who sunk his hands in firmness down thy sides . . . (*CP* 69)

These questions, as in 'The Tyger', are rhetorical, celebrating the dynamic, artistic process of creation. The final stanza of an earlier draft describes the imparting of breath with particular vividness before urging Adam, 'kissed' into life by God, to keep that 'kiss from the adultress' theft' (933). This draft appears to be so early as to guard moralistically against such 'theft', to accept the conventional contrast between the love of God and the love of other human beings. The later version alters the last two lines, making them less moralistic and altogether more sceptical. God imparts the less unambiguously wonderful gift of 'dim breath's hastening hiss', leaving the persona of the poem to ask, 'Whence cometh this, that thou must guard from theft?' An additional stanza stresses the mysterious nature of this gift of existence, about whose source and purpose it is less clear. These alterations are significant; what began as a straightforward rendering of the wonder of creation gains in scepticism about the 'unknown moulder' whose 'trace' has survived in the curves of Adam's form.

'Eve', another early poem printed among Lawrence's 'Juvenilia' (*CP*), is altogether uncritical of conventional doctrine, providing a theologically straightforward if stylistically mannered retelling of the biblical narrative of the fall. It begins with a Miltonic Eve 'swinging her dusky limbs disconsolate', straying into the forest of Eden, eating the apple to assuage her hunger and 'discontent', and giving the unnamed 'man' a taste of her 'sorrows' before walking 'Out of Eden, weary with the wistfulness of her silent tomorrows' (866–7). The very absence of narrative augmentation or even interpretation, combined with the presence of too much verbal colouring, confirms the likelihood of an early dating for this poem. The mature Lawrence is never content simply to reproduce biblical material without giving it some interpretive slant. Even in 'The Cherry Robbers', written by January 1909, where 'an Eastern girl' is depicted with 'crimson cherries' hanging like jewels in her hair, surrounded by the bodies of three dead birds, 'robberlings / Stained with red dye', there is an intriguing ambiguity about the challenge she offers in the final stanza:

> Against the haystack a girl stands laughing at me,
> Cherries hung round her ears.
> Offers me her scarlet fruit: I will see
> If she has any tears. (36–7)

The poem, only obliquely about Adam and Eve although the girl's offering of fruit does suggest the biblical model, leaves it open to what extent her proffered gift is dangerous. The circumspection of the male persona, the Adam figure in the poem, not quite sure if he should indulge himself, if the dead birds represent a bad omen, or if tragic consequences will necessarily follow, is comically self-deprecating. Not for the first time, Lawrence displays an endearing ability to laugh at himself in the role of Adam, reluctant to commit himself to 'sin'.

Three more volumes of Lawrence's early poetry were published during the war: *Amores*, 'a sort of inner history of my life, from 20 to 26' (*Letters* II 521), published in 1916, *Look! We Have Come Through!*, an equally autobiographical account of his elopement with Frieda, published the following year, and *New Poems*, 'mistitled, apparently by Secker, since the contents are largely from his earliest years' (*Letters* III 11), published in 1918. *Amores*, like so much of Lawrence's work, is transparently autobiographical, describing the impact of identifiable events in Lawrence's early life such as the death of his mother and the struggle with Jessie Chambers. 'Monologue of a Mother', for example, first published in 1914, presents the persona of the poem struggling to accept that 'the lips and the eyes of God are behind a veil', failing to provide comfort at death (*CP* 48), while 'Brother and Sister' has the bereaved son resolving like the Israelites, to bear 'the ark / Of the covenant onwards' (131–2). 'Last Words to Muriel', an earlier version of a poem retitled 'To Miriam' in *Amores*, laments the sadness he has caused his lover, who has as a result become 'a God-joy diminished' (945). The later version describes the face 'hardening, / Warping the perfect image of God' (946). 'A Spiritual Woman' (depersonalised and retitled 'These Clever Women' in *Collected Poems*) is more aggressive towards her, attacking her cold concept of 'God like geometry / Completing his circles and working cleverly' (949). Like Blake, however, Lawrence resents a mechanical Newtonian view of the universe.

Biblical images in these poems are relatively rare, incidental rather than central to their meaning. 'Mating' (retitled 'Come Spring, Come Sorrow' in *Collected Poems*), gives the conventional attempt to persuade his coy mistress to join the rest of the natural world in fertility a biblical twist, pointing in particular to a drake 'proud/As Abraham, whose seed shall multiply' (126). There are frequent celebrations of the grandeur of creation, as in 'The Wild Common', where 'All that is right, all that is good, all that is God takes substance' (34). The version of 'Dreams Old and Nascent' which appeared in *Amores* celebrates somewhat Whitmanesquely 'the quick, restless Creator moving through the mesh / Of men, vibrating in ecstasy through the rounded flesh' (925). Even the boys in the persona's class reveal 'the unseen Shaper', 'the melting, fusing Force', 'the great Thing labouring through the whole round flesh of the world' (926). Other poems such as 'Discipline', first published in 1912, reveal some of the frustrations of teaching, the difficulty of learning not to 'trespass' on the children, who 'draw their sap from Godhead' (93). The first version of 'The Schoolmaster', published in the same year, depicts a scripture lesson, with the boys 'muttering the psalms' while 'furtively from among the texts / Forbidden things and thoughts come fluttering' (911). 'The Punisher', also published in 1912, describes the guilt he feels at causing his pupils pain in terms of a reversal of Moses' experience before the burning bush:

> The fire rose up in the bush and blazed apace,
> The thorn-leaves crackled and twisted and sweated in anguish;
> Then God left the place.

He likens himself to a 'desolate . . . church whose lights are put out / And doubt enters in' (94). Like Nietzsche in *Human, All Too Human*, Lawrence portrays others being drawn by bells to a 'Weeknight Service' while he and nature look on indifferent: 'The wise old trees / Drop their leaves with a faint, sharp hiss of contempt' until the 'damned bells cease'and 'the droning church / Is peopled with shadows and wailing' (54). Conventional Christianity in these poems fails to reflect their strong sense of the grandeur of creation.

Look! We Have Come Through!, while equally autobiographical in origin, makes the Bible much more central to its narrative. Some of Lawrence's friends found his dramatisation of himself and Frieda as Adam and Eve unintentionally funny. Bertrand Russell famously refused to look while Cynthia Asquith wrote in embarrassment of 'some poems all about bellies and breasts which he gave me to read' (Kinkead-Weekes 1996: 411). Others were shocked. The publishers Chatto and Windus sent Lawrence's agent J. B. Pinker a list of 'proposed modifications' and questioned 'the good taste of the titles 'Candlemas' and 'Eve's Mass' as applied to poems of an amorous character' (*Letters* III 145n). This, of course, was to miss the point. *Look! We Have Come Through!* both 'mimes the religious year of the soul from the Day of the Dead to Candlemas' and 'at the same time rewrites Genesis', its Eve being 'reborn , not from the rib but by exchanges of blood with Adam' (Kinkead-Weekes 1996: 361). Lawrence, according to Catherine Carswell, wanted originally to call it 'Man and Woman' (*CP* 1007), advertising the typical rather than the typological qualities of the deuteragonists. The 'Foreword' describes theirs as 'an essential story' while the 'Argument' emphasises the positive twist he gives to the biblical account of Adam and Eve, referring to their final attainment of 'some condition of blessedness' (191). This Adam and Eve, in other words, are not content passively to accept their expulsion from Eden.

Many of the poems in the sequence allude specifically to the Book of Genesis. 'She Looks Back', for example, tentatively dated May 1912 (Kinkead-Weekes 1996: 741), develops the theme of guilt, discussing Frieda's misery over abandoning her children with reference to Lot's wife, turned into a pillar of salt in Genesis 19: 26 because she disobeyed the angels' instructions not to look back on the destroyed city of Sodom. 'How I know that glitter of salt', writes Lawrence, 'Not tears, but white sharp brine / Making hideous your eyes.' Frieda is cursed for being like Lot's wife, for turning back to the past, to her children, and so bringing down upon Lawrence a sense of guilt at being the cause of her tears, which are described as the 'pillar of salt, the whirling, horrible column of salt, like a waterspout / That has enveloped me!' (207). Later in the poem Lawrence tries to soften his anger, remembering that she never looked 'quite back'. The biblical story, it could be argued, simply supplies the frame within which Lawrence explores his own resentment at Frieda's 'disobedience' (208). But these biblical images persist, consistently undermining conventional Judaeo-Christian morality. The following poem in the sequence, for example, 'On the Balcony', written later that summer, restages some of the elements in the Flood narrative. The two lovers look down from their balcony on a scene which includes a storm, 'a faint, lost ribbon of rainbow' and a departing boat. The persona asks, in Arnoldian vein, as at the end of 'Dover Beach', 'what have we but each other?' (208–9), a question which seems to imply a rejection of the divine covenant, a refusal to join Noah in the ark of salvation. This would also appear to be the significance of another poem which contains a rainbow, 'Manifesto', probably written in the summer of 1916 and inserted towards the end of the sequence, which resolves in the final section not to 'look before and after' but to '*be, now*'. Even this poem, however, continues to quote the Bible apparently without irony, asserting with St Paul (1 Cor.13: 12) 'We shall know in full' (268). The apostle's celebration of charity is here transferred to a more earthy form of love.

Other poems in this sequence which develop the characterisation of Adam and Eve against the grain of their portrait in the Bible include 'Why Does She Weep?', also probably dating from 1912, which presses the question in its title further ('Are you afraid of God / in the dark?') before the persona of the poem asserts, 'I am not afraid of God', confidently rewriting Genesis 3 so that it is now God who is commanded to 'come forth':

Now in the cool of the day
it is we who walk in the trees
and call to God 'Where art thou?'
And it is he who hides. (*CP* 231)

The point of the biblical story has been totally changed to become
an irreverent challenge to God, as in Nietzsche's version of Genesis 3
in *The Anti-Christ.*

'Lady Wife', probably written in the winter of 1912, rewrites
another part of Genesis, the visit of the angels announcing to
Abraham the imminent birth of a son in chapter 18. Only this time
the angels are dismissed and the woman is told to forget 'the fruit of
your womb' 'and put them / Into the fire / Of Sodom' (235).
Lawrence characteristically combines the typological (the annunciation first to Sarah and later, of course, to Mary) with the personal
(his continuing resentment of Frieda's regret at losing her children
along with her husband). The angels who visited Abraham return in
'Song of a Man Who Has Come Through', dated '1914 or later,'
which also begins with a clear echo of Nietzsche: 'Not I! Not I! but
the wind that blows through me', a line which gives a Shelleyan
accent to *The Gay Science*'s 'Not I! Not I! but a *God* through my
instrumentality!' (Sagar 1982: 46). It proceeds with a Whitmanesque
celebration of 'the wonder that bubbles into my soul' before ending
with a biblical knocking at the door at night: 'it is the three strange
angels. / Admit them, admit them' (*CP* 250). The rewriting of
Genesis here is characteristic of Lawrence: the poem from which
Frieda took the title of her celebration of his individual genius draws
attention to its complex intertextuality, re-accenting Genesis through
Nietzsche, Shelley and Whitman. In Derrida's terminology,
Nietzsche is 'grafted' on to Genesis to produce an explosion of
meaning different from both.

Perhaps the most aggressive retelling of material from the Book of
Genesis occurs in 'Paradise Re-entered', tentatively dated early 1913,
in which the exiled lovers pass through the 'flames of fierce love'
back into the 'sinless being' from which they were unfairly discarded,
storming 'the angel-guarded / Gates of the long-discarded /
Garden'. They refuse to accept that they have done anything wrong,
defying conventional morality with a confidence that again
advertises its Nietzschean genealogy: 'Back beyond good and evil /
Return we.' Eve is encouraged to resist God's control, deliberately to
'dishevel' her hair for their 'bliss-drenched revel' (242–3). Another

poem tentatively dated February 1913, originally entitled 'Eve's Mass' but changed to 'Birth Night' under pressure from the publisher, develops the typological connection between Eve and Mary in order to describe Eve being 'born again' through Adam's 'veins of fire' (239). Their sexual union, it is claimed, amounts to a rebirth, a birth eclipsing Christmas itself:

> This is Noël for me.
> To-night is a woman born
> Of the man in me. (240)

'Elysium', initially entitled 'Eden', claims to have found a place 'Lovelier than Paradise', in which Eve waits for 'watchers to shut the gate' before approaching and taking him by the hand in order to 'set me free' (261). It would be a dull reader who had not grasped by the end of the sequence that Lawrence was casting himself and Frieda as a new Adam and Eve who had freed themselves from the chains of conventional morality and found rebirth in sexual fulfilment.

Adam and Eve, as we have seen, give way typologically at moments in the sequence to Mary and Joseph, opening up an additional fund of biblical resonance. 'Ballad of a Wilful Woman', first called 'Trier' presumably because that was where it was written in May 1912, casts Frieda as Mary descending from her donkey, saying goodbye to Joseph (Ernest Weekley) and giving him her child before entering the arms of 'a dark-faced stranger'. Poor Joseph is left 'watching evermore' (200). This somewhat triumphalistic reversal of the biblical tale is repeated in the 'Third Part' of the poem in which Mary, still wearing 'her blue, blue mantle', tells Joseph that she's been to Cythera (in other words, encountered Venus), before joining her lover, who is waiting with a suggestively 'lifted oar' on a 'heaving sea' (201). Lawrence, to be fair, portrays himself more modestly later in the poem as a beggar attempting to scrape a living by selling 'curious liquors' distilled from the berries and 'flowers of pain', a clear recognition of the autobiographical nature of his writing (202–3).

One of the most powerful poems of the sequence, written in 1912, first published in 1914, but omitted from the first edition of *Look! We Have Come Through!* on the insistence of the publishers (1009–10), portrays Weekley more sympathetically as a Christ-figure. 'Meeting Among the Mountains' describes an encounter with a crucifix, the 'beautiful young man's body' hanging 'White and loose at last, with all the pain / Drawn on his mouth, eyes broken at last by his pangs'. The persona is disturbed while gazing at this suffering figure by a peasant whose 'accusing eyes . . . black with misery and hate' he conflates with those of both Christ and Weekley, feeling 'a chill of anguish, trying to say / The joy I bought was not too highly priced' (225). Lawrence's earlier devotion to the suffering Christ here adds depth and resonance to the guilt he feels about the misery he has inflicted on Weekley. He leaves the carved Christ 'breathing the frozen memory of his wrong', harbouring 'clenched in his fists the shame, / And in his belly the smouldering hate of me' while the persona suffers disturbingly consumptive symptoms turning his 'lungs to stone' and making him feel 'the dead Christ weighing on my bone' (226). Later in the sequence, in 'New Heaven and Earth', as later in his career, he cannot resist the temptation to play the role of Christ himself, writing of the awakening of desire as a form of resurrection, 'rising from the tomb' (260). The sequence ends with a poem called 'Craving for Spring', not written until February 1917, which celebrates the renewal of the whole of the natural world, imposing a positive ending upon its liturgical year. Even this poem, however, introduces a note of personal doubt, praying at the end not to 'die on this Pisgah blossoming with violets' nor to be deprived like Moses of possession of the Promised Land (273–4).

Mark Kinkead-Weekes argues that the biblical framework imposed upon these autobiographical poems for their appearance in volume form improves them, that the 'simpler 1912 poetry has been deepened and supplanted by later understanding'. Even the earlier poems, he suggests, should not be read as 'a too-intimate confession' since Lawrence shapes his own experience by creating a 'dramatic *mythos*', a plot borrowed from the biblical original (Kinkead-Weekes 1996: 359).This may be so but the flashes of autobiographical emotion, whether, anger, love or guilt, make the retelling of the biblical narrative of the expulsion from Eden more intense. Lawrence and Frieda had experienced what exclusion, isolation and guilt felt like, which gives a real edge to the cycle. They had also, Lawrence claimed, experienced paradise, an autograph draft of his poem 'Elysium' recently discovered inside a copy of *Love Poems* celebrating 'Eve discovered' as the 'perfect consummation, / The final paradisal One' (*Independent* 21/11/98, p. 9). The framework, in other words, is biblical but the feelings are personal.

Some of Lawrence's early short stories play similar variations on the same myth. Two stories written between 1911 and 1913, although not published until they were collected in *A Modern Lover* in 1934, parade their biblical references in their titles. 'The Old Adam', written in 1911, tells the story of a young man surprised to discover violent impulses within himself. There may well be an allusion here to St Paul wanting to crucify 'the old man' in Romans 6: 6 and to the baptismal prayer to bury 'the old Adam in this child' (*LAH* 233) but there is also the Lawrentian point that men deny their animal nature, their derivation from 'sinful' Adam, at their peril. 'New Eve and Old Adam', written in 1913, may derive its title from a German novel translated into English as *The Old Adam and the New Eve*, which Lawrence gave to his friend Alan Chambers in 1910, a novel in which 'the new Eve . . . finds it hard to bear the fetters of her dependence on Man, but is lost when she attempts to shake them off' (247). Lawrence's story involves a row between newly-weds (written within a year of his own elopement with Frieda) in which the wife makes the feminist point, to be repeated by Anna Brangwen in *The Rainbow*, that her husband's conception of her (moulded, of course, by Genesis 2: 21–2) is inadequate: 'Your idea of your woman is that she is an expansion, no, a *rib* of yourself, without any existence of her own. That I am a being by myself is more than you can grasp' (*LAH* 182). These stories, it should be acknowledged, fall more into the category of significant allusion than wholesale rewriting of biblical material. But Lawrence uses the allusions to subvert traditional biblical interpretations of human nature in the first story and to suggest a realignment of relations between the sexes in the second.

Biblical allusions perform a similar function in some of the stories collected in *The Prussian Officer and Other Stories* in 1914. 'Daughters of the Vicar', the first draft of which, composed in July 1911, was entitled 'Two Marriages', presents a rather obvious contrast between one of the eponymous daughters, Louisa, who marries a miner and is physically fulfilled, and another, Mary, who attempts to deny the 'flesh', the body, in favour of the 'spirit' (*PO* 55–7). Lawrence's hostility to orthodox Christianity is all too evident in his portrait of the vicar Mary is forced by her parents to marry, described in the first draft as 'an abortion, a foetus of a man' (214) and in the final version as 'a perfect Christian' who prays with a 'fine lucidity' (49–50). It is not altogether clear which Lawrence regards as the more damning description. In the first draft, Mary realises that there is 'a lack of reverence', a lack of genuine respect for the parishioners he serves (217). Her decision to marry him is entirely based on the 'religious ideal' of 'self-sacrifice' (218), to undermine which the story is patently written. By contrast, her sister Louisa is seen to be a more admirable type of Mary, valuing the 'flesh' of her husband and of the child she is carrying even if she only realises this on his death. The comparison with the mother of Jesus is achieved by the slightest of allusions: Louisa is 'troubled in her heart' (73) as her precursor was 'troubled' at the annunciation (Luke 1: 29). The subtlety of this reversal of traditional Christian views both of Mary and of the relative value of body and spirit which she demonstrates contrasts with the cruder anti-Christian polemic of the rest of the story.

'The Thorn in the Flesh', first written in June 1913 with the title 'Vin Ordinaire,' also involves a re-awakening to the value of physical instinctive love, young Emilie being awakened by the soldier Bachmann to 'a new world' in which 'she moved and had her being' (36). This is clearly *not* what St Paul had in mind when assuring the citizens of Athens that it is in Christ that 'we live, and move, and have our being' (Acts 18: 27). It is St Paul too who is subverted in the title of the story, the allusion being to 2 Corinthians 12: 7, where he glories in his infirmities, in particular the unspecified 'thorn in the flesh'. Again these allusions are mostly subversive, Christianity being seen to have forgotten the importance of the flesh as celebrated in Genesis. Christianity is associated by Lawrence with an attempt to spiritualise this, as in Christ's own use of Genesis 2: 23–4 not to celebrate the 'flesh' but to preach the indissolubility of marriage (Matt. 19: 5–6).

A similar contrast between Old and New Testament values informs another early story collected in *The Prussian Officer*, 'The Christening,' written in June 1912. In this case, however, the narrative is more finely balanced between the two (or rather, against both). As Brian Finney describes him in the Introduction to the Cambridge edition, the father in this tale is 'an Old Testament patriarch whose vitality . . . negates the "vague tenderness" (175: 36) of the New Testament vicar come to christen the innocent bastard child' of the old man's daughter (xix). The vicar rejoices that a 'man-child is born unto us' (177), echoing the words of Jeremiah 20: 15, themselves, of course, appropriated by Christians for celebrating the birth of Christ. The father, who retains elements of his prophetic vitality to the end, certainly has the last word, echoing

Isaiah's celebration of the joy with which 'the trees of the field shall clap their hands' (Isaiah 55: 12) while his daughters shrink back, 'sullen' (180). The 'meaning' of this story (apart from the Nietzschean contrast between Old Testament vitality and New Testament morality) is mercifully unclear, as is that of 'The Shades of Spring', a story which went through much revision and many different titles between its first draft of 1910 and the final version of 1914. Common to all the versions is the return of a young man to the girl and the paradisal surroundings of his youth, only to find his entry barred by her new lover. He is forced not only 'to recognize that he has become no more than a trespasser in this former Garden of Eden' but that his Eve now 'reproaches him for being unnaturally bodiless and failing to consummate their love affair sexually' (xxiv). Again, Lawrence can be seen to undermine conventional Christian readings of Genesis which play down its celebration of the flesh.

Adam and Eve continue to play an important role in Lawrence's first three novels, the first of which, originally called 'Laetitia', he began at Easter 1906. The final version, published as *The White Peacock* in 1911, is a lament for lost innocence which plays heavily on the myth of the expulsion from the Garden of Eden, with chapters rather pointedly entitled 'Dangling the Apple' and 'The Fascination of the Forbidden Apple'. But the point of the fall as it is re-marked in the novel is that its lovers, its Adams and Eves, finding themselves subject to sexual attraction in a rural paradise, become self-conscious and guilt-ridden about their bodies, developing a harmful knowledge of what they *mistakenly* see as evil. The first-person narrator Cyril Beardsall, the first of many autobiographical characters in Lawrence's fiction, develops the imagery of Genesis, complaining to his friend Emily, like Paul Morel to Miriam in *Sons and Lovers*, that her spirituality is too bodiless: 'You think the flesh of the apple is nothing, nothing. You only care for the eternal pips. Why don't you snatch your apple and eat it, and throw the core away' (*WP* 69). Later in the novel Emily is depicted at one with nature: 'Like Eve in a meadow in Eden,' says George, 'and Adam's shadow somewhere on the grass', to which she responds, playfully perhaps but still revealing a distrust of the other sex, 'No – no Adam' (208). She clearly resents the complications of sexuality disturbing her self-contained tranquillity. Not that their surroundings are entirely Edenic; nature is depicted in the novel as wasteful when they see that 'the great red apples were being shaken from the Tree [*sic*] to be left to rot' (211), the biblical allusion being even more obvious in the manuscript reference to 'the Tree of Life' (521). The whole world, it seems, has fallen and this is nowhere more evident than in the relations between men and women in the novel, none of which bear healthy fruit.

The symbolism throughout this novel is perhaps too obvious, whether biblical, as in these allusions, or in the episode which gave the novel its eventual title in which a shrieking white peacock leaves its mark on a statue of an angel in the graveyard of a rotten church. The violently anticlerical gamekeeper Annable, himself once trained as a clergyman, does not fail to draw his conclusions about the state of the church, conclusions reinforced by the way in which some of the most sympathetic characters in the novel find their vitality sapped by religion: George has to suffer his daughter's pious lecturing about God loving nice church-goers like her mother and herself (312) while Alice has to trot to chapel with her husband 'like a lamb' (316). In the original manuscript her complaint had been even more specific: 'He's a deacon at the Congos, and lugs me to chapel twice every Sunday' (395). The final version of the novel erases such traces of the bitterness Lawrence felt about his own particular tradition but retains evidence of his continuing fascination with biblical myth, which emerges even in slight references, as when Lettie is presented expressing her moods on the piano, playing 'the little trills as if she were waltzing up the ladder of Jacob's dream like the damsels in Blake's pictures' (25), a reference to a small water-colour by Blake entitled *Jacob's Dream* and subtitled 'Vide genesis, chap. xxviii, ver. 12' (359). With Lawrence, as in Blake, a reader most definitely does need to 'see Genesis', to pick up the biblical references, in order to appreciate the extent of its Blakean re-marking of Genesis.

Sexual relations in a fallen world are also central to Lawrence's second novel, *The Trespasser*, published in 1912, although once more the fall, as far as Lawrence is concerned, lies not so much in the taking of the apple but in the failure to enjoy it. Based upon the tragic experiences of his friend Helen Corke, whose lover had hanged himself the previous year, this novel enjoyed the Wagnerian title 'The Saga of Siegmund' when it was first written in 1910. It laments the failure of its hero Siegmund, living at a time in which the old order, based upon conventional Christian morality, is collapsing but still powerful, to free himself of the guilt incurred in breaking the commandment against adultery. The label 'Trespasser' is one that advertises the failure of a nominally Christian society actually to follow the advice of its founder to 'forgive . . . that your Father . . . may forgive you your trespasses' (Mark 11: 25). In terms of the old order his 'trespass' is that of adultery; the doomed love affair on the Edenic Isle of Wight is presented as a battle between conventional Christian morality, symbolised by a crucifix which makes Siegmund feel 'very heavy, sad and at fault in presence of the Christ', and a Nietzschean 'will to life' which momentarily lights up the world and makes him feel like 'a happy priest of the sun' (*T* 87–9). When he can escape the feelings of guilt at abandoning his wife, Siegmund enjoys the beauty of the natural world, worshipping like Haeckel in 'the nave of the night' as if it were a cathedral: 'it was all sacred, whatever the God might be' (127–8). Helena, his lover, seated among the rock-pools, also experiences the sacredness of the world in an echo of Moses' experience of the burning bush (Exod. 3: 3) although it is the sea which she feels blazing with 'the fire of God', with 'his white incandescence' (*T* 138).

The implicit comparison of the two lovers with Adam and Eve is reinforced by references to the long poem *Adam Cast Forth* by Charles Doughty which, as we have seen, Lawrence had himself sent to Jessie Chambers on its publication in 1908. This 'Sacred Drama in Five Songs refers in its epigraph to a particular *"Judaeo-Arabian Legend"* or midrash in which "Adam and Hawwa, cast forth from PARADISE, fell down in several places of the Earth: whence they, after age-long wandering, meet together again upon a Mountain"' (Doughty 1908). Doughty is probably referring to 'The Life of Adam and Eve', a Latin text of which was published in 1878, although there are a number of other 'Adam books' which would also fit his description (Sparks 1984: 141–3). The 'list of persons' in Doughty's sacred drama informs readers that Adama, Adam's wife, was renamed Hawwa after giving birth, which explains why Siegmund is made to mutter 'Hawwa, – Eve – Mother!' when he wakes like Adam to see Helena in all her beauty standing before him (*T* 103). It certainly helps to explain how Helena, herself closing her eyes from the oppressive sun,

felt a sympathy with Adama in 'Adam Cast Forth.' Her mind traced again the tumultuous, obscure strugglings of the two, forth from Eden through the primitive wildernesses, and she felt sorrowful. Thinking of Adam blackened with struggle, she looked down at Siegmund. (118)

The narrator, here referring to a retelling in English verse of a Latin version of an ancient Jewish legend which was itself a reworking of the original biblical myth, has grafted several layers of interpretation upon the original biblical narrative.

Lawrence develops these layers of interpretation in his own anti-Christian manner, once more retelling the story of creation and fall with more sympathy for the trespassers. When Siegmund fails to sympathise with Helena's guilty reaction to their breaking of the commandments, she begins to wonder whether her love is an illusion, whether she (rather than God) has not created him in her own image: 'Was he the real clay, and that other, her beloved, only the breathing of her soul upon this?' (125). Unable to cope with her sobbing, Siegmund, like Adam in Genesis 3: 7, feels, 'It was all exposed. He wanted to hide, to cover himself from the openness; and there was not even a bush under which he could find cover' (127). Lawrence here alters the motivation of Adam's shame: Siegmund is unable to cope with emotional rather than physical nakedness. Later in the novel, when he comes to Waterloo to see her off on another trip to the Isle of Wight, Helena recovers for a moment 'some of her old protective grace, her "Hawwa" spirit' (196). But the moment passes and she travels to their Eden without him. Unable to cope with the role of moral trespasser in which conventional religion has cast him, Siegmund hangs himself. Readers are clearly encouraged not to do likewise but to throw off the yoke of Judaeo-Christian morality and thereby regain both Eve and paradise.

Lawrence's third novel, *Sons and Lovers*, has not been widely recognised as a novel about religion. But Charles Rossman finds within it a Lawrencian gospel which reverses the Johannine emphasis on the spirit, reverting to a celebration of the flesh to be found in the opening chapters of Genesis (1970: 31–4). Avrom Fleishman also claims that the 'dominance of patriarchal and prophetic elements from the Bible is less obvious but no less prominent in *Sons and Lovers* than in *The Rainbow* or *The Man Who Died*'. *Sons and Lovers* certainly illustrates the same 'preoccupation with the cycle of the generations, sibling rivalries, and parental preferences for younger and older sons' as the book of Genesis. Moreover, the 'groundwork for the Scriptural references,' according to Fleishman, 'is well prepared by the fact that the characters . . . are themselves imbued with the Bible-centered' Protestant tradition, so that it is entirely realistic for Lawrence to present them as thinking in biblical terms

(Fleishman 1988: 70). Paul Poplawski sees the novel as revolving 'quite literally around religion', which is not only the main focus for Paul and Miriam's discussions but the framework, in terms of the liturgical year, for many of the key events, the family gatherings at Christmas and the excursions at Easter (Poplawski 1993: 72–3).

Sons and Lovers, of course, began life as 'Paul Morel', which itself went through three different versions, the first dating from October 1910, the second from mid-1911 and the third from the end of that year to mid-1912 (*SL* xxiv–xxxi). The second, which survives in truncated form in the Humanities Research Center at Texas (and will be the basis for the forthcoming Cambridge edition) is highly critical of orthodox Christians, presenting the Congregational minister Mr Revell as 'dreamy and speculative' (PM 123), entirely dependent on Paul's mother both for his sermons and for emotional support. Like Robert Reid in relation to Lawrence himself, he becomes Paul's 'spiritual father' as well as his tutor in languages (125). He continues to visit even after his resignation although, 'profound egotist that he was, he talked to her of nothing but his own nebulous states of soul' (176). Miriam's parents in this version of the novel, Mr and Mrs Staynes, are equally unsympathetic: she 'chooses to become an invalid out of Christian piety' while he remains officious and condescending (Brunsdale 1978: 261). The young Paul himself, as in later versions of the novel, spends much of his time in prayer. When he gets the job at Jordan's, for example, the narrator somewhat scathingly reports, 'Like any devotee, he thanked Almighty Heaven for this great beneficence' (PM 191). Miriam too is described 'as one of those spiritual women whose passion . . . becomes a religious service rather than a carnal thing' (223). Paul, however, proceeds to engage in a form of higher criticism for her benefit, explaining naturally what the Bible records as supernatural: he likens some flowers lit up by the sun to the time 'when God appeared in a fiery bush to Moses'. Their harsh scent, he speculates, was enough to induce fear in them as it had in Moses, thereby (supposedly) explaining away the miraculous elements in Exodus (228).

Paul's criticism of traditional Christianity of the kind Miriam represents reaches its climax in a scene which the narrator illustrates their different temperaments. He, brought up as an Independent, is critical even of his own tradition while she is 'fervent, rhapsodic, what is called intensely spiritual':

It was a thousand pities that Paul had ever started to batter at her creed. For him, Nonconformist Christianity as his mother accepted it was a stiff, narrow thinking which would not fit his life. Somehow or other, the true Christianity was walled in, like a monastery, to keep out life. Paul wanted to get out of the four high walls of ordinary dogmatic Christianity and the only way was to break and tear a breach in the enclosure. (242)

This image of traditional doctrine as a wall or sheet of ideology, obscuring rather than revealing truth, is one to which Lawrence frequently returns. Here the narrator recognises that Miriam, who needs 'the security of established religion', is shocked by Paul's critique of it. This version of the novel, however, gives Paul's side of their correspondence as well as hers: 'Does it really seem terrible,' he asks her, 'when I say the bible-religion is cloth which you can cut your coat from to fit you just as you please' (243). A later letter has him urging her to be 'gay' (presumably in Nietzsche's sense), to read Homer (to recover pre-Christian attitudes towards the body) and to be more critical of traditional christological formulations. 'It would be cruel,' he argues along Renanian lines, 'to give up the resurrection, yet the Christ-*man* is so much more real, so inspiring . . . .You see people have such small ideas of the Divine, such indulgent parent notions' (282). Paul refuses to be so small-minded about God, perhaps because his own father, who proceeds to kill his younger brother Arthur in a family row, is so lacking in indulgent parenthood. The manuscript ends, however, before he can develop his theology any further.

It is characteristic of the Christo-centric Lawrence that when this version of the novel was rejected by Heinemann, he reacted with the most savage of curses, imagining himself in the role of the crucified Christ without his heroic resignation to suffering:

God, how I hate them! God curse them, funkers. God blast them, wish-wash . . . .Why, why, why was I born an Englishman! – my cursed, rotten-boned, pappy hearted countrymen, *why* was I sent to *them*. Christ on the cross must have hated his countrymen. 'Crucify me, you swine,' he must have said through his teeth. It's not so hard to love thieves also on the cross. But the high priests down there – 'crucify me, you swine.' – 'put in your nails and spear, you bloody nasal sour-blooded swine . . . ' (*Letters* I 422)

This is perhaps the most extreme example of Lawrence's continuing tendency to identify with Christ while investing him with Nietzschean misanthropy.

Crucifixion continues to loom large at the beginning of the next attempt Lawrence made at the novel which was eventually to become *Sons and Lovers*, six surviving fragments of which are reproduced in the facsimile of the manuscript edited by Mark Schorer. The first of these presents Mrs Morel listening to the sound of her husband's drunken 'bawling' of hymns as he returns with other miners from the pub, setting her bitter reflections against the backdrop of three stunted oak trees on the hill opposite, which 'reminded Mrs Morel of Calvary'. The miners turn from 'Lead, Kindly Light' to 'There is a Green Hill Far Away', prompting her too to identify somewhat bitterly with the crucified victim of whom they are singing:

'Not so very far away, my sirs,' she said to herself, half in wonder, half in bitterness. She began to realise the crucifixion. She herself was being slowly crucified. She was waiting, all the time in pain, to say 'It is finished': and then she could be free . . . (Schorer 1977: 7).

Traces of this intense identification on her part with the crucified Christ survive in the final version of *Sons and Lovers*, for example when her husband's shearing of their son's curls is described as 'the spear through the side of her love for Morel' (*SL* 24). By then, however, Paul Morel has come to reject such identification with suffering as self-indulgent.

The third of these fragments (in what is only a fragmentary manuscript, amounting to fifty-six pages, all from the beginning of the novel) introduces more hymns, this time sung by the travelling yeast-salesman, 'Barm-O', a convert who intersperses his cry for custom with such pious choruses as 'Jesus loves me this I know? / For the Bible tells me so' and 'At the cross, at the cross, where I found . . . ' (Schorer 1977: 48a). This leads into a scene in which Mrs Morel is seen to mother the young minister who visits her, Mr Revell, whose own mother died at childbirth but who ponders now for the first time in the expectant Mrs Morel the pain and danger involved in giving birth, the curse pronounced upon Eve in Genesis 3 (48). As in the final version of the novel itself, Mrs Morel is seen to be much more in touch with the life of the community than the poor minister whom she helps with his sermons.

The final manuscript of *Sons and Lovers*, the basis for the New Cambridge Edition, written between July and November 1912 before being significantly cut by Edward Garnett for publication by Duckworth the following year, gives full prominence to the religious dimension of the novel. Mark Schorer claims that all Garnett's deletions were 'to the novel's advantage' (9), a judgement disputed by those 'interested in the religious Lawrence' like Mark Spilka, who shows that Garnett cut many of the discussions of religious issues in accordance with his Jamesian criteria as not supposedly relevant to the characterisation and deleterious to the 'form' of the novel (Spilka 1992: 42). He pruned, for example, the scene in which Mrs Morel brings her young minister, now called Mr Heaton, 'judiciously to earth', telling him how he ought to preach about the miraculous changing of water into wine in John 2: 1–11:

'No,' she said aloud, 'don't make things into symbols. Say: "It was a wedding, and the wine ran out. Then the father-in-law was put about, because there was nothing to offer the guests, except water – there was no tea, no coffee, in those days, only wine. And how would he like to see all the people sitting with glasses of water in front of them. The host and his wife were ashamed, the bride was miserable, and the bridegroom was disagreeable. And Jesus saw them whispering together, and looking worried. And He knew they were poor. They were only, perhaps, farm-labouring people. So He thought to himself 'What a shame! – all the wedding spoiled.' And so He made wine, as quickly as he could." – You can say, wine isn't beer, not so intoxicating – and people in the East never get drunk. It's getting drunk makes beer so bad.' (*SL* 45–6)

Garnett presumably found Mrs Morel's insistence on 'his making the bible real to the people' (46) too reminiscent of a nonconformist preaching manual. Her concern with the issue of drink, however, is not only in character and relevant to a major cause of her marital problems (her husband's drinking) but vital to the novel's search for the 'real' truth of religion.

Mrs Morel is described from the outset of the novel as 'deeply religious' (17). She still has the Bible given to her by a former admirer, John Field, whose memory she 'kept . . . intact in her heart' just as Mary 'kept all these things, and pondered them in her heart' (Luke 2: 19). Later in the novel, she unburdens herself to Paul 'of all she had pondered' (*SL* 142). These would in themselves be slender textual grounds on which to build a Marian reading of her character were it not for a passage in the manuscript which Lawrence himself decided to omit in which she dreams that her son William will achieve something great in the world, fulfilling some of the 'as yet unused . . . vitality' of her own soul: 'She wanted to get it forth, to give it to the world, through the medium of her son. Mary first, and then Jesus' (524). She harbours similar ambitions for Paul, at one point holding him up in the evening sun by a field of corn and imagining his older brothers 'bowing: perhaps her son would be a Joseph' (50), a theme continued in William calling the much-mended patchwork shirt she gives him 'My Joseph's-Coat' (72). Later in the novel she still hopes that Paul 'was going to alter the face of the earth, in some way that mattered' (261). Her repeated cry, 'Oh, my son – my son!' on William's death (169) is likened by Carl and Helen Baron (editors of the Cambridge edition) to that of David lamenting the death of Absalom in 2 Samuel 18: 33 (533) but it can also be seen to carry at least some of the resonance of Mary lamenting her dead son.

One of the central themes in *Sons and Lovers*, of course, is the way in which Mrs Morel's religious aspirations place impossible burdens not only on her sons but on her husband. This is played down slightly in the final text, Lawrence himself (presumably following Garnett's example), cutting an extended analysis of the resentment she feels about her husband being 'strictly irreligious', living only for pleasure, in contrast to herself: 'She was deeply religious. She felt that God had sent her on an errand, that she must choose for God from her sense of right and wrong' (*SL* 514). Some of this survives in the final version of the novel, although Morel is now seen to have no 'grit' rather than no 'religion'. She still sees him as 'purely sensuous', however, and 'strove to make him moral, religious' (22), enlisting the rest of the family in this project. The young Paul internalises his mother's attitudes so strongly that he includes praying for his father's death as part of his 'fervent private religion' (85).

Sons and Lovers charts the effect of this parental pressure on Paul. Not only does his mother regard him as a potential Joseph, even perhaps a Jesus, but she decides impulsively to name him Paul, supposedly without knowing why (51). But we are told at the beginning of the novel that her father, a proud and unapproachable man, 'drew near in sympathy only to one man, the Apostle Paul' (18) while her son, whose nickname is 'Postle' (73, 242), submits to bronchitis in the manner worthy of his precursor in Acts 11: 5: 'it was no good kicking against the pricks' (91). Again, the biblical typology is clear, although in this case it operates as an indication of the religious attitudes foisted upon him. The young Paul cannot avoid seeing life through biblical lenses, as when, noticing a big red moon shining in the sky after a fight with his friends, 'he thought of the bible, that the moon should be turned to blood' (101), dredging up images from Joel 2: 31 and the Book of Revelation 6: 12. He later, of course, reads the Bible in the light of his experiences, telling Clara later in the novel that he used to think that the reference to 'a pillar of cloud by day and a pillar of fire by night' of Exodus 13: 21–2 'was a pit, with its steam, and its lights and the burning bank – and I thought the Lord was always at the pit-top' (364). At this stage he can look back with a certain detachment at his boyhood saturation in the Bible, but he continues to describe Clara to his mother in biblical terms as 'already singled out from the sheep', a reference to Christ's parable of the separation of the sheep from the goats in Matthew 25: 32. The reference in this instance is ironic, since he clearly admires her difference from the rest of the Christian flock. When his mother lies dying towards the end of the novel, however, the reference to their being 'afraid of the veils that were ripping between them', like the signs accompanying the crucifixion in Luke 23: 45, is far from ironic. When Paul later feels his identity almost disintegrating after her death, so that he seems 'less than an ear of wheat lost in the field', the image here also recalls Christ's promise in John 12: 24, 'Except a corn of wheat fall into the ground and die, it abideth alone: but if it die, it bringeth forth much fruit.' The traditional consolation of Christian belief in the resurrection is no longer available to him but he nevertheless draws comfort at the thought that his mother's life (and death) has not been in vain. He wants her still to be with him, 'to touch him, to have him alongside with her' (464) like the disciples on the Emmaus Road and St Thomas after the resurrection. That, of course, is denied him but, as in Renan's account of belief in the resurrection being a moral victory of love over suffering and death, he derives some strength to continue from her memory.

Paul's gradual development away from the conventional Christianity first of his mother and then of Miriam is central to the novel (along with the emotional development which accompanies this). Miriam, the Hebrew form of Mary and the name of Moses' sister, inherits some of his mother's Marian characteristics, including a tendency to 'ponder these sayings' after Paul has made them (183, cf. Luke 2: 19). She is introduced in Part II of the novel as intensely 'mystical' (173), as 'cut off from ordinary life, by her religious intensity, which made the world for her either a nunnery garden, or a Paradise where sin and knowledge were not' (179).

Mrs Leivers and her children are described as 'almost his disciples' (179), Miriam in particular having a brooding appearance that makes her look like 'one of the women who went with Mary when Jesus was dead' (184) This is reinforced by a passage which Garnett cut from the original published version of the novel in which, as Paul rehearses the Good Friday sermon to the whole Leivers family, Miriam is portrayed watching him

with deep satisfaction. She loved him in the same way that Mary loved at Bethany. Only when the man came up in him was there war between them. And which was stronger in him, the Disciple or the man. She believed the former, and by the former she held him. (263)

The Barons, commenting on this passage in the explanatory notes of their edition of the novel, point out that Bethany was the place outside Jerusalem to which Jesus went to relax, quoting a passage from Renan's *Life of Jesus* celebrating Bethany as the place where this Mary, seated at the feet of Jesus, 'forgot, in listening to him, the duties of real life' while Jesus 'forgot the vexations of public life' (551). The implication clearly is that the Haggs Farm is Paul's Bethany and Miriam his Mary, hoping all the time that he will remain a disciple, an imitator of Christ.

Miriam herself has indeed been brought up to imitate Christ. When she resents both the housework she is forced to do and the roughness of her treatment by her brothers, she is told by her mother to put up with it 'even for my sake', a conflation of Matthew 5: 11 with John 13: 38, the 'blending of pseudo-biblical phraseology,' according to the Barons, being 'common in the evangelical churches' (534). So, of course, was theological discussion but this did not prevent Garnett cutting most of it, including a passage in the manuscript in which Paul challenges Jesus' view that not one sparrow falls to the ground without the Father knowing, for 'the very hairs of your head are numbered' (Matt. 10: 29–30). 'I used to believe that about a sparrow falling,' Paul explains; 'Now I think that the race of sparrows matters, but not one sparrow: all my hair, but not one hair', evolution caring for the species more than the individual (193). Miriam continues to worship Paul, quivering 'as at some Annunciation' at the discovery of his 'rare potentiality' (201), keeping his sayings 'graven in her mind, as one of the letters of the Law' (202) and praying that she will continue to love him 'as Christ would, who died for the souls of men' (202). In her company, whether painting pine trees in the sunset and commenting, 'There's God's burning bush for you, that burned not away' (183), or visiting a church with her on Easter Monday, his own 'latent mysticism', his own sense of the 'fascination of shadowy religious places . . . quivered into life' (203). But his intellect examines the 'religion in which she lived and moved and had her being' (230), like the disciples in Acts 17: 28, and finds it wanting. Miriam, of course, resents this, claiming that he has 'no anchor of righteousness' (265), a conflation of Hebrews 6: 19, which refers to the 'anchor of the soul', and Ephesians 6: 14, which describes the 'breastplate of right-eousness'. Her Pauline images, however, in Paul Morel's eyes, simply reveal her continuing entrapment in conventional Christian modes of thought.

It is sex, of course, portrayed as the 'serpent in her Eden', which brings about the final separation between Miriam and Paul. Reading her a chapter of St John's Gospel, Paul finds himself growing self-conscious about the reference to a 'woman in travail' (John 16: 21), which he omits, much to her mortification (268). The 'Defeat of Miriam', however, the title of chapter nine, involves a rejection of her religion as well as its attitude towards sex. Paul complains,

'It's not religious to be religious,' he said. 'I reckon a crow is religious when it sails across the sky. But it only does it because it feels itself carried to where it's going, not because it thinks it is being eternal.

But Miriam knew that one should be religious in everything, have God, whatever God He might be, present in everything.

'I don't believe God knows such a lot about himself,' he cried. 'God doesn't *know* things, He *is* things – and I'm sure he's not soulful.' (291)

His long discussions with his mother at this time also indicate the extent to which 'Religion was fading into the background': 'he had shovelled away all the beliefs that would hamper him', coming to 'the bedrock of belief that one should feel inside oneself for right and wrong, and should have the patience to gradually realise one's God' (298). Again, one can argue, the novel as a whole displays Lawrence himself 'realizing' his theology, becoming fully conscious of it by embodying it in his fiction.

Even the turning from Miriam, who offers Paul sex as a sacrifice, to Clara, who is much less inhibited sexually, rejecting the notion that it makes them 'sinners' (358), is represented in biblical terms, as a return by Paul to his 'old Adam', a recovery of the natural man. He teases Clara, imputing to her whole sex a taste for guilt: 'I

believe Eve enjoyed it, when she went cowering out of Paradise.'
Garnett characteristically cut Paul's development of this biblical
episode, so important in all Lawrence's early writing, which continued: 'And I guess Adam was in a rage, and wondered what the
deuce all the row was about – a bit of an apple that the birds could
peck if they wanted to' (358). As in *Look! We Have Come Through!*,
Lawrence rewrites Genesis to create an Adam in his own image (or
rather, the image of what he would like to have been), released from
inhibition and at ease with his body, at one with the natural world.
The 'final loss of innocence is depicted . . . as the gain of full
humanity' (Fleishman 1988: 70), the fall retold as fortunate not in
Augustine's sense (as requiring a redeemer) but in Nietzsche's (as a
successful rebellion against a slave morality).

That Lawrence saw himself as rewriting the Bible in this aggressive Nietzschean manner is apparent in the 'Foreword to *Sons and
Lovers*', written in January 1913, after the completion of the manuscript of the novel, and enclosed in a letter to Edward Garnett, to
whom he explained that it was not for publication, something he
'wanted to *write* . . . not to have printed' (*Letters* I 510). As well as
attempting to show Garnett what the novel was about, how
profoundly religious it was supposed to be, it reveals a great deal
about his inner motivations and beliefs. He was to tell Garnett a
year later, 'I am a passionately religious man, and my novels must be
written from the depth of my religious experience . . . I can only
work like that' (II 165). The foreword, as the Barons acknowledge,
represents 'a sustained account of the relationship between Man,
Nature and God', sketching a 'new religious cosmology' which is
also a 'subversion of biblical texts' (*SL* li). It begins with an inversion
of St John's Gospel:

John, the beloved disciple, says, 'The Word was made Flesh'. But why
should he turn things round? The women simply go on bearing talkative
sons, as an answer. 'The Flesh was made Word.' (467)

John's Gospel is seen as irredeemably phallogocentric, presenting
the male principle of reason as responsible for the female body,
thereby reversing the natural order, in which women give birth to
men. Lawrence, according to Martin Green, may be drawing here
on the work of Johann Bachofen, who believed that the earliest
societies were matriarchal and that 'Woman exists from everlasting',
giving birth to sons in whom she recognises 'the very image of that

fecundating power to which she owes her motherhood' (Green 1974: 83–4). Whether drawing on Bachofen or not, Lawrence here creates an opposition between the Word, which is male and linked with the Son, and the Flesh, which is female and linked (somewhat paradoxically) with the Father. Christ is the 'Uttered Word' as opposed to God 'the unutterable Flesh'. Adam, Lawrence continues, in a reversal of traditional Christian typology, is 'the first Christ: not the Word made Flesh, but the Flesh made Word'. The Word, Lawrence continues, is human and 'finite', as opposed to the Flesh, which is 'infinite and has no end . . . The Flesh is beyond us' (*SL* 467). To follow Christ and to 'love our neighbour as our self' is to proclaim allegiance to the Word but to remain below the level of the Flesh: 'For the Son is not greater than the Father' (467), as Jesus himself had recognised (John 14: 28).

What Lawrence is challenging, here as in his short story, 'Daughters of the Vicar', is the Christian interpretation of the Book of Genesis, as when Christ in Matthew 19: 5 quotes from Genesis 2: 24 in defence of marriage but omits the previous verse which focuses on the flesh ('And Adam said, "This is now bone of my bones, and flesh of my flesh"'). The 'Foreword' asks, 'And who shall say, "That woman shall be Flesh of my Flesh. I, the Word, have said it"?' (*SL* 468). Lawrence, as Helen and Carl Baron argue, is 'challenging the literal, legalistic interpretation of Genesis' (578), which tones down, tames and would altogether emaciate the power and the glory of the flesh. Again, Lawrence uses the Bible against itself, producing a pastiche of Paul's famous celebration of charity in 1 Corinthians 13: 'For the Word hath neither passion nor pain . . . It has charity, which we call love. But only the Flesh has love, for that is the Father, and in love he begets us all'. He proceeds to quote the authoritative narrator of Genesis 2: 24, 'They shall be one flesh', before commenting, 'Thus did the Word usurp the Father' (469). Lawrence denies the power of the Word to unite the sexes, 'for the Flesh is not contained in the Word, but the Word contained in the Flesh'. So 'if a man shall say, "This woman is flesh of my flesh"', as Adam does, 'let him see to it that he be not blaspheming the Father. For the woman is not flesh of his flesh, by the bidding of the Word; but it is of the Father.' Similarly, Lawrence subverts the claim of the Word to 'have dominion over the flesh of my neighbour' (a conflation of Genesis 1: 26, in which God gives man 'dominion' over all creatures with the evolution in Exodus of a set of moral commands). Lawrence, in other words, opposes his own reading of Genesis to Christ's, at least the Christ of conventional Christianity.

The 'Foreword to *Sons and Lovers*' continues to rewrite Genesis, again giving voice, as so many of Lawrence's female characters do, to the feminist objection to the biblical claim that 'the Word created Man, and Man lay down and gave birth to Woman. Whereas we know the Woman lay in travail, and gave birth to Man' (470). It is the woman throughout who is aligned with the Flesh, closer to nature and the natural cycle, represented here as in *The White Peacock* by the apple and its pip. The Word tries to make 'the pip that comes out of the apple, like Adam's rib, . . . the mere secondary product, that is spat out'. But the pip, the seed, is 'responsible for the whole miraculous cycle'. In Lawrence's radically feminist theology, 'the Father – which should be called the Mother' comes first while 'the Son, who is the Utterer, and then the Word', can be 'tossed away' (470). The sexual fulfilment he had recently found in Frieda presumably contributes to the grand claims he proceeds to make, that 'God the Father, the Inscrutable, the Unknowable, we know in the Flesh, in Woman' (471), that it is 'in the flesh of the woman' that God enacts Himself (472). The final paragraph, with its recognition that a mother cannot make a proper lover (473), is perhaps the only ostensible reference in the whole piece to the central plot of *Sons and Lovers*, but the Foreword as a whole reflects the spirit of Nietzschean rebellion against orthodox Christianity in which the novel was written.

The mistaken understanding of religion evident in conventional Christian readings of Genesis is clearly a recurrent target in much of Lawrence's early work. The story of Adam and Eve and their supposed fall into sexual guilt will continue to play an important part in his later writing as well, tranformed from a narrative about disobedience into one which involves a failure to enjoy the gift of life to the full. Much of human misery and evil, these works suggest, is attributable not to the taking of the apple so much as to the conventional Christian morality which forbids its full enjoyment. In the words of Nietzsche's prophet, Zarathustra, man's real 'sin' is to 'have enjoyed himself too little' (*TSZ* 112). Similarly, in Lawrence's early work the real 'trespassers' are those who lack the courage to rebel against God's commands. Those who dare to take the apple do not 'fall' but 'come through' to a higher level of existence, a paradise of sexual fulfilment.

CHAPTER 6

Re-marking Genesis: 'The Rainbow' as counter-Bible

The Rainbow is perhaps the most obviously biblical of Lawrence's novels. John Worthen has written of its ambition to *become* a sacred text, a 'kind of "Bible of the English people"' (Worthen 1981: 21), while Mark Kinkead-Weekes claims that Lawrence derived from sacred history 'a hint of the shape his own "bible" ought to have', a threefold pattern outlined in the *Study of Thomas Hardy* from an 'Old Testament' dominated by Law through a 'world of transition in which . . . the promised land is seen but not entered' to 'a new world' modelled on the Book of Revelation (*R* xxxiv). The biblical symbol of the rainbow, of course, first shown by God to Noah after the flood as a sign of the new covenant in which 'the waters shall no more become a flood to destroy all flesh' (Gen. 9: 15), reappears in the Book of Revelation both as a glory-cloud around the throne of heaven (Rev. 4: 3; 10. 1) and as a symbol of the new world of which St John is given a glimpse. The flood of Genesis is a type of the destruction of the corrupt world in the Book of Revelation, bringing into being 'a new heaven and a new earth' (21. 1). Similarly in *The Rainbow*, Ursula, whose grandfather perishes in the flood, achieves at the very end of the novel a rainbow-vision of the replacement of the 'old, brittle corruption' with a new 'world built up in a living fabric of Truth, fitting to the over-arching heaven' (*R* 459). It is not just the symbolism of this novel, in other words, but its plot and structure, which reflects the Bible.

There are, however, significant differences, one of which is the fact that Lawrence completely overturns many of the values of the Books of Genesis and Revelation as conventionally understood, in particular the fear of the body, of sexuality. Genesis, as we have seen, appears at times to celebrate the sacredness of the flesh. Noah, for example, is instructed by God to 'Be fruitful, and multiply, and replenish the earth' after the flood (Gen 9: 1). It is hard, however, not to see a causal connection between 'the sons of God' coming in 'unto the daughters of men' (Gen. 6: 4) and God's anger at 'the wickedness of man' and his 'evil' imagination in the following verse. Lawrence, as we shall see, makes Ursula refashion the significance of this episode, re-marking the union between the sons of God and the daughters of men as entirely positive. Lawrence's later commentary on the Book of Revelation will also reject out of hand the layers of Christian asceticism and fear of the body which he argues were superimposed upon an original pagan celebration of the glory of the flesh. For this reason, it seems more appropriate to label *The Rainbow* a 'counter-Bible', a term employed by Robert Fraser, editor of Sir James Frazer's classic of religious anthropology *The Golden Bough*. A 'counter-Bible' is a book written in direct antagonism to a sacred text responsible for the ossification of a religious system. Without such stabilising texts, Fraser claims, religions would more easily change, progressively adapting themselves to the advances of their culture. When a religion is 'enshrined in a book', however, this reforming process is made 'much more difficult because the opponents can always cite chapter and verse in support of their conservativism'. Hence the need for 'counter-books' or 'counter-Bibles' such as *The Golden Bough* (Frazer 1994: xxv). I will discuss Lawrence's reading of *The Golden Bough* shortly; now I want simply to suggest that the *The Rainbow* too is a kind of counter-Bible, designed to loosen up interpretation of the Bible, to develop Christianity beyond its unnecessarily rigid dogma and morality. Lawrence, in Bakhtin's terms, 're-accents' familiar biblical narrative, replacing the 'slave morality' imposed upon it by Christian interpreters with a more generous celebration of the body. In Derrida's words, he 'supplements' the Bible, not simply adding to it but at times attempting to supplant it, to replace the traditional text with his own.

One of the characteristics *The Rainbow* shares with the Hebrew Bible is that it went through many layers of revision and rewriting before the final text was established. Lawrence began work on what became *The Rainbow* in March 1913, although at that time it was known as 'The Sisters' and included material later to be part of *Women in Love*. A second version of 'The Sisters', which 'seems to have been the "Ur-Rainbow"' (Kinkead-Weekes 1968: 376) was begun in August, continuing through the winter until the end of January 1914, at which point Lawrence began yet another draft, this time entitled 'The Wedding Ring', which he finished in May. This brought the second 'Sisters' nearer to *The Rainbow*, although its narrative still covered events later to be included in *Women in Love* (378). In September he began a 'Study of Thomas Hardy', a sustained and in places deeply religious meditation for which Hardy's novels act as a springboard for Lawrence's own thought rather than the object of conventional literary criticism. This was finished in October, a month before Lawrence began the final rewriting of *The Rainbow*, which was completed in March 1915. Further extensive revision of the novel took place from mid-March to the end of May, to be followed by considerable changes to the proofs in July and August. The novel that was finally published on the last day of September, only to be suppressed by Court order in November, was thus the result of complex layers of writing and rewriting, a textual history as complex as the Book of Genesis itself.

Before analysing the novel, however, I want to consider some of Lawrence's reading during this period along with some other examples of his own writing, most importantly the *Study of Thomas Hardy*. These are all significant intertexts, books which share ideas and symbols to be found in the novel. In some cases it is clear that they are direct sources, feeding into Lawrence's writing. Even where this is not certain, however, they serve at least to shed light on what 'comes to pass' in *The Rainbow*. Not all these books are as well-known or as monumental (either in size or in impact on contemporaries) as *The Golden Bough*. Katharine Jenner's *Christian Symbolism*, for example, which Lawrence recorded having 'liked very much' when he read it in December 1914, was 'a little half-crown vol. – in the *Little Books on Art* series' published by Methuen. But it helped put him 'more into order', giving him a new respect for the whole framework of Christian symbolism (*Letters* II 250). The 'old symbols', he now realised as a result of reading Jenner, were 'a great attempt at formulating the whole history of the Soul of Man' which required understanding 'in their whole context'. The Crucifix and even Christ himself he now came to see as of symbolic and psychological rather than of historical value (II 248–9). This reflects not quite what Jenner herself says but how Lawrence read her.

Jenner's book is mainly known for having provided Lawrence with the symbol of the phoenix. Its poor black-and-white reproduction of a medieval bestiary depiction of a 'Phoenix Rising from the Flames' appears opposite an explanation of the origin of this symbol in the first Epistle of St Clement, where it represents 'the resurrection of the dead and its triumph over death' (Jenner 1910: 150). This appears to have provoked Lawrence into drawing his own phoenix in a letter to his friend Samuel Koteliansky early in 1915, in which he suggests that it could be the 'badge' for their new religious community, to be called Rananim after the opening Hebrew words of a musical version of Psalm 33, 'Rejoice in the Lord, O ye righteous' (*Letters* II 252) . Lawrence makes Will Brangwen put it on a butter-pat in *The Rainbow*; he was later to reproduce it on the cover of the first edition of *Lady Chatterley's Lover*, much to the distaste of his publisher Orioli, who thought it looked like 'a pigeon having a bath in a slop-basin' (Nehls 1959: 186). Later still, of course, it would appear on the covers of a whole generation of Penguin editions of Lawrence. What is not so widely appreciated is that it was 'a recognised symbol of the Resurrection of Christ' (Jenner 1910: 150). His appropriation of a key element of Christian symbolism accurately represents the way his own writing functions as a counter-Bible.

The phoenix, as Mark Kinkead-Weekes notes, was by no means the only symbol in Jenner's book which seems to have 'lodged' in Lawrence's mind. Among the many paintings reproduced by Jenner are Fra Angelico's *Entry of the Blessed into Paradise*, Van Eyck's *Adoration of the Lamb*, and a representation of the risen Christ as a Lamb with a banner, the symbolism of which becomes the subject of dispute between Will and Anna in *The Rainbow* (Kinkead-Weekes 1996: 796). More important than these individual details, however, is the understanding of the role of symbolism in religion which Lawrence appears to have picked up from Jenner, who makes no attempt to disguise her high church allegiance, writing rather dismissively of the failure of 'the "Reformed" Churches' to appreciate the complexity and necessary indirectness of theological representation (18). The process Lawrence refers to as being put 'more into order' by her book (*Letters* II 242) involved the clarification in his own mind of some of the details of Christian symbolism which had been neglected in his decidedly protestant upbringing.

Jenner's central argument is that Christianity, like all religions, relies upon symbolism. Since it 'is not possible to express spiritual things adequately in words . . . even the words used for religious purposes must be largely metaphorical and symbolical'. A 'certain element of the esoteric and mystical' was therefore 'a necessary characteristic of early Christianity'. No religion starts from scratch

but necessarily appropriates 'the conventions of existing religions
. . . sometimes invested with slightly varied or wholly new signifi-
cances' (Jenner 1910: xiii). Like her contemporary Saussure, she
divides symbols into two classes: 'fixed and arbitrary'. As an example
of the latter, in which 'the relation . . . to the thing signified is not
always traceable', she explains that there is 'no reason . . . why a
Fish should signify Christ' but once such an arbitrary association is
made, it can become particularly powerful to a persecuted minority
(xiv-xvi). Jenner refers to a wide range of esoteric religions contemporary with early Christianity, taking examples from gnostic,
Greek, Egyptian and kabbalistic Jewish sources, celebrating the
richness and variety of the Christian tradition as a product of its
eclectic and synthesising tendencies (xx).

A chapter on 'The World of Spirits', as well as providing
Lawrence with his knowledge of some of the more obscure angels
(*Letters* II 242), discusses the seraphim in Isaiah (also to find their way
into *The Rainbow*) and the winged divinities of two races whose
religion was to fascinate Lawrence, the Etruscans and the Egyptians.
He would also have learnt much of which his mother would have
disapproved in Jenner's chapter on 'The Saints', which explains the
'description of Our Lady in the Apocalypse (Rev 12: 1)' (Jenner
1910: 98). Among the 'Lesser Symbolisms' explored by Jenner in
chapter eight of her book are not only the phoenix but other animals
to assume great significance in Lawrence's work, such as the serpent,
'partly the emblem of evil, and partly that of wisdom' (147–8), the
peacock, 'emblem of eternal life' (149), the lion and the dragon.
Jenner also explains 'the significance of the *Crown*', denoting rank
and sovereignty, and devotes space to the history of Saint Ursula,
again suggesting that this little book fed into *The Rainbow* in a variety
of ways. A final chapter on 'Old Testament Types' deplores modern
ignorance of the Bible, pointing up the irony that 'Such a minute
knowledge of Scripture does not obtain in these days of cheap Bibles
as in the days when the Bible was taught and fixed in figures of stone
and blazoned in colours on walls and windows' (168). Jenner
expresses a much firmer belief in the 'perfect continuity' between
God's revelation to the Jews and to the Christian Church than
Lawrence could probably have mustered but he seems to have
shared (and made Will Brangwen display) her enthusiasm for the
Old Testament and its typological significance for medieval art.

Another book Lawrence read in December 1914, which had a

much bigger profile among his contemporaries, was James Frazer's *The Golden Bough* (*Letters* II 470), a book which has been described as 'a foundation stone of the modern sensibility' (Frazer 1994: x). It synthesises 'many strands of nineteenth-century thought and feeling', balancing 'the scientific temper' with an appreciation of 'the imaginative, spiritual, myth-making impulses of mankind' (Vickery 1973: 3–5). Vickery suggests that Lawrence may have read Frazer as early as 1911 (280) but it is typical of Lawrence's rather casual reference to sources that it is unclear either when he first read *The Golden Bough* or which edition he read, the first two-volume edition of 1890, the second three-volume edition of 1900 (the most radical and subversive of Christianity), or the twelve-volume edition of 1906–15. The only citation of Frazer by Lawrence, in the foreword to *Fantasia of the Unconscious*, using a sentence from 'the already-old-fashioned "Golden Bough"' as an example of scientific embarrassment at the superstitions of primitive man, is from the second edition (*Fant.* 14). There is another disparaging reference to modern man being able only to 'twiddle-twaddle about golden boughs' because he is 'empty, hollow, deficient, and cardboardy', incapable himself of any 'living relation in *sacredness*' in *Reflections on the Death of a Porcupine* (*Phoenix* II 480). But, as so often with Lawrence, such detraction may well conceal a recognition of debt, even down to the names of three racehorses in 'The Rocking Horse Winner' (Fitz 1974: 199–200). *The Golden Bough* would certainly have provided a classic example of a 'counter-Bible'. The second edition in particular, which begins, like the first, 'in an Edenic Grove', reaches its climax in the chapter entitled 'The Crucifixion of Christ' (reduced to an Appendix in the third edition) before providing an alternative, more 'sceptical apocalypse' at the end. In the third edition

this counter-Biblical typology grows still more ornate: so we have a Passover sequence; an Immaculate Conception sequence; a Nativity sequence; a Baptism sequence; a sequence on fires followed by a Resurrection sequence – all of which are embedded within the text. (Frazer 1994: xxv–vi)

Frazer's main point, implicit rather than explicit in the book itself but expressed in a private letter of 1889, is the 'striking . . . resemblance of the savage customs and ideas [of primitive religion] to the fundamental doctrines of Christianity' (xx). Like Jenner, he anticipates structural anthropology and linguistics in this respect, focusing on the elementary structures of the human mind to be found in all religion. The final paragraph of Book II, 'Killing the God', locates these similarities not in the 'fleeting and evanescent' details of 'religious consciousness' or 'elaborate theologies' but in its 'simpler forms' which are 'comparatively stable and permanent, being rooted deep in those principles of common minds which bid fair to outlive all the splendid but transient creations of genius' (554). Details from Frazer will be found in much of Lawrence's writing, especially the Mexican novels for which he appears to have reread *The Golden Bough*, and, of course, *The Escaped Cock*, which will be found to pick up material from Book II, 'Killing the God'. John Vickery attributes to Frazer, either directly or indirectly, through the work of other anthropologists themselves influenced by Frazer, much of the material from ancient myths to be found in Lawrence's work. *The Literary Impact of 'The Golden Bough'* has chapters on Lawrence's poetry, picking up many of the references to sacred symbols, totemic animals and 'dark Gods', and another on 'The Mythic Elements' in the short stories, outlining six areas in which Lawrence can be said to have embodied in his work the insights of Frazer's anthropology: the myth of the scapegoat, sacrificial death, totemic myth, sacred marriage, the reviving God and ghosts or spirits of the dead (Vickery 1973: chs 8 and 9). In all these areas, Lawrence's thinking can be said at the very least to overlap with Frazer's.

Lawrence was also familiar with the work of other members of the Cambridge School of Anthropology such as Jane Harrison and Gilbert Murray. He read Harrison's study of *Ancient Art and Ritual* in 1913, reporting in his characteristically grudging way that it was a 'scrubby book . . . stupidly put, but it lets one in for an idea that helps one immensely' (*Letters* II 114). He had earlier recorded, 'It just fascinates me to see art coming out of religious yearning' (90). When he finally completed the book, in December, he again stressed 'how much I got out of that *Ritual and Art* book' even though it had been written by 'a school marmy woman' (119). The point of Harrison's book is that although the 'modern mind' may associate ritual with 'fixed forms and ceremonies' as opposed to the greater freedom from convention attributed to artists, they share a 'common root'; it is 'one and the same impulse that sends a man to church and to the theatre' (Harrison 1927: 9–10). She describes details of the festival of Osiris, for example, 'the prototype of the great class of resurrection-gods who die that they may live again', with reference to the Bible, the account of Ezekiel finding the women 'weeping for Tammuz', type of Adonis and Osiris, and due acknowledgement of the relevant volume of *The Golden Bough* (15–18). Art and ritual, she insists, are 'closely linked . . . not only in Greece but in Egypt and Palestine' (21), a clear hint that Christianity displayed the same symbolic forms as other ancient religions.

Another member of the Cambridge School of Anthropology whom Lawrence read with interest was Gilbert Murray, whose study of Greek religion he was lent by Lady Ottoline Morrell. Again Lawrence complained about the style of the book, the 'layers of flannel' Murray placed 'between him and his nakedness. But the stuff of the book interests me *enormously*' (*Letters* II 558–9). Murray's *Four Stages of Greek Religion*, later revised to *Five Stages* by the simple expedient of splitting the third stage (and chapter), is another attempt to explore the 'uncharted region of human experience' represented by religion. Murray insists that 'man must have some relation towards the uncharted, the mysterious, tracts of life which surround him on every side' (22) but which conventional theology fails fully to capture, even our word 'God' being 'too stiff, too personal, and too anthropomorphic' (27), unlike those of Greek religion, which represented its Gods quite self-consciously as symbols of something beyond themselves rather than essential beings. The point to emphasise here is that Lawrence was familiar with these arguments, more widely read than is often recognised.

Some of this reading filters into Lawrence's letters throughout this period, which are unremittingly religious in tone, the horrors of the war exacerbating his conviction that his society needed complete renewal. They are also full of biblical allusions. Many refer explicitly to the Flood, placing hope for the future in the destruction of the old world and the foundation of the new. In the imagery of refracted light which he often associates with the rainbow, Lawrence tells Lady Ottoline Morrell in April 1915, 'All the beauty and light of day seems like a iridescence [*sic*] on a very black flood. Mostly one is underneath: sometimes one rises from the ark: but there is no olive branch.' He immediately retracts this 'sentimental simile: myself as a dove' (*Letters* II 330) but returns to the same theme in a letter to her the following month (II 338). He repeats the idea in a letter to Catherine Carswell the following October, raising hopes of a renewed life after the war: 'We shall be like Noah, taking all the precious things into the ark, when the flood comes, and disem-

barking on a new world' (II 663). Even Bertrand Russell, part of a
Cambridge circle whose irreverence Lawrence deplored when he
visited them in April 1915, is treated to a sermon on the resurrection,
complete with text from 1 Corinthians 15: 36: 'Except a seed die, it
bringeth not forth. Only wait. Our death must be accomplished first,
then we will rise up' (II 347–8). The two of them planned a series of
lectures for that autumn with Russell focusing on ethics and
Lawrence on 'Immortality' (II 359). It soon became apparent,
however, that Lawrence saw the lectures as much more centred
upon religion than Russell. Having followed Russell's suggestion that
he read some early Greek philosophy, he was soon acknowledging, 'I
have been wrong, much too Christian, in my philosophy . . . I must
drop all about God' (II 364). Not that he did, as the rest of this book
will demonstrate, but the biblical images that dominate both the
Study of Thomas Hardy and *The Rainbow* became a little less evident in
'The Crown', written later in the year.

Lawrence's most sustained attempt to express his views on religion
during this period occurs in the *Study of Thomas Hardy*, begun in
September 1914 and finished the following month, though published
only posthumously in *Phoenix*. The typescript, as we have seen, has the
Nietzschean title, 'Le Gai Savaire', which gives some indication of the
radical twist Lawrence gives to conventional religion. The opening
chapter, like Nietzsche, presents religion as a reflex of primitive
ignorance of cause and effect, involving the 'propitiation of the
Unknown God who controls death and the sources of nourishment'.
More positively, as Lawrence had read in Harrison, religion is seen to
share with art the basic impulse to express feelings illustrated by
primitive man 'scratching pictures on the walls of his cave, and
making graven images of his unutterable feelings' (*STH* 3).
Lawrence's characteristic strategy in this as in other pieces of non-
fictional prose is a kind of perverse or hostile midrash: he will often
begin by quoting a biblical passage before proceeding to demolish or
at best to re-interpret it. He disagrees entirely with Jesus, for example,
over lilies, which, far from taking no care for the morrow, can be
found to lay down stores of food for the future continuation of the
natural cycle. Lawrence celebrates the resulting beauty, whether of
lilies or poppies, as representative as they are of the 'excess' of nature,
its profligate but glorious beauty (7; 27). He again follows Nietzsche
in warning of the dangers of Christ's commandment to love one's
neighbour, which can simply encourage tears of self-pity (13).

Perhaps the most important of Christ's commands which Lawrence picks up is his injunction, 'Ye must be born again' (40), which he sees as fundamental to all human development, requiring the individual to break with the past, with parents and with society. Hardy is criticised (perhaps unfairly) for standing with the community against the aristocratic individual who rebels against it (45), unlike Christ, who was prepared to depart from the Jewish tradition, replacing the epoch of Law, the embodiment of a female principle rooted in the body, with that of Love, the male principle which emphasises spiritual values. In this, of course, Lawrence is developing themes raised in the 'Foreword to *Sons and Lovers*', although he now displays more sympathy with the male spirit than he had done in the earlier essay. Both, he argues, are necessary. For, as he says at the beginning of chapter VII, 'no new thing has ever arisen, or can arise, save out of the impulse of the male upon the female, the female upon the male'. This process, he recognises, cannot be 'frictionless' (52), requiring the kind of conflict depicted in *The Rainbow* between the male idealism of Will Brangwen and the female rootedness in the physical exemplified by Anna.

Chapter VII gives perhaps the clearest account of the interdependence of desire, religion and art. The idea of God, although based on lack, the impossibility of finding 'a perfect mate', is seen as an essential part of the male drive to spiritual development. Tragic art is the expression of the loss of completeness, of oneness with the female, a communion which, when achieved, produces 'a joyful utterance of religious art', as evinced in the Bible, which presents three ages: God's approach in David, the rapture of contact in Solomon, and the anguish of separation in Job (57–8). The Jewish God, the object of all this desire, is, according to Lawrence, intensely female, very much a 'God of the body'. His jealousy too is female, as is the desire for unity in 'the whole of flesh', the 'complete Monism of the female' as opposed to the male desire for multiplicity and diversity (59).

The opening of Genesis fits into Lawrence's gender stereotypes as a typically female story:

Cunning and according to female suggestion is the story of Creation: that Eve was born from the single body of Adam, without intervention of sex, both issuing from one flesh, as a child at birth seems to issue from one flesh of its mother. And the birth of Jesus is the retaliation of this: a child is born, not to the flesh, but to the spirit: and you, woman, shall conceive, not to the body but to the Word. 'In the beginning was the Word', says the New Testament. (60)

As in the 'Foreword to *Sons and Lovers*', the New Testament is seen as the 'great assertion of the male', producing a Christ who is begotten of the spirit, whose body 'must be destroyed . . . to testify that he was Spirit, that he was Male, that he was Man, without any womanly part.' All this contrasts with the beginning of Genesis, which shows how 'consciousness of the body came through woman' (60). The argument continues on a broad historical level with the 'male utterance of Christ' ushering in a prolonged 'fight against the body' apparent in the religious art of the medieval period when 'the collective, stupendous emotional gesture of the Cathedrals' expressed this spirituality in 'concrete form' (61). Even in these buildings, however, Lawrence detects a counter-movement,

the denial of the Monism which the Whole uttered. All the little figures, the gargoyles, the imps, the human faces, whilst subordinated within the Great Conclusion of the Whole, still from their obscurity, jeered their mockery of the Absolute, and declared for multiplicity, polygeny. (62)

This tension between monism and multiplicity (Bakhtin's monologism and multiplicity) will be echoed in the arguments between Will and Anna Brangwen in *The Rainbow*, which also focus upon the details of medieval cathedrals.

Chapter VIII of *Study of Thomas Hardy* constructs another elaborate set of binary oppositions: God the Father is aligned with the Law (the Old Testament) while the Son ushers in the age of Love. Since the Renaissance, according to Lawrence, 'the northern races have sought the consummation through Love; and they have denied the Father' (76). He sees no future, however, in continuing this opposition between the Father and the Son, the flesh and the spirit, and introduces the Holy Spirit as the conciliator, the mediator between them. Hardy's novels, to which the book somewhat belatedly turns, are seen, like those of Dostoevsky, to tell the tragedy of Love in conflict with Law. Lawrence analyses the way in which Hardy's male characters are made to deny their female side, their bodily passions, while his female characters are made either to despise their bodies (as Tess eventually does) or to destroy themselves (as in the case of Sue Bridehead) through the overdevelopment of their male qualities, 'the Love, the Spirit, the Mind, the Consciousness', at the expense of their female characteristics, 'the Law, the Soul, the Senses, the

Feelings' (117). Again, these oppositions will be found to play a significant role in *The Rainbow*, the very title of which involves not only an allusion to the sign given by God as a covenant to Noah in Genesis 9 but an association with the qualities of multiplicity which Lawrence saw as breaking down the pure white light of monological truth. Lawrence's thinking here is again very similar to Bakhtin's, the novel being promoted as a dialogical or internally persuasive discourse in opposition to the authoritative Word of monological theology. Later essays such as 'Morality and the Novel', not written until the 1920s but reprinted in the Cambridge edition of *Study of Thomas Hardy* because of shared themes, contrasts the way in which philosophy, religion and science are 'busy nailing things down' with the novel, in which 'If you try to nail anything down . . . either it kills the novel or the novel gets up and walks away with the nail.' Lawrence, like Bakhtin, celebrates the novel as 'the perfect medium for revealing to us the changing rainbow of our living relationships'. It is the novel, he proceeds, which 'can help us to live, as nothing else can: no didactic Scripture, anyhow' (*STH* 150, 154).

Another essay from the 1920s , 'Why the Novel Matters', also to be found in the Cambridge edition of *Study of Thomas Hardy*, rescues the Bible from accusations of dogmatism, didacticism or monologism by calling it

a great confused novel. You may say, it is about God. But it is really about man alive. Adam, Eve, Sarai, Abraham, Isaac, Jacob, Samuel, David, Bath-Sheba, Ruth, Esther, Solomon, Job, Isaiah, Jesus, Mark, Judas, Paul, Peter: what is it but man alive, from start to finish? Man alive, not mere bits. Even the Lord is another man alive, in a burning bush, throwing the tablets of stone at Moses's head. (*STH* 169)

Here, in a nutshell, are Lawrence's favourite bits of the Bible, most of which surface in the text of *The Rainbow*. The point, emphasised later in the essay, is that Lawrence refuses to accept 'any dazzling revelation, any supreme Word, any absolutes: things flow and change' in a manner captured better by fiction than by the more authoritative sections of the Bible (536). Yet another essay on 'The Novel' contrasts the gospels, which are 'wonderful novels' written by authors 'with a purpose', with Old Testament books such as Genesis, which are 'greater novels' because written 'by authors whose purpose was so big it didn't quarrel with their passionate inspiration' (157). After again denying the possibility of absolutes, Lawrence returns in this essay to the meaning of the rainbow as a symbol of relative truth: 'the gods,' Lawrence argues, 'are all like the rainbow, all colours and shades. Since light itself is invisible, a manifestation has got to be pink or black or blue or white or yellow or vermilion, or "tinted".' None of these manifestations can claim fully to represent God, who can only be known through the 'flame-life in all the universe; multifarious, multifarious flames, all colours and beauties and pains and sombreness' (426). It is this 'multifarious' quality which Lawrence sees as the most important characteristic of the novel. *The Rainbow*, as Joan Peters has argued, is misread if taken as a monological embodiment of Lawrencian metaphysics. Its differing narrative voices and focalisers (not only the narrators but the characters through whose eyes the action is seen) present a series of 'epiphanies, stratified in the novel through the symbol of the rainbow', all of which interrogate the biblical narratives while none can claim to have a monopoly of truth (Peters 1996: 205, 217).

The opening chapter of *The Rainbow* reproduces a number of features from the Book of Genesis, including an interest in genealogy, the 'succession of familial generations' which 'establish a significant parallel between the Brangwens . . . and those ancient biblical families . . . which carried God's promise in its table of genealogy' (Moynahan 1963: 147). In what appears to be a reversal of the gender stereotypes in the *Study of Thomas Hardy*, however, the men of the early Brangwen generations described in this chapter can be said to belong to the era of Law, content with the body and the satisfaction of its needs: 'It was enough for the men, that the earth heaved and opened its furrows to them.' Like Adam too, they enjoy having 'power over the cattle' (*R* 10). The women, identified by George Ford as the Eves in this garden of plenitude (Ford 1965: 118), want more, 'another form of life than this, something that was not blood-intimacy', facing outward, 'having turned their back on the pulsing heat of creation, . . . to enlarge their own scope and range and freedom' (*R* 11). They also symbolise 'religion and love and morality', standing as 'the restraining hand of God'. The men ask her to be their 'conscience-keeper', the 'angel at the doorway guarding my outgoing and my incoming' (20), a reference to the final verse of Genesis chapter 3, substituting Eve for the angel as the guardian of morality.

The women of all three generations of the Brangwen family whose stories are the subject-matter of the novel are certainly involved in a quest which they take to be religious. In the first generation it is Lydia, with her memories of the Polish convent of her youth, who represents a spirituality, an 'otherness' and an otherworldliness which fascinates Tom. To him she is an 'awful unknown, . . . the unaccountable and incalculable' (58). She worships 'God as a mystery, never seeking in the least to define what He was' (97). The language of their union, described as 'this transfiguration' which 'burned between him and her' (38), is also invested with biblical resonance. Sometimes this use of religious language, as Andrew Kennedy complains (Kennedy 1982: 222), can appear forced, even blasphemous, as when their sexual union is called Tom's 'trial and his admittance, his Gethsamene and his Triumphal Entry in one' (*R* 56). But other biblical references are more firmly grounded, as when Anna is born and Tom identifies so strongly with his wife that he feels 'the child was being brought forth out of their one flesh' (71), a clear echo of Genesis 2: 24. Chapter 3 ends with the first of the bow / arch symbols in the novel: Anna is described as 'at peace' between her parents, playing 'between the pillar of fire and the pillar of cloud in confidence' like the Israelites in their journey through the desert, her parents forming an 'arch' which 'met to the span of the heavens' (91). The narrative of each Brangwen generation in fact concludes with this image, which increases in importance as the novel progresses.

The young Anna, it should be noted, is also deeply religious. She learns Latin prayers and how to say the rosary. She becomes 'an assiduous church-goer', although 'the language meant nothing to her', seeming 'false' in comparison to the mysterious reality it attempts to express (99). The relationship between her and Will, as Poplawski observes, is articulated from the outset in religious terms (Poplawski 1993: 90). She first meets him on a Sunday and accompanies him to church, being both 'elated' and amused by his strangeness, by the sense in him of 'an unknown Presence' (*R* 106). He in turn feels that the 'veils had ripped,' that 'the hand of the Hidden Almighty. . . had . . . gripped him' (112). Each of the lovers is compared to Moses: Anna draws 'the very fountain of life' from rock while Will experiences the burning of the bush: 'The flame flowed up his limbs . . . till he was consumed' (121). Will begins a carving of Adam and Eve immediately after Anna's declaration of love for him, which makes him feel gripped by the 'hand of the Hidden Almighty, burning bright', the Blakean phrase at the end suggesting the grandeur of all creation. Will works on this carving, 'a panel in low relief', with 'a passion' which makes the connection between divine and human creation, divine and human love, quite clear:

Adam lay asleep as if suffering, and God, a dim, large figure, stooped towards him, stretching forward His unveiled hand; an Eve, a small, vivid, naked female shape, was issuing like a flame towards the hand of God, from the torn side of Adam. (112)

He trembles with passion as he touches her figure in the glory of creation. The additional details in his carving are also biblical: 'a bird on a bough overhead, lifting its wings for flight, and a serpent wreathing up to it', the two animals perhaps representing the ambivalence of the so-called Fall, since Eve's motives are the quest for wisdom, the desire to soar higher, while the serpent's evil intentions towards the bird suggest the death which will be the punishment for her disobedience of God's command. At the sides of the carving are two more biblical symbols: 'two Angels covering their faces with their wings' (113), symbolic of God's presence, like those which surround the Ark of the Covenant (Exod. 26: 18–21) or those Isaiah describes around the throne of the Lord (Isa. 6: 2), about which Lawrence had read in Jenner. Will, who lives in a world lit up by the glory of creation, sees angels everywhere: 'he felt that the Angels, with covered faces, were standing back as he went by' on his way to the Marsh in the twilight (*R* 113). He is described later as basking in the light of Anna's love 'as if his soul had six wings of bliss . . . , feeling the radiance from the Almighty beat through him like a pulse'. He appears to Anna as similarly transfigured: 'his face lit up, he seemed like an Annunciation to her' while she 'was subject to him as to the Angel of the Presence' (158). Again, this appropriation of traditional Christian symbolism can irritate both more orthodox Christians and more resolutely secular readers. Lawrence, like the Cambridge anthropologists, treads a narrow line, risking the alienation of readers who do not share his understanding of religious language as a necessarily inadequate attempt to express religious experience.

Will and Anna's Eden, of course, is not without its flaws. Even on their honeymoon, while Anna hurries round the cottage tidying up in preparation for their father's visit, Will dwells upon the inability of his carving fully to embody his vision. He cannot find words for what is wrong with his Eve, breaking off in the attempt to explain it, reduced to 'a gesture of infinite tenderness' and causing her 'a pang of disconsolate sadness' (149). For a time their love continues to override their differences, Will watching with joyful abandon while what his Nietzschean narrator calls 'his Tablets of Stone' go 'bounding and bumping and splintering down the hill, dislodged for ever'. He does not abandon religion altogether, however, retaining some of the vocabulary of the Book of Exodus: they kindle to each other 'like the Lord in two burning bushes that were not consumed' (Exod. 3: 2) while, in the language of the Book of Revelation (21: 1), language to be taken up again in the final vision of the book, they 'stand in a new world, a new earth, naked in a new, naked universe' (*R* 140).

Already, however, the first seeds of Will's disillusionment have been sown. A lengthy passage in the manuscript develops Will's fear of losing that sense of wonder which Lawrence thought essential to religion, focusing on the Christmas tree, which would need to be

undressed and thrown away. It was all a lie. He was beside himself with frantic rage. The time had come for disillusion. This magnificent, gleaming Tree of Life, this bush blazing with the Presence of God, was only a Christmas tree decked up, with the candles now gone out, and sordid dust upon it, waiting to be untrimmed and thrown on the rubbish heap. (579)

Like Carlyle, that other great worshipper of trees and discarder of outdated clothes (ancient forms which have lost their vitality), Will is forced to recognise that the great symbols of Genesis and Exodus, the Tree of Life and the burning bush, no longer mean what they did. The manuscript also gives more detail of Anna's scorn for such pieties as 'a reproduction of St Veronica's Kerchief' and depictions of 'sacred hearts' beating in their open chests, which seem to her 'horrid' (581). In the final text too Will and Anna continue to struggle over their different attitudes towards the church. She had been, we are told, 'a regular attendant at morning service' and 'had never questioned any beliefs' before. Now, with Will, she is 'still in the eternal world' (146) but resents having her life ordered by the Church.

Will's response to the Church illustrates the kind of idealism Lawrence had associated with the male in *Study of Thomas Hardy*, although it is emotional rather than intellectual: 'The Church teaching in itself meant nothing to him.' He luxuriates, to Anna's annoyance, 'in his dark emotional experience of the Infinite, of the

Absolute' (147). Anna's more pragmatic female temperament rebels agains this soulfulness and celebration of the mysterious, a rebellion which takes shape in objections to the symbolism of the stained-glass windows, particularly the figure of the triumphant lamb with the banner of victory (a symbol of the resurrection taken from the Book of Revelation chapter 5, as Lawrence would have read in Jenner). Against her inclinations she finds herself succumbing for a moment to the appeal of this lamb and experiencing 'a powerful mystic experience' as 'the power of the tradition seized on her' but pulls herself up, reacting with anger against the 'silly lamb' and her 'soulful' husband (160). She scoffs at his reverence for religious art as he pores over his pictures from Bamberg Cathedral and scorns his credulity in continuing to accept such miracles as the turning of water into wine, which could not, according to the higher critics, have happened precisely as St John recounts:

'Whether it turned into wine or whether it didn't,' he said, it doesn't bother me. I take it for what it is.'
'And *what* is it?' she asked, quickly, hopefully.
'It's the Bible,' he said. (160)

This answer angers her but satisfies him, since he is 'not a dogmatist' and doesn't 'care about the Bible, the written letter', taking what he finds 'of value to him' without having to accept it as literally true (160). Will's faith, however, is gradually eroded by her criticism and he finds himself unable to complete the carving. Like the wife in 'The New Adam and Eve', Anna objects to the notion of Eve as a spare rib and to his making Eve 'like a little marionette, . . . like a doll' in comparison to his Adam, who is 'as big as God'. ' "It is impudence to say that Woman was made out of Man's body," she continued, "when every man is born of woman. What impudence men have, what arrogance!" ' It is a complaint which causes Will to destroy his carving (162).

The chapter title, 'Anna Victrix', is sometimes taken as suggesting a defeat not only for Will but for the religious aspirations he embodies. But, as Poplawski argues, the conflict between them arises 'not simply because he is religious and she is not' but because his 'is a religious attitude guided and controlled by a conventional, abstract, and inflexible creed' while hers 'derives from spontaneous living experience within the natural world' (91). Poplawski perhaps overstates the case; Lawrence had learnt from Jenner the theological value of a coherent symbolic framework. The debate between Will and Anna, I suggest, reflects ambivalences within Lawrence himself, both attracted to Christian symbolism and critical of its limitations (especially when understood literally). Anna herself, for example, displays a tendency to stage biblical scenes of her own. One of the reasons for the suppression of the first edition of *The Rainbow* was the scene in which she dances naked before the Lord, exalting in her conception, a scene which combines Mary's exultation at being chosen to bear the Lord with David dancing before the Ark. That Anna is to be seen as a type of Mary is clear from the reference to her walking 'glorified' while 'the sound of the thrushes, of the trains in the valley, of the far-off faint noises of the town, were her "Magnificat"' (*R* 166). And that her dance in the bedroom, naked before the mirror, is analogous to that of David is made explicit in the manuscript description of her spirit being like David's: 'It had haunted her, how he danced naked before the Ark, and the wife had taunted him. And David had said "It was before the Lord: the Lord hath chosen me, therefore will I play before him."' (585) The final text reinforces the Marian comparison as she dances, 'lifting her hands and her body to the Unseen, to the unseen Creator who had chosen her, to Whom she belonged' (169–70). Just as Michal despises David for his 'leaping and dancing before the Lord' (II Sam. 6: 15) and Joseph too feels slighted by Mary, so Anna's exultation excludes and provokes Will: 'she danced exulting before her Lord, and knew no man' (*R* 171). This is not, of course, because she is a virgin but because she refuses to accept his domination. The manuscript has her acknowledge with Mary that a woman needs male protection: 'The sun knew, and the moon knew, that she could not go alone, since the man took her, as Joseph took Mary to Egypt' (588). Even the sun and moon here refer to the symbols surrounding the Virgin in Revelation 12: 1, suggesting her power over the universe (Hyde 1992: 87) while Anna regards her daughter Ursula as blessed with the kind of divine protection accorded to the three Israelites whom the furnaces of Nebuchadnezzar fail to consume in Daniel chapter 3. She feels confident that 'she might toss the child forward into the furnace, the child might walk there, amid the burning coals and the incandescent roar of heat, as the three witnesses walked with the angel in the fire' (*R* 181). She transfers her prophetic hopes, in other words, from her husband to her daughter.

The conflict between Will and Anna reaches its climax in Lincoln

Cathedral, where Will is portrayed swooning in an ecstasy which combines both the religious and the sexual. In one of the most extended passages of the manuscript cut from the final text, presumably because he recognised its openness to ridicule, Lawrence elaborated even further on what remains in the final text a 'swooning consummation' for Will as he enters the 'timeless ecstasy' of the building at 'the apex of the arch' (187–8). The arch, of course, relates to two other prominent symbols in the novel: the rainbow, which bridges heaven and earth, and the womb, source of life. The correspondence between the cathedral and the female body is made even more explicit in the manuscript, where Will's soul is portrayed 'swooning forever, locked there in the swooning, upper ecstasy, forever in the clasp of consummation . . . up, up, to the climax, the eternal embrace . . . on, on, and on, surging always upward' (591). Will could be said to be enacting the process described in *Study of Thomas Hardy* in which David objectifies his lack, constructing an ideal object for his unsatisfied desire. It is hardly surprising therefore that Anna should feel somewhat jealous of the cathedral, before which she too feels some 'reverence and fear and joy' but which she mistrusts (188).

Anna's reaction had been very different in the manuscript, in which she too is seen to respond initially to the call of the sacred as 'the power of the cathedral swept her up and carried her out of herself'. She hears the injunction to take off her shoes which Moses received before the burning bush in Exodus 3: 5, 'for this is holy ground' (591). Her initial response, like his, is to obey, her soul stooping 'to the latchet of its sandals'. She turns to the cathedral, 'a postulant' like her husband, and only later suffers a sense of unease, a feeling that 'the goal was missing, even in her rapture of her holy, awful height'. The first day of their visit to the cathedral ends with her dwelling on this religious impulse and having the equivalent of Jacob's dream in Genesis 28 of angels which 'quivered in flames of praise' around 'the Most High' (591–2). The difference is that when Jacob awakes from his dream in Genesis he retains a sense of awe, saying, 'Surely the Lord is in this place; and I knew it not . . . this is none other but the house of God.' He takes the stone that he had used as a pillow and sets it up 'for a pillar', pouring oil upon it in consecration (Gen. 28: 16–17). Anna, by contrast, suffers a sense of dreadful disappointment at the disappearance of her angelic vision. When she returns to the cathedral 'hoping to see, down the vista of shadowy, progressive ecstasies, the flickering lights of the angels, who should use the altar as an alighting-stone', she discovers that 'they were not there. Only the columns soared up in all their power', no longer lit up by divine radiance (*R* 592–3). The manuscript proceeds with a detailed analysis of Anna's disillusionment with conventional religion, presenting her as a risen Christ not sure what to do. She yearns to be united with 'the Mystery' but the cathedral has 'no flickering altar and no door', making her feel 'shut in', forced to go beyond the ecclesiastical building to the world outside, where 'the sky was infinitely high'. It is at this point in the manuscript that she notices 'the little human faces carved in stone across the screen' of the cathedral, faces which 'with their nice and nasty traits . . . made sly little mockery of the church's grand impulse of goodness . . . They winked and jeered' (594). This, as we have seen, dramatises the passage in *Study of Thomas Hardy* in which the gargoyles of medieval cathedrals are seen to subvert the 'monism' of absolute truth (*STH* 62).

Both the manuscript and the text record the same interchange between Anna and Will:

'Oh look! cried Anna, 'Oh look, how adorable, the faces! Look at her.'
Brangwen looked unwillingly. This was the voice of the serpent in his Eden.
She pointed him to a plump, sly, malicious little face carved in stone.
'He knew her, the man who carved her,' said Anna. 'I'm sure she was his wife.' (*R* 189, 594)

In the manuscript this leads to a huge argument in which he is possessed by 'devils of rage' while she jeers at his 'gothic ecstasies and his cathedral religion', which she reduces to 'mere architecture, museum things, relics of bygone history' (594). As in Bakhtin, belief in an absolute monological truth founders in the face of the modern demand for multiplicity. Will tries to cling to the church, although he recognises that its 'gloom' compares poorly to the brightness of the natural world outside. Anna places her hopes in this world, specific- ally in the child she is expecting, represented somewhat obscurely as a door 'under the foot of the rainbow', a gateway towards the new covenant (595). In both the final text and the manuscript, Anna's pointing to the human elements in the carvings has a devastating effect on Will, undermining his faith in the Church's claims to absolute truth. He continues to attend the church 'for what it tried to represent' although he no longer believes that it succeeds fully in that representation (191). 'He was like a lover who knows he is betrayed, but who still loves, whose love is only the more tense. The Church was false, but he served it the more attentively' (193). This part of the novel ends with her triumphant in her destruction of his belief in the Absolute, mocking his pretence of prayer to a personal God.

The spiritual battle between Will and Anna, however, continues within the mind of their daughter Ursula, named after one of Will's (and Jenner's) saints. Anna's concern for her is expressed in terms of the vision of the Promised Land from her 'Pisgah mount', as granted to Moses in Deuteronomy 34. From there Anna can just glimpse 'a rainbow like an archway, a shadow-door with faintly coloured coping above it (181). Earlier generations had failed to reach the goal, her grandfather Tom perishing in the flood, calling out drunkenly to his horse, 'which of us is Noah?' (227) while Will, as we have seen, has his faith undermined by Anna. That Ursula is to be regarded as the last of the Brangwen patriarchs (in spite of her gender) is also suggested by the blurb on the spine of the first edition which describes her as 'the leading-shoot of the restless, fearless family, waiting at the advance-post of our time to blaze a path into the future' (*Letters* II 402) although there are also suggestions here of a Nietzschean Superman (again with change of gender). The novel can thus be read as 'the story of the ancestry, birth, development, suffering, trials and triumphs of a prophet, . . . Ursula Brangwen, whose mission it will be to show the way out of the wilderness into a Promised Land' (Ford 1965: 130).

To begin with, Ursula's spirituality, like that of her father, is very other-worldly, having little to do with the flesh. She hears voices in the night like Samuel and her Jesus is 'the shadowy Jesus with the Stigmata,' not the 'actual man, talking with teeth and lips, telling one to put one's finger into His wounds' (*R* 255). She has earlier been presented meditating upon the relationship of the spirit to the body as it appears in the account of the sons of God coming in unto the daughters of men in the opening verses of Genesis chapter 6. Ursula, who is 'stirred as by a call from far off' by this narrative, identifies with the daughters of men and wonders about the nature of these suitors, whether 'these Sons of God, had known no expulsion, no ignominy of the fall'. She lives, at least in her imagination, 'in the essential days, when the Sons of God came in unto the daughters of men . . . these were such as should take her to wife' (257). She also dwells on passages from the New Testament, for example Jesus' reply to the rich man, 'It is easier for a camel to go through the eye of a needle, than for a rich man to enter into heaven' (Mark 10: 25). She has clearly read her Renan, recognising like him a tendency to hyperbole on the part of the 'Eastern mind'. She ponders the strangeness of this saying before concluding with a Bakhtinian distinction between 'the Absolute World' and 'the relative world' which can never hope fully to understand it. The passage cannot be interpreted literally, so she reverts to 'the non-literal application of the Scriptures' (*R* 258). The whole Brangwen family continue to live their lives in the light of the liturgical year, 'the epic of the soul of mankind', being born with Jesus at Christmas, crucified with Him on Good Friday and rising on Easter Sunday. The chapter ends with a long meditation on the risen Christ refusing to touch Mary Magdalen, culminating with a series of challenges to the fleshless spirituality of conventional Christian teaching:

Why shall I not rise with my body whole and perfect, shining with strong life? Why, when Mary says: Rabboni, shall I not take her in my arms and kiss her and hold her to my breast? Why is the risen body deadly, and abhorrent with wounds? (262)

These questions could perhaps be read as free indirect discourse filtered through Ursula's mind but the voice, besides being distinctly masculine in desire, seems too authoritative for her at this stage of the novel, proceeding to hammer home the answers: 'The Resurrection is to life not death' and requires 'living in the flesh, loving in the flesh, begetting children in the flesh' (262). It is a voice in direct continuity with that of the 'Foreword to *Sons and Lovers*'.

Ursula herself is shown gradually to appreciate the significance of the flesh. She soon abandons her faith in the literal truth of miracles and also rejects Christian teaching about giving to the poor and turning the other cheek, 'this humble side of Christianity' appearing to her (as to Nietzsche) 'unclean and degrading' (265). She even begins to think of Jesus as a lover rather than a teacher, leaping 'with sensuous yearning' to his invitation, 'Come unto me all that labour and are heavy-laden, and I will give you rest' (Matt. 11: 28). She fantasises about laying her head on his breast and being 'caressed like a child', receiving 'a sensuous response' from Jesus. She does not abandon her religion but wants it to become more physical. She suffers a momentary sense of guilt at taking 'his words of the spirit' and making them 'pander to her own carnality' (*R* 267) but when the glamorous Skrebensky appears she immediately sees him as one of 'those Sons of God who saw the daughters of men, that they were fair', not 'servile', like Adam and his descendants. Skrebensky's divinity, his Sonship of God, as Ursula has now come to understand that term, is asserted in terms of the passage in Genesis 18 when Abraham is visited by three angels standing in his doorway, who 'greeted him, and stayed and ate with him, leaving his household enrichened for ever when they went' (271). As in the oldest strands of the Book of Genesis, when God appears it is in a very physical form.

One of the first scenes of lovemaking between Ursula and Skrebensky takes place significantly in a derelict church, 'filled with scaffolding, fallen stone and rubbish' (275). The clear implication is that the old covenant, propped up and repaired though it may be, must eventually give way to the new. When Skrebensky kisses her, the narrative blasphemously echoes that used by the Creator in Genesis 1: 'And it was good, it was very, very good' (282). Lawrence again uses the image of 'transfiguration' (284) although, as with the earlier generations of lovers, their path is not completely smooth; Ursula receives some of Skrebensky's kisses 'cold and unmoved as a pillar of salt' (297), presumably an indication that she is still looking backward, like Lot's wife, not yet ready for the new covenant. Her development (and *The Rainbow*, like so many of Lawrence's novels, does turn into a *Bildungsroman*) is marked once again by her reflecting the following morning in church upon 'her favourite book in the Bible', the Book of Genesis, at which she glances during the service, significantly apart from the rest of the worshippers, whose activities pass 'unnoticed'. She reads the first three verses of chapter 9, again in the King James version, which contain God's instructions to 'Be fruitful and multiply', finding herself unmoved, bored even by this 'vulgar and stock-raising sort of business'. Her interest, however, is aroused by verses 9 to 15, which record God's promise, sealed in the token of the rainbow, never again to 'destroy all flesh'. She picks up these last three words, indulging in some rather fanciful midrashic speculation upon possible developments after the flood in which she imagines a few dryads and naiads escaping to tell 'amusing tales of Noah in his ark', and herself as a nymph 'flicking drops of the flood at Noah' before escaping to 'people who were less important in their Proprietor and their Flood'. Ursula's irreverent speculation reveals her rejection of the conventional Judaeo-Christian deity: 'She was surfeited of *this* God' (my italics), though not of the source of all life (301–2).

At this point in the manuscript, Ursula is made to turn once more 'to the New Testament, to the Sermon on the Mount' in Matthew's Gospel, which she subjects to increasingly severe interrogation. Her eye is caught by key verses which are interspersed in the manuscript by her own comments. She objects in turn to being 'the light of the world', to possessing treasure and to being enjoined not to take thought for raiment. She reacts violently to Christ's injunction not to give 'that which is holy unto the dogs, neither cast ye your pearls before swine' (Matt. 7: 6): 'Is not my body holy, and my flesh more precious than pearls?' (*R* 629). When, later in Matthew 7, she comes across the parable of the man who built his house upon the sand, she reacts with similar violence, launching into a diatribe against conventional notions of God, the Fall and the Church. Instead of enjoying the security of divine protection, the man who built his house upon a rock, in Ursula's version of the parable, sees the floods come and destroy it; 'and great was the fall thereof,' she adds, in her best biblical pastiche (629). She proceeds to an astonishing prophecy of the new covenant in which,

The fauns shall run in your parks and the dryads shall play among the pews of your churches, and Jesus, whole and glad after the Resurrection, shall laugh when evening falls and the nightingale sings, and he shall give himself to the breasts of desire and shall twine his limbs with the nymphs and the oreads, putting off his raiment of wounds and sorrows, appearing naked and shining with life, the risen Christ, gladder, a more satisfying lover than Bacchus, a God more serene and ample than Apollo. (629–30)

If Britain in 1915 was to find the idea of Anna dancing naked before the mirror obscene, it was certainly not ready for the manuscript version of Ursula's vision of a proud dryad who describes how Jesus 'came starting through the leaves last night, and flung away his garments, and caught me with wonderful hands, more exquisite and lover-like than the hands of Bacchus', proceeding to kiss and embrace her. Jesus, she insists, 'is the only perfect lover, since he is risen from the grave, the only perfect lover in heaven or earth' (630).

Such a radical vision of Jesus the perfect lover would not, of course, see print until *The Escaped Cock*, when Lawrence was past caring or relying financially upon the reception of his work. In the version of *The Rainbow* published in 1915 Skrebensky not only fails to share Ursula's vision but fails utterly to live up to her lofty expectations. The embraces of Winifred Inger, similarly unacceptable to the British public in 1915, also fail to satisfy, though she learns from Winifred to rid religion 'of its dogmas, its falsehood', revealing 'universal' religion beneath the regional differences along theosophical lines (317). She also suffers disillusion in her dream of knowledge as a substitute for religion. She goes to college in Nottingham with a wide-eyed belief in its 'black-gowned priests' but is soon disabused of this faith too. Only botany retains its glow as a route 'to the source of the mystery', a route long since abandoned by her other teachers. In a vision deeply critical of modernity and its belief in scientific explanation she sees the inhabitants of Nottingham, lit by electric lamps, as sleepers by a camp fire refusing to admit that there can be anything beyond their limited circle of vision. They insist that there is nothing beyond 'our light and our order'. She and Skrebensky, however, choose to walk in the darkness outside the glare of the 'stupid lights' and the 'stupid, artificial town', their kisses being 'their final entry into the source of creation', passing for a moment 'into the pristine darkness of paradise' (450–1). They also cavort unashamedly naked in the open air, like the prelapsarian Adam and Eve.

Eventually, in the final chapter of the novel, it is the Book of Revelation which supplies Ursula with a positive vision of the future. There is the encounter with the mysterious horses, the falling into a trance, the painful labour of childbirth (Rev. 12: 2) and, of course, the rainbow of Revelation 4: 3 and 10: 1, recalling the sign given to Noah. Recovering from her miscarriage, Ursula, like St John, has a vision of the 'new creation', 'the new germination' which will arise out of the old, 'a band of faint iridescence colouring in faint colours a portion of the hill'. Gradually the rainbow gathers strength and clarity, leading to the triumphant final paragraph of the novel in which, lit up by the rainbow, the people whose lives had been sordid 'cast off their horny covering of disintegration' and assume 'new, clean, naked bodies'. The 'old, brittle corruption of houses and factories' are swept away, to be replaced by a new 'world built up in a living fabric of Truth, fitting to the over-arching heaven' (*R* 458–9). There is still the possibility of Truth with a capital 'T' but it has to be fabricated, constructed by men and women, and mediated by the rainbow, that symbol of disseminated, multivocal and dialogical truths.

Lawrence's reworking of biblical elements in this novel, I want to suggest, was an outpouring of the profound religious impulse which continued to drive much of his writing but which was to turn increasingly bitter, partly as a result of the reception and suppression of this novel (Delany 1979: 156–9) after which his ongoing wrestling with the Bible was to become increasingly aggressive and blasphemous, assuming a predominantly hostile readership which he deliberately provokes. His rewriting of the Book of Genesis in *The Rainbow*, while attempting to bring out what conventional Christian reading had long suppressed, its dominant concern with creation, sexuality, fertility, husbandry and brotherhood, working towards a spirituality that does not deny the body, could be said to retain a respect for the biblical original which was to disappear in much of his later writing. It continues the battle begun in the earlier work with 'the flesh-denying religion of the Son' (*STH* 80). But it also embodies a vision of a risen Christ (even more prominent in the manuscript) who assumes some of the characteristics of the 'Sons of God' of Genesis 6, going into the daughters of men and making them happy. It is certainly what Harold Bloom would call a 'strong' reading of the original text, 're-accenting', in Bakhtin's terms, a text Lawrence believed to have been falsely appropriated by a timid and unimaginative Christian orthodoxy. The novel provides an ambivalent supplement to the original, one which not only completes but in some ways supplants the original, re-marking conventional Christian symbols in a self-consciously fictive 'counter-Bible'.

CHAPTER 7

Double-reading the Bible: esoteric 'Studies' and 'Reflections'

Lawrence had finished *The Rainbow* with a flourish, a letter to Viola Meynell enclosing a sketch of an industrial town lit up by a rainbow, confiding his dreams of finding 'pots of gold at its feet', and referring optimistically to a new 'book about Life – more rainbows, but in different skies' to be published first in a magazine called *The Signature* (*Letters* II 299). Other letters drumming up subscribers for *The Signature* liken himself to 'the prophet in the wilderness' (II 389) announcing 'the beginning of a new religious era' (II 399). The suppression of *The Rainbow*, however, and the collapse of the magazine after only three issues, along with the continuing nightmare of the war, quickly destroyed this optimism, giving a darker tone to his apocalyptic vision, a tone which dominates much of his writing of this period, not only the essays written for *The Signature*, eventually published as 'The Crown' in *Reflections on the Death of a Porcupine* in 1925, but also *Twilight in Italy*, published in 1916, and a series of essays written from 1917 to 1919, some of which were published at the time in *The English Review* under the title 'Studies in Classic American Literature'. This remained their title when they were heavily revised for publication as a book in 1923. The essays reflect rather more than the book Lawrence's developing interest in theosophy, in particular its deconstructive 'double-reading' of the Bible as a not-completely-successful attempt to cover over the traces of an earlier ancient wisdom. Blavatsky and her followers read between the lines of the 'exoteric' Bible (the Bible as canonised by the Church) in an attempt to recover the earliest layers of esoteric wisdom within it. This, they claim, is the 'real' meaning of the Bible. Lawrence, I claim, while remaining characteristically detached from theosophical orthodoxy, can be found to practise a mode of 'double-reading' of the Bible similar to that of Blavatsky and her followers, a mode of reading which was to culminate in *Apocalypse*.

Lawrence's letters throughout the war years, as we saw in the introduction, are dominated by apocalyptic fears, full of warnings of the end 'of the Christian era' and its replacement with new religious ideas, 'a new Word' (*Letters* II 433 and 526). He even compared himself to Noah, 'taking all the precious things into the ark, when the flood comes, and disembarking on a new world' (II 663). By July 1917, however, he could see 'no Rainbow' but only 'the deluge of iron rain' which he thought would 'destroy the world here, utterly: no Ararat will rise above the subsiding iron waters' (III 142–3). There are other gloomy references to the desired 'destruction of mankind, as in Sodom' (II 650) and to his continuing belief that 'There ought to be a flood to drown mankind' (III 20). The Flood, of course, functions in the New Testament as a type of the final destruction: Christ warns his disciples that 'as the days of Noe were, so shall also the coming of the Son of Man be', with the profane 'eating and drinking, marrying and being given in marriage' right up to the final judgement (Matt. 24: 37–9). The punishment is even worse in the Book of Revelation, where the wicked are plunged into 'the lake which burneth with fire and brimstone: which is the second death', worse even than water (Rev. 22: 8). Lawrence still harboured hopes of escaping all this, setting up 'a sort of Garden of Eden of blameless but fulfilled souls, in some sufficiently remote spot' (*Letters* III 65), but his vision had darkened considerably.

Crucifixion also provides a key symbol for the suffering of the war years. One of the most powerful poems Lawrence produced during the war, 'Eloi, Eloi, Lama Sabachthani?', published in *The Egoist* in May 1915, presents its crucified Christ-figure as a reluctant soldier, who has dreamt of love but is forced to kill, using the bayonet on his 'bride', the enemy soldier, 'that other, / The enemy, my brother'. 'Why should we hate,' he asks, and why does the war command such support:

> why do the women follow us satisfied,
> Feed on our wounds like bread, receive our blood
> Like glittering seed upon them for fulfilment? (*CP* 741–3)

The poem combines Lawrence's hatred of conventional religion, presenting the eucharist both as a perverted sublimation of sexual instincts and as a contributing factor in the continuation of the war, with a characteristic identification on Lawrence's part with Christ, the supreme victim. Although, as he told Catherine Carswell in

1916, he was no longer a Christian he wanted people 'to be more Christian rather than less', fulfilling their 'deepest desire' for 'living truth' (*Letters* II 633).

The essays which comprise 'The Crown', the first three of which were published in the only issues of *The Signature* to reach the public in 1915 (in October and November), reveal a continuing preoccupation with biblical themes even though Lawrence had announced that he was going to rewrite his philosophy from a different, less Christian perspective than that of *Study of Thomas Hardy* (II 367). Notions of eternal flux, of unity beneath apparent chaos, which recur in the essays, have been traced to Heraclitus filtered through John Burnet's *Early Greek Philosophy* (*Ref.* xxii). Blavatsky too may have contributed to his belief in the necessary marriage of opposites, *Isis Unveiled* citing 'several pairs of mythic antagonists', including Cain and Abel and Christ and Satan, who display 'a mysterious connection' with each other (Whelan 1988: 155–6). A more obvious model, however, is Blake, whose celebration of 'The Marriage of Heaven and Hell' also involves pastiche of the Bible. There are, as ever, a range of mediating intertexts between the Bible and Lawrence's own writing.

'The Crown' begins with the struggle between the lion and the unicorn, 'the king of beasts and the defender of virgins', which is taken to symbolise the dualism Lawrence wants to overcome. Neither pagan celebration of the senses nor Christian asceticism, he argues, can ever win the struggle or claim to possess the whole truth. The unicorn, as Lawrence would have read in Jenner, had already been a 'symbol of purity . . . in pre-Christian times' before its appropriation as 'an emblem of chastity and strength' in medieval 'representations of Our Lady' (Jenner 1910: 148) while the lion is introduced in biblical terms 'roaring after his prey', as in Psalm 104: 21 (*Ref.* 253). The problem, according to Lawrence, is that most people tend to adopt either one side or the other, either proclaiming with Jesus, 'I am the light', or opposing him altogether (255, 257). Lawrence attacks both these extremes. St John's portrait of Jesus as the light shining in uncomprehending darkness, for example, in the opening chapter of his Gospel, characteristically overlooks the positive role darkness has to play, which is given greater recognition in the first chapter of Genesis (for Lawrence, as we shall see in the next chapter, Genesis and John, like the lion and the unicorn, are opposites). The Old Testament is seen to celebrate the way in which 'the flesh develops in splendour and glory out of the prolific darkness, begotten by the light it develops to a great triumph, till it dances naked in glory of itself, before the Ark' (257).

Lawrence insists that this battle between the flesh of Genesis and the spirit of John can only be resolved by a balance of opposites, not a victory for either side:

Love and hate [1925: power], light and darkness, these are the temporary conquest of the one infinite by the other. In love, the Christian love, the End asserts itself supreme: in hate, in wrath [1925: in power, in strength] like the lion's, the Beginning re-establishes itself unique. But when the opposition is complete on either side, then there is perfection . . . the perfect balance of light and darkness. (258–9; see 469 for the textual variants between 1915 and 1925)

John, unsurprisingly, is aligned by Lawrence with the End, his Book of Revelation ushering in the end both of the world and the Bible, uttering a curse against anyone who 'shall add unto these things' (Rev. 22: 18). Genesis is associated, naturally enough, with the Beginning both of life itself and of the Bible. Love and power will be identified in *Apocalypse* as Nietzsche's 'two divine things in life' (*A* 165). Both are here seen to be necessary, to be held, if possible, in a balanced and fruitful tension.

'The Crown' proceeds with a prolonged meditation on the significance of the rainbow as a symbol of the interpenetration of light and darkness in a truth which is multiple rather than mono-logical, developing themes to be found in *Study of Thomas Hardy* and *The Rainbow*. Lawrence's language becomes increasingly poetic as he celebrates this evanescent 'foam, this iris between the two floods', the rainbow combining the 'spray of earth and the foam of heaven' in a Blakean consummation, a 'fight of opposites which is holy' (*Ref.* 262). It is in the marriage of sexual opposites, however, that man comes closest to God; it is then that 'I melt and am gone into the eternal darkness . . . and at last *I am*' (265, cf. Exod. 3: 14).

'The Crown' continues to attack all forms of what Lawrence labels 'Monism', all attempts by 'the unconsummated soul' to 'seek to make itself whole by bringing the whole world under its one order' (267). All such attempts at interpretive mastery are seen to be motivated by a Nietzschean will to power, as in the career of the egoistic David: 'slaying the preposterous Goliath, overthrowing the heroic Saul, taking Bathsheba and sending Uriah to death'. Even David dancing naked before the Ark, so celebrated in *Study of Thomas*

Hardy and *The Rainbow*, is now presented as a means of 'asserting the oneness, his own oneness, the one infinity, *himself*, the egoistic God, I AM' (268). Such 'monism' is presented as the product of a sterile and stagnant spirituality: 'the course of the barren spirit is dogmatically to assert One God, one Way, one Glory, one exclusive salvation'. This is 'the sham Crown', when either the lion or unicorn is made victorious: 'This is evil, when that which is temporal and relative asserts itself eternal and absolute' (272). Lawrence's opposition to dogmatic Christianity emerges most strongly at this point. He turns Christ's cry on the cross, '*It is finished!*', against the religion founded in his name, calling it 'a fatal half-truth', for 'It is never finished' (292). He launches a savage attack on 'deadened forms' and 'the static ego, with its will-to-persist' (293). Such confidence in the absolute truth of one's position is seen as leading to violence and war, driving men to 'destroy life for the preserving of a static, rigid form, a shell, . . . the glassy envelope of the established concept' (294). The beliefs for which the war was being fought are cited as an example of such hypocrisy, a 'whited sepulchre' (296), itself another example of Lawrence using Jesus's own words (Matt. 23: 27) against Christianity. What is required is a combination of the two perspectives, the flesh and the Word, Genesis and John. 'The Crown' ends with Lawrence advocating a new notion of God as a revelation which 'vanishes as the rainbow' (*Ref.* 304), never static or finished but always developing and in flux. The 'one glorious activity of man' becomes, in words taken from Revelation 21: 1, ' the getting himself into a new relationship with a new heaven and a new earth' (306).

Many of the concerns and much of the imagery of 'The Crown' find their way into *Twilight in Italy*, published in June 1916. Some of the material, of course, was first written much earlier. The first version of 'Christs in the Tirol', for example, dates from early September 1912, while 'A Chapel Among the Mountains' was probably drafted that August. Most of the other essays, however, date from the late summer of 1915. What Lawrence finds impressive about the crucifixes described in 'Christs in the Tirol' and the paintings of biblical scenes described in 'A Chapel Among the Mountains' is the sincere attempts of their creators 'to get at the meaning of their own soul's anguish', at the experience of death and suffering (*TI* 44–5). He clearly prefers the more realistic depictions of Christ, miserable though some of them are and 'in need of a bit more kick', as he tells one of them, to the florid and ornate crucifixes with 'great gashes' and 'streams of blood' to be found on the Italian side of the Brenner Pass (46). The essay ends by meditating on the multitude of Christs depicted, from the sentimental to the rebellious. In a final twist to the essay, Lawrence considers the failure of the English to carve such Christs, 'afraid lest they should be too like men, too like ourselves' (47). By creating a metaphysical abstraction rather than focusing upon his humanity, he argues, we lose the very qualities that make the Christs in the Tyrol so appealing. Among the English Christs mentioned at the end of this first draft of the essay is *Jude the Obscure* (233), a recognition that his precursor Hardy was involved in a similar process of representing Christ, re-presenting him (and rewriting the gospels) by setting his Christ-figure Jude in a contemporary setting.

Yet more Christs appear in 'The Crucifix Among the Mountains', which celebrates the creative imagination of the Bavarian peasants, evident not only in their crucifixes but in their relish for liturgical processions and festivals and their continuing to 'act the mystery plays with instinctive fulness of interpretation' (93). It is in discussing the Italians in an essay 'On the Lago di Gada' that Lawrence develops the familiar theme of conflict between innocent enjoyment of the flesh characteristic of the Book of Genesis and ascetic denial of it demanded by Christ in the gospels. Like Nietzsche, Lawrence deplores the medieval 'striving, out of a strong, primitive, animal nature, towards the self-abnegation and the abstraction of Christ, . . . towards the elimination of the flesh' in the service of 'The Word'. Like Nietzsche too he sees the Renaissance as a turning-away from Christ and 'back to the flesh', celebrating how 'God the Father created man in the flesh, in His own image' (116).

The mixture of discourses to be found in this essay, however, creates a certain dissonance. Blake's tiger, for example, finds itself burning in a strange biblical environment, supposedly symbolic of 'the supremacy of the flesh, which devours all, and becomes transfigured into a magnificent brindled flame, a burning bush indeed' (116). Christ is depicted as 'the lamb which the eagle sweeps down upon, the dove taken by the hawk, the deer which the tiger devours' (119), a series of oppositions similar to those in 'The Crown'. As in that work Lawrence is advocating a balance of 'Northern' and 'Southern' attitudes: 'The Infinite is two-fold: the Father and the Son . . . And man must know both' (125–6). If we can achieve this, the original typescript claims, 'we shall have re-created Paradise' (315).

The third section of 'On the Lago di Garda' develops this conflict between the two infinites, the 'Christian Infinite' and 'the old pagan Infinite' in terms similar to 'The Crown', referring again to David dancing before the ark as an example of one extreme, and 'the Christian ecstasy' of the monks as the other (146). 'We are tempted,' Lawrence writes, 'like Nietzsche, to return back to the old pagan Infinite', but what is required once more is the reconciliation of 'the Holy Ghost that relates both natures of God' (148). Finally, in 'Italians in Exile', he sees the position as changing, with Northern Europe 'turning back on its own Christianity, denying it all' and 'whether it hates Nietzsche or not, . . . crying out for the Dionysic ecstasy' while Southern Europe is struggling against its 'sensuous spirit . . . breaking free from Dionysos' (200). Lawrence's assessment of these sweeping changes in national temperament are less important for the current argument than his clear desire to return to the paradisal celebration of the flesh which he associates with the Book of Genesis.

Lawrence's essays through the latter period of the war and in its immediate aftermath continue to draw upon biblical originals, often eclectically, as in an essay on 'Love' published in the *English Review* in 1917, a characteristically heady mixture of Old and New Testament material in which the Song of Solomon is brought together with Pauline celebration of sacred love as 'selfless, seeking not its own' (*Ref.* 9, cf. 1 Cor. 13: 5). A series of essays on 'The Reality of Peace', which appeared in the *English Review* from May to August 1917, continues to wrestle with the way we relate to our religious traditions, deploring the tendency to cling tenaciously and uncritically to old habits and beliefs. These essays are really sermons, Lawrence taking his biblical texts as the basis for his own highly personal preaching in which images from Isaiah (the lion and the lamb), Exodus (the burning bush) and the Psalms (on true peace) are juxtaposed with others from St John's Gospel (the corn of wheat that must die) and the Book of Revelation (the river of life). The biblical material is welded into the Lawrentian message that true peace must accept the impossibility of the lion ever lying down with the lamb: 'the peace of the lamb is to be devourable' (47). Here, as in *The Rainbow*, the conventional Christian symbolism of the lamb is given a Blakean twist. Even when he celebrates the joys of nature, the springtime renewal of all forms of life, as in 'Whistling of Birds' in the *Athenaeum* in 1919, he does so with reference to the Song of

Solomon (the voice of the turtle), St Matthew's Gospel (on letting the dead bury their dead) and the Book of Revelation (celebrating a new heaven and a new earth).

Some of these last essays are already beginning to reflect Lawrence's growing interest in theosophy, which is reported to have begun in his Nottingham days, when he went with William Hopkin to at least one meeting of the Theosophical Society (Cobau 1976: 133–4). He may also have attended lectures on the subject in London in 1917 (Kinkead-Weekes 1996: 832). He is also likely to have encountered theosophy in *The New Age*, which published nine articles on theology and theosophy in 1911. Whether or not he read these particular articles, 'theosophy and esotericism generally were in the air at the time' (Whelan 1988: 104), the most nebulous of the forms intertextuality can take. We know, however, that Lawrence occasionally read *The Occult Review* and was soon reading Madame Blavatsky's main works, *Isis Unveiled* and *The Secret Doctrine*, reporting to David Eder in 1917 that the latter was 'in many ways a bore and not quite real. Yet one can glean a marvellous lot from it' (*Letters* III 150). He had similarly announced in July of that year that he was 'not a theosophist' but found 'the esoteric doctrines . . . marvellously illuminating' (III 143).

Blavatsky, of course, has much to say about the Bible, reflecting the contemporary reawakening of interest in all ancient eastern religious texts including the apocrypha, pseudepigrapha and the kabbala, along with Buddhist and Hindu sacred texts such as the Vedas, many of which were properly edited for the first time in the nineteenth century (Washington 1993: 36). For Blavatsky the 'real Hebrew Bible was a secret volume, unknown to the masses', not to be confused with the 'exoteric' volume carefully constructed by a later priestly caste in Israel (*IU* II 471). She finds traces of that ancient text in the kabbala, printed portions of which contained 'ruins and fragments, much distorted remnants still of that *primitive system which is the key to all religious systems*' (*SD* II 461). Extant texts of such pseudepigrapha as the Books of Enoch were merely copies of 'some scripture of a prehistoric religion' while the Book of Revelation had simply adapted some of this material to Christianity (II 483). *Isis Unveiled* describes the Book of Revelation as 'the product of an initiated Kabalist [*sic*] taking material from the Books of Enoch' (*IU* 147), an argument which other theosophists such as Carter and Pryse (not to mention Lawrence himself) were to develop.

Reading the Bible for Blavatsky is a matter of reading between the lines in order to detect traces of an older strand of sacred wisdom now lost. She attacks the naivety of 'accepting the narratives literally, and as a whole', insisting that 'the Hebrew Scripture wears on its face the mark of its double origin', a surface level produced by redaction at the time of the Babylonian captivity and a deeper level containing much older material, some of which could be traced back to the Chaldeans (I 575–6). This is the point of her repeated insistence that the Hebrew Bible requires a special kind of double reading:

> Read by the light of the Zohar, the initial four chapters of Genesis are the fragment of a highly philosophical page in the World's Cosmogony. . . Left in their symbolical disguise, they are a nursery tale, an ugly thorn in the side of science and logic, an evident effect of Karma. To have let them serve as a prologue to Christianity was a cruel revenge on the part of the Rabbis, who knew better what their Pentateuch meant. It was a silent protest against their spoliation . . . (*SD* I 10–11).

To accept 'the dead-letter of the Bible' is therefore to be guilty of naivety and superstition (I 303–5). The core truth, the secret inner meaning of scripture, has to be uncovered through layers of distortion and misinterpretation, whether Patristic impositions of Platonic metaphysics upon Jesus and his initiates or rabbinic mis-readings of Moses and his teaching, itself derived from Egypt.

The symbolic significance of the Bible is the subject of chapters in *The Secret Doctrine* such as 'Tree and Serpent and Crocodile Worship', which discusses the Book of Genesis in terms of phallic symbolism and mysterious sources of energy. After quoting a kabbalistic manu-script which discusses the womb as 'the MOST HOLY PLACE, the SANCTUM SANCTORUM, and the *veritable* TEMPLE OF THE LIVING GOD', Blavatsky deplores the way 'the Hebrew Bible, and its servile copyist, Christian theology' made this merely metaphorical. The Genesis account of the Fall, she insists, needs to be read on a deeper level. While it may on the surface, or 'exoterically', appear to describe 'a temptation of flesh in a garden of Eden' which God curses, '*esoterically* he regarded the supposed *sin* and FALL as an act so sacred, as to choose the organ, the perpetrator of the *original sin*, as the fittest and most sacred symbol to represent that God' (I 382–3). To choose circumcision, in other words, as the identifying mark of the chosen people was to erect the phallus to a status which succeeded only in undermining its sexual morality. In passages such as this Blavatsky's double reading of the Bible appears uncannily to anticipate Derrida, a result perhaps of their shared interest in the kabbala.

Blavatsky herself was generally less enthusiastic than Lawrence about what she called the 'phallicism' of the rabbis, preferring Hegel's notion of a 'God (the Universal Spirit)' who *objectivises himself as Nature*, and again rises out of it' (I 257n). She finds the rabbis guilty of dragging the divine into the animal. At one point she labels Judaism 'this sexual religion' (II 274) while at another she complains of the 'gross . . . realism of the Jews', explaining David's uncovering himself before the ark in sexual terms, the ark being an 'emblem of female generative power' (II 459). One of the main differences between theosophical and more orthodox readings of Genesis lies in their treatment of the Fall, which is seen by Blavatsky in terms of a descent from the spiritual to the physical. Creation itself, incarnation in the flesh, is itself a descent from spiritual existence. The biblical Eve in Genesis 2, according to Blavatsky, represents Nature or matter while Adam represents the Spirit, although, following the kabbala, she separates the heavenly Adam, Adam Kadmon, from the second Adam, who produces Eve out of his side. Jehovah, Blavatsky explains, as 'embodied' in the opening chapters of Genesis, 'is but a *human* god', in contrast with 'the Supreme and Unknown God' adored by the Jewish kabbalists, in common with their initiated masters, the Chaldeans and the Hindus. Jehovah, whom Christians worship as 'the exoteric deity', 'the 'father' of the initiated Jesus', is known to esoteric wisdom as 'half-spiritual and half-material', a lesser figure than the 'universal Spirit', the ultimate Godhead (*IU* II 267–9).

The first chapters of Genesis, as retold by Blavatsky, herself drawing upon kabbalistic texts, represent an allegorical account of the process by which mankind degenerated from an earlier state that was purely spiritual. Midrashically reading Genesis through the light of I Corinthians and its distinction between the heavenly and the earthly man (I Cor. 6: 3), Blavatsky finds there not only evidence that St Paul too 'must be recognized as an initiate' but also hope for man's eventual recovery of the spiritual state forfeited in Eden. The role of the serpent in the 'fall' of man is totally reversed by Blavatsky in a manner which will be shown to have fed into the symbolic significance of much of Lawrence's writing, in particular *The Plumed Serpent*. Rather than seeing the serpent as responsible for evil, Blavatsky insists that it should 'be thanked for the signal service it had rendered humanity. For it taught Adam that if he ate of the fruit of the tree of knowledge of good and evil, he would raise his being immensely by the learning and wisdom he would thus acquire' (*SD* I 404). Symbolically, Blavatsky claims, the serpent is connected with the tree of life, both being 'a glyph of Immortal Being'. The 'winged serpent' who emerged from the original mundane egg was 'the symbol of the All-wisdom', represented by the 'flying or fiery serpents' and brazen serpent of the Book of Exodus (I 364). Blavatsky also reverses traditional interpretations of the sons of God going into the daughters of men in Genesis chapter 6 (the passage so dear to Ursula in *The Rainbow*). These sons of God, demonised by orthodoxy, she insists, should be celebrated as initiates, like the angels in the Book of Enoch who teach the daughters of men the secrets of heaven. They fell into sensuality and 'became the "Fallen Angels" only after perceiving that the daughters of men were fair' (I 412).

Blavatsky has her own esoteric view of Jesus, claiming that he too, like Moses, would have been initiated into the esoteric mysteries by the Egyptians (*IU* II 305). She rejects Renan's Jesus as a 'sentimental ninny', presenting her own portrait of him as a 'Jewish philanthropist', an adept and mystic, 'who preferred even to risk death than withhold some truths which he believed would benefit humanity' (II 340). Her reconstruction of the supposed 'originals' of biblical texts, of course, is often plainly fictitious. Not content with references in Jerome to an original secret Gospel of St Matthew (II 182), she refers at various points to 'the ORIGINAL Acts of the Apostles' (*SD* II 481), 'the real original text of I Corinthians' (II 153) and a whole host of speculative pseudepigrapha and midrashim. The biggest fiction of all is her supposed Book of Dzyan, on which *The Secret Doctrine* is an extended commentary. This text 'utterly unknown to philologists', whose doctrines were scattered through 'thousands of Sanskrit MSS.' (I xxii–iii), as Lawrence himself must have realised, was as imaginative a construct as any of his own novels.

Blavatsky was by no means the only theosophist Lawrence read at this time. The letter to David Eder of August 1917 which refers to *The Secret Doctrine* as 'in many ways a bore, and not quite real' also discusses 'the physiological . . . interpretations of the esoteric doctrine' to be found in such books as James Morgan Pryse's *The Apocalypse Unsealed*. He is as irreverent about these as about Blavatsky: 'The devils won't tell one anything, fully. Perhaps they don't understand themselves – the occultists – what they are talking about, or what their esotericism really means . . . Yet one can gather enough' (*Letters* III 150). What this means in practice is that Lawrence feels free to take what he likes from these books while denying any allegiance to them. Among other books into which he delved at this time were Eliphas Levi's *History of Magic*, which suggests that the Sons of God in the Book of Enoch were initiates of secret wisdom, and (according to Frieda) 'many of Mrs Besant's works' (Whelan 1988: 105–10). Annie Besant, at this stage of her career, was peddling what she called *Esoteric Christianity*, which claimed that Christ himself was an initiate, preaching 'the mysteries of the Kingdom of God' to a privileged inner circle of disciples, a secret wisdom which Christianity needed to regain (Besant 1898: I 11). Like Blavatsky, Besant believed the Bible to contain 'fragments' of that wisdom, which discerning readers could recover (IV 20).

Pryse's *Apocalypse Unsealed* is probably the most important esoteric book Lawrence read, the one from which he drew most. He completely overturns its central argument, that the physical should be subsumed in the spiritual, but adopts some of its concepts, for instance its belief in 'chakras', a series of distinct nerve-centres or ganglia extending on each side of the spinal chord whose energy needs to be liberated or unlocked. Pryse explains that the purpose of his book is to show that the Book of Revelation is 'a manual of spiritual development and not, as conventionally interpreted, a cryptic history or prophecy'. Important to his argument is the new translation he provides of the original Greek, which is significantly different from the Authorised Version. He takes his epigraph, for example, from Luke 11: 52, which he translates, 'Woe unto you, conventionalists, for you took away the key of the sacred science, *you* did not go in and those who were about to go in you prevented.' The Authorized Version, of course, has Jesus addressing 'lawyers', a more normal translation of the Greek *nomikois* than 'conventionalists', and referring to 'the key of knowledge', for which the Greek genitive *tes gvoseos* is more plausibly seen to refer to a more arcane gnosis, a secret wisdom, suggesting to Pryse that Jesus himself was an adept, an initiate, a teacher of gnostic wisdom.

Pryse's opening chapter proceeds to explain this phrase, 'The Key of the Gnosis', claiming that the Bible, read aright, contains 'very clear intimations of a secret traditional lore, an arcane science, handed down from time immemorial' and that this secret science 'was guarded with jealous care' in the primitive church, 'being imparted only to a comparative few who were deemed worthy of initiation' (Pryse 1910: 1). Again, that there were gnostic sects in the early church is confirmed both by surviving gnostic gospels and by letters from orthodox leaders denouncing the circulation of gnostic versions of the canonical gospels (Pagels 1979). For Pryse this gnosis was the 'real' meaning both of the gospels and of the Book of Revelation, an esoteric wisdom replaced in later centuries by 'a selfish and decadent priesthood' who subsituted 'a system of dogmatic theology formulated from the literal interpretation, the dead letter, of the books of the *Old* and *New Testaments'* (2).

For Pryse the secret wisdom, in order to remain secret, to protect the 'sacred science' from those 'morally unworthy to receive it' and to prevent its destruction or removal from the canon (3), had been carefully encoded in the Book of Revelation. He combines this with a belief in a latent force known as the *kundalini*, 'which in the *Upanishads* is said to lie coiled up like a slumbering serpent', but which becomes in theosophic interpretation the agent of the perfecting work:

As it passes from one ganglion to another its voltage is raised, the ganglia being like so many electric cells coupled for intensity; and moreover in each ganglion, or *chakra*, it liberates and partakes of the quality peculiar to that centre, and it is then said to 'conquer' the *chakra*. (16)

Lawrence, as we shall see, makes use of this theory both in his essays and in his novels, but alters the significance, rejecting the whole moral and spiritual framework within which it is set. For Pryse and the other theosophists, the process of spiritual birth requires 'the most rigid purificatory discipline, which includes strict celibacy and abstemiousness'. The 'sacred trance of seership' or union with the paraclete does not come to 'the man who is gross and sensual' who 'can arouse only the lower psychic forces of his animal nature, forces which are cruelly destructive and never regenerative'; they only come to 'the man or woman who has attained a very high state of mental and physical purity' (21–2).

Pryse proceeds to unravel 'The Riddles of "Revelation"' (the title of chapter 3) in terms of the 'four animal-symbols or beasts' which are its *dramatis personae*: first the Lamb, or conqueror, identified with Jesus, secondly 'a beast resembling a leopard', thirdly 'a red Dragon' who is 'the Devil and Satan' and lastly a beast that looks like a lamb but speaks like a Dragon, the 'Pseudo-Seer, or false teacher' (25).

With the help of a complicated mathematical code Pryse achieves a reading of the Book of Revelation as a symbolic account, 'portrayed with poetic imagery of exquisite beauty' of the conquering of the lower forces of the body in which the 'deathless solar vesture' or spiritual body 'is symbolized as a city which comes down out of the sky, enveloped in the radiance' of God (29). He has nothing but scorn for those 'sentimental literalists' who read the Apocalypse as 'a record of visions actually seen by "the seer of Patmos"'. In his reading, the leading character of the drama that is the Book of Revelation is

the neophyte himself, the sacrifical 'Lamb,' who awakens all the slumbering forces of his inner nature, passes through the terrible ordeals of the purificatory discipline and the telestic labours, and finally emerges as the Conqueror, the self-perfected Man who has regained his standing among the deathless Gods. (35)

The seven Asian cities supposedly addressed by St John are merely disguises for the seven ganglia whose energies are harnessed to such spiritual ends while Lucifer, 'the fallen "son of the morning"', is a symbol of 'the *debased psychic mind of man*, which is indeed the ruler over the abysmal depths of desire, the bottomless pit of the passional nature' (47). When the Dragon is 'hurled down from the sky' these base passions are destroyed and 'the *mind* is now purified from the taint of impure thoughts' (50). And when the Conqueror appears, 'mounted on a white horse' and treading the grapes of wrath, with the title of the 'supreme ruler' inscribed on his thigh, a euphemistic representation of 'the *phallos, membrum virile*' (60), it means that this unruly member is conquered once and for all.

It is difficult to imagine Lawrence swallowing this part of Pryse's argument, but he does seem to have accepted much of his general account of the Book of Revelation. His essay on Fenimore Cooper of 1919, for example, in the version published in the *English Review,* announces with great confidence,

It is certain that St John gives us in the Apocalypse a cypher-account of the process of the conquest of the lower or sensual dynamic centres by the upper or spiritual dynamic consciousness, a conquest affected centre by centre, towards a culmination in the *actual* experience of spiritual infinitude. (SM 75)

He may not himself have approved of this Christianising of earlier 'pre-Christian' or pagan understanding of the consciousness, in

particular its privileging of the spirit over the body, its outlawing of
the passions. As with Blavatsky, however, what he appears to have
taken from Pryse was not this 'spirituality' so much as the possibility
of reading the Book of Revelation as an allegorical account of a way
of integrating the self, releasing its internal energies. This will
emerge clearly in his correspondence with Frederick Carter, begun
in Mexico in 1922, in his Mexican novels and, above all, in
Apocalypse.

Lawrence's interest in theosophy, in particular its reading of the
first and last books of the Bible, is also reflected in the series of essays
entitled 'Studies in Classic American Literature' some of which
appeared in the *English Review* in 1918 and 1919, the first surviving
versions being published in 1962 as *The Symbolic Meaning*. These
present America as 'a refuge, a paradise compared with England'
(*SM* 6), although becomes less paradisal in the final version, *Studies in
Classic American Literature* of 1923, after he had actually moved there.
Then it becomes a site of conflicting emotions: an unfulfilled desire
to throw off the shackles of old European ideals, held back in many
of the writers by an inability fully to escape from their puritanical
legacy. The texts themselves, according to Lawrence, undermine
their authors' intentions, which is the point of his celebrated
injunction, 'Never trust the artist. Trust the tale' (*SCAL* 8). This
motto, however, can be turned against Lawrence himself, for his
analysis of their attempt in some ways to escape and in other respects
to develop an inherited religious and moral tradition betrays more
about himself than he presumably intended. A double reading of
Lawrence himself will discover that the tale told by these 'Studies'
involves a pervasive concern with the sacred canon as well as with its
American literary supplement.

The first contradiction Lawrence finds in the traditional tale told
about America is in the Pilgrim Fathers themselves, who did not, as
they claimed, 'sail to America in search of religious freedom', which
they could have fought for at home, but in pursuit of power and
property, for which 'the Christian religion served as a word, a
weapon, an instrument' rather than a check (*SM* 24–5). A second
contradiction, apparent in Benjamin Franklin, is between conscious
and unconscious beliefs. It is Lawrence's central theme and the
principle of his critical practice that 'the source of creation is central
within the soul' and 'proceeds without any choice or knowledge on
our part. The creative gesture, or emanation, for ever precedes the

conscious realisation of this gesture' (37). This, he argues, is true of religion as well as art and makes all conscious creeds a mockery, especially those surrounding the benevolent businessman Franklin worships as God. The revised chapter sets out Lawrence's alternative 'creed', presenting the soul as 'a dark forest' in which 'my known self' is never 'more than a little clearing', into which 'gods, strange gods, come forth from the forest' and return (*SCAL* 22). It also introduces the notion that each person has his own 'Holy Ghost' within, an inner core of being which is denied at his peril (25), a belief reiterated in the chapter on Edgar Alan Poe.

The chapters on Crèvecœur and Fenimore Cooper develop the contrast between their conscious adherence to idealistic European values and their unconscious imaginative recognition of the complexity of nature. Cooper is presented as having almost, or partially, succeeded in sloughing off his idealistic European skin. *Deerslayer*, for example, captures the absurdity of Hetty's 'Wandering with her Bible into the hostile and dangerous camp of the Red men' and lisping to them 'of the God of immaculate love, the beauty of holiness and humility' (109) in contrast with Deerslayer himself, who recognises the Red Man's values, 'the opposite mystery – the mystery of the other' (110). Hawthorne is similarly divided between conscious idealism and unconscious sensuality. Lawrence reads *The Scarlet Letter* as an artistic reworking of the myth of Genesis, although his exposition of the esoteric significance of the story of the Garden of Eden owes as much to Blavatsky and Pryse as it does to the Bible (Carter 1932: 8–9). For Lawrence, as for the theosophists,

The Eve myth symbolises the birth of the upper mind, the upper consciousness which, the moment it becomes self-conscious, rebels against the physical being, and is sensible of shame because of its own helpless connection with the passional body. The serpent is the symbol of division in the psyche, the knife, the dagger, the ray of burning or malevolent light, the undulating line of the waters of the flood, the divider, which sets spiritual being against sensual being, man against woman, sex against sex, the introducer of the hostile duality into the human psyche. (*SM* 139)

But while the theosophists saw the solution to the problem of dualism as the recovery of harmonious spirituality, Lawrence pleads for a fuller recognition of the physical. He casts Hester Prynne as an Eve/Mary, a 'Mary of the Sacred Heart', her 'sensual body' pierced 'through the seven gates of the body, in the seven great passional centres' of which Pryse had given so detailed an account, and

Hawthorne as the serpent, speaking with a forked tongue to deliver a contradictory message: 'Openly he stands for the upper, spiritual, reasoned being. Secretly he lusts in the sensual imagination, in bruising the heel of this spiritual self and laming it for ever' (141). Lacking the courage to allow Hester to become a second Eve, to initiate another rebellion against Puritan morals, he makes her return to 'the old life of self-abnegation and spiritual purity' (144).

The final version of this chapter develops the argument through a similar reading of the novel as a retelling of the Book of Genesis, paying particular attention to its 'diabolic undertone' (in Blake's positive sense). Adam's fall is seen to lie not in lying with Eve but in the 'knowledge-poison' which came with 'that beastly apple':

When Adam went and took Eve, *after* the apple, he didn't do any more than he had done many a time before, in act. But in consciousness he did something very different. So did Eve. Each of them kept an eye on what they were doing, they watched what was happening to them. They wanted to KNOW. And that was the birth of sin. Not *doing* it, but KNOWING about it. Before the apple, they had shut their eyes and their minds had gone dark. Now, they peeped and pried and imagined. They watched themselves. And they felt uncomfortable after. They felt self-conscious. So they said, 'The *act* is sin. Let's hide. We've sinned.'

No wonder the Lord kicked them out of the Garden. Dirty hypocrites. (*SCAL* 90–1)

Lawrence can be seen here to practise his own subversive brand of theosophical midrash (complete with the italicised and capitalised emphases so beloved of Blavatsky), double-reading the original biblical narrative, retaining some of the original details but giving them a very different symbolic meaning. He also, for good measure, reverses the theosophical account of the Fall, seeing self-consciousness not as part of the way back to spirituality, a recovery of the state from which becoming incarnate was a fall, but as the root of the problem.

The most transparently theosophical essay of the original series, entitled 'The Two Principles', the only one to be omitted altogether from the final version of *Studies in Classic American Literature*, retells the creation narrative of the opening chapter of Genesis in terms of the hermetic quest to reconcile 'the material cosmos and the human soul' (*SM* 176). Lawrence, again anticipating Derrida, accepts from the outset that 'There never was a beginning' but that we have to postulate one 'to fix a starting-point for our thought'. He proceeds to interweave phrases from the opening verses of Genesis with his own esoteric interlinear commentary. His version of verse 6, for example, presents 'the waters . . . divided by the firmament' of verse 6 in terms of 'perpendicular' and 'horizontal' divisions of Chaos comprising the Rosy Cross (177). He must, however, have suspected that his readers were unlikely to appreciate the extended discussion of the plexuses and ganglions of esoteric awareness with which this essay closes, which is presumably why he omitted it from the final version.

The first of two essays on Melville, written for the original *English Review* series but not published in it, returns to the subject of the widespread loss in the modern world of the sense of wonder basic to religion. Melville is seen to have gone to the South Sea islands in an attempt to recapture this primitive sense of wonder, but could not 'remain in the Eden' he described because he was still subservient to the 'tablet of stone, on which the old ethic is engraved' (228). His unpreparedness for paradise is further emphasised in the final version of this essay. For a time he basks in the edenic qualities of his island, which is a paradise:

> He insists on it. Paradise. He could even go stark naked, as before the Apple episode. And his Fayaway, a laughing little Eve, naked with him, and hankering after no apple of knowledge, so long as he would just love her when he felt like it. Plenty to eat, needing no clothes to wear, sunny, happy people, sweet water to swim in: everything a man can want. Then why wasn't he happy along with the savages? (*SCAL* 144)

The answer, according to Lawrence, is that modern white men, the product of years of historic struggle, cannot go back in time, cannot undo the result of centuries of moral endeavour. Melville 'didn't really want Eden'. He was 'much happier in his miseries' (147). The second essay on Melville reads *Moby Dick* as an allegory of the final destruction of 'the deep, free sacral consciousness in man', the whale itself being a relic from 'the pre-Flood worship' which dwelt on sensual rather than cerebral understanding (*SM* 235–6). The final version of this essay ends with an even clearer depiction of the end of Christianity; 'To use the words of Jesus, IT IS FINISHED' (*SCAL* 170). Not for the first time, Lawrence turns Christ's words on the cross against him, placing them in an entirely different context so that they bear an utterly different meaning. The concluding essay focuses upon Whitman as inaugurating the final phase of the process through which Christianity set out 'to *annihilate* the sensual being in man' (*SM* 255). The final version again takes the words of Christ on the cross to indicate the end of the road for Christianity and its attempted spiritualisation of the body (*SCAL* 179) although Whitman is also celebrated as 'a strange, modern, American Moses' (180).

Throughout these essays Lawrence can be seen to oscillate between blaming the religious traditions for failing to modify to meet the modern world and the modern world for failing to be open to religion. He believes both to be mistaken. He is clearly critical of orthodox Christian reading of the Bible, its imposition of an ascetic morality upon it, but he remains equally critical of modernity for losing touch with its 'primitive' roots. If the theosophists can be said to have aimed at a double-reading of the Bible, rejecting its superficial, exoteric meaning and attempting to uncover its symbolic meaning, the ancient wisdom embedded deep within its texts, Lawrence in turn can be said to have deconstructed them, reversing their privileging of the spiritual over the material. The ancient wisdom he finds embedded in the Bible, especially in the Book of Genesis, involves not a gradual ascent from matter to spirit but a full-blooded celebration of the flesh. His is a double reading not only of the Bible but of its theosophical interpretation.

CHAPTER 8

Genesis versus John: 'Women in Love', 'The Lost Girl' and 'Mr Noon'

Many of the ideas developed in Lawrence's essays during and immediately after the war find their way, as one might expect, into the novels written over the same period. *Women in Love*, of course, spanned more years than most, beginning in 1913 with the first draft of 'The Sisters', the few surviving pages of which end with Gerald experiencing 'a wave of faith, warm, strong, religious faith' (Kinkead-Weekes 1968: 376; *WL* xxii). As the different versions of the novel were written and rewritten, however, mainly through 1916 and 1917 with a final revision in 1919 prior to publication the following year, the religious dimension of the novel grew ever bleaker. In the 'Foreword to *Women in Love*' which he wrote on the publisher Thomas Seltzer's suggestion in September 1919, Lawrence, after defending himself against the charges of obscenity levelled at *The Rainbow*, encapsulates his residual religious vision, urging his readers to nourish 'a deep respect, even reverence, for all that the creative soul, the God-mystery within us, puts forth'. He insists, however, on the need for change, for the abandonment of outdated religious forms, for we live 'in a period of crisis' in which 'the new idea' will only come into being at the expense of the old. Those who 'fix themselves in the old idea,' he warns, 'will perish with the new life strangled unborn within them' (*WL* 485–6). Like its predecessor, in other words, *Women in Love* presents itself as a radical but profoundly religious work.

If *The Rainbow* had been 'a kind of Genesis', *Women in Love* is his Apocalypse (Kermode 1968: 20), combining a concern with the recovery of paradise with an altogether grimmer awareness, partly as a result of the war, that the new world can only emerge out of an apocalyptic destruction of the old. 'I think I'll call it "Noah's Ark"', Lawrence wrote in November 1917, at the height of his identification with that lonely survivor in a wicked world (*Letters* III 183). Other titles considered by Lawrence for this novel include 'The Latter Days' and 'Dies Irae' (Kinkead-Weekes 1968: 398). It has been linked with Fra Angelico's fresco of *The Last Judgment*, described by Lawrence in a letter as embodying 'a whole conception of the existence of man – creation, good, evil, life, death, resurrection, the separating of the stream of good and evil, and its return to the eternal source'. This fresco, which depicts 'sinners tumbling hell-wards' while the blessed, 'joining hands, wind in colourful procession through the flowering meadows of Paradise', is translated by Birkin into his own terms, which contrast the decadent sensuality of Halliday and his statues with what he calls 'another way, the way of freedom . . . the paradisal entry into pure, single being' (Urang 1983: 247).

Birkin is in many ways a Messianic figure. The opening scene has been seen to subvert the parable about the Second Coming in which the foolish bridesmaids fall asleep while 'the bridegroom tarried' (Matt. 25: 5–8). Here both groom and best man (Birkin) are delayed, Hermione and the rest of the congregation becoming increasingly agitated at their non-appearance (Hyde 1992: 104–5). The apocalyptic rage of Matthew's Messianic Jesus, however, is caricatured in the Lawrentian figure of Birkin, whose 'dislike of mankind, of the mass of mankind' is expressed in terms of a desperate desire for 'the end of the world' in his conversation with Gerald Crich on the train to London towards the beginning of the novel. 'You've got very badly to want to get rid of the old,' he tells Gerald, 'before anything new will appear' (*WL* 54). So mankind itself should be 'destroyed like Sodom' (61). Gerald Doherty argues that Birkin goes through the five stages which Blavatsky and others saw as characteristic of such Messianic figures: first he preaches what others laugh at as 'a new gospel' (54). 'He is as bad as Jesus', complains Halliday, who poses as a repentant sinner, asking 'Lord, *what* must I do to be saved' (382). Second comes a period of retreat, of regrouping to gather strength, third the instruction of disciples (in Birkin's case just Ursula), fourth a 'ritual initiation' and finally the defeat of a false prophet or pseudo-seer, in this case the aesthete Loerke (Doherty 1982: 54–5). Birkin at one point quotes the angry Matthean Jesus (*WL* 131; Matt. 7: 20) while Ursula, of course, resents what she describes as Birkin's 'Salvator Mundi touch', mocking his belief in what amounts to two things, 'the end of the world, and grass' (129). Halliday's Russian friend Libidnikov makes the same complaint, that 'He thinks he is the saviour of man' (384, 'Saviour' capitalised in the first American edition). One of the redeeming features of the Messianic typology of this novel, in fact, is the way in which Birkin's pretensions are constantly undermined by the other characters in this genuinely polyphonic novel.

One of the many voices in *Women in Love* is certainly the Bible, upon which Birkin draws a great deal for his apocalyptic vision of a world grown so wicked that it needs to be destroyed and begun again. To Ursula as to Gerald Crich he paints a grim picture of a generation grown so corrupt, so far short of its edenic origins, that it deserves, like the generation of the Flood, to be annulled. The young men and women of their period, who 'look very nice and rosy', he tells her, are in reality 'apples of Sodom . . . Dead Sea Fruit, gall apples'. For him 'there would be no *absolute* loss, if every human being perished tomorrow. . . The real tree of life would then be rid of the most ghastly heavy crop of Dead Sea Fruit.' Ursula cannot believe that he is setting himself up as such a patriarchal figure (in both senses of the word, modelled upon the patriarchs of Genesis and unsympathetic to women). 'So you'd like everybody in the world destroyed?' she asks, to receive the provocative answer that the earth would indeed be a better place 'cleaned of *all* the people', leaving only some animals, some grass and a few angels (126–8).

The loss of paradise, the eating of the forbidden apple of knowledge, and the attempt to recover the innocence of Eden are further motifs in the novel which derive from the Book of Genesis. The sisters, for example, watch Gerald dive naked into Willey water on a morning 'full of a new creation' (46) while Birkin's Bohemian friends are also attracted to nudity, to the idea of throwing off the corruption of civilisation along with their clothes (77). His own wallowing naked among the flowers after being struck by Hermione could be said similarly to echo the striving after lost innocence to be found in Edward Carpenter. There is a terrible fall from innocence, he explains to Hermione, implicit in her false kind of knowledge, which he traces back to Eve, who chose the wrong fruit from the wrong tree. She and her generation are 'imprisoned in a limited, false set of concepts' without 'any real body, any dark sensual body of life'. They have to learn to abandon their 'mental-deliberate' will, 'to lapse into unknowingness' (41–4).

Ursula too wants to modify the biblical account of the fall. She sees Gerald Crich's mistreatment of his horse as an abuse of the power granted in Genesis 9: 2: 'however man is lord of the beast and the fowl,' she says, 'I still don't think he has any right to violate the feelings of the inferior creation' (143). She complains to Birkin about the male desire for power, which she calls 'the old Adam', prompting on his part an ill-advised return to the theme of paradise (150). She mocks his 'paradisal unknowing', which she interprets as her being 'your thing, never to criticise you or to have anything to say for myself' (250). She advocates greater respect for otherness, the separate existence of the other, in a passage which picks up the references to Genesis 6 in *The Rainbow*, considering Birkin as 'a strange creature from another world', close but still 'separate', and recalling 'the old magic of the Book of Genesis, where the Sons of God saw the daughters of men, that they were fair' (312). Her celebration of the 'mysterious life-flow . . . the strange mystery of his life-motion' (313) may derive some of its metaphors from James Pryse's location of the sources of cosmic energy or 'kundalini' in the seven centres of the body, energy released by the meditative stroking of his loins (566). But the sexual union of this son of God and daughter of men is portrayed not as a fall into corruption, a degeneration into wickedness which will necessitate the flood, but as a recovery of an originally proud sensuality.

Other strands of the Book of Genesis find their way into *Women in Love* with their significance similarly mediated by a range of theosophical and other intertexts. Gerald Crich, for example, is portrayed from the beginning as a Cain figure. When Gerald's mother tells Birkin that she wants her son to have a friend, Birkin's flippant reply, 'Am I my brother's keeper?' recalls to his mind that Gerald had accidentally slain his brother in a shooting accident (26). Later in the novel, in the chapter in which his sister drowns, he is described as still feeling guilt about the earlier accident, 'set apart, like Cain' (172). The two men develop a strange relationship that is part hatred, part love and develops into a blood-brotherhood sealed by their naked wrestling, which echoes Jacob's wrestling with the angel (275). The Cain–Abel, Jacob–Esau theme of rivalry, which will be more systematically developed in *The Boy in the Bush*, flickers into the text here without attaining any substantial significance, though Gerald remains a murderous threat throughout the novel, attacking both Gudrun and Ursula before committing what amounts to suicide in the snow.

It is the Book of Revelation, however, rather than Genesis, which becomes the dominant biblical intertext in this novel, which portrays a world approaching nearer and nearer to destruction and dissolution. The two sisters are introduced in the opening chapter as 'confronted by a void', a terrifying chasm of meaninglessness, 'as if they had looked over the edge' (10). Hermione too suffers from a 'bottomless pit of insufficiency', like that from which Satan emerges and back into which he is cast in the Book of Revelation (Rev. 20: 3), her identity being 'established on the sand' (*WL* 17) like the 'foolish man' in the apocalyptic parable, whose house fell when 'the floods came, and the winds blew, and beat upon' it (Matt. 7: 26–7). She is frequently likened to the fallen angels, with a look which 'seemed spiritual, like the angels, but which came from torture', and 'the face of an almost demoniacal ecstatic' (*WL* 21). Birkin, breaking into one of his long apocalyptic speeches about the world being 'drowned in darkness' and 'the deluge', talks of her as 'a palpable body of darkness, a demon' and finally 'the real devil who won't let life exist' (43).

Hermione, however, is not the only fallen angel in the novel, banished like Lucifer to the 'bottomless pit'. 'Don't you feel like one of the damned,' Birkin asks Gerald as they travel in the train to London (61), while when they get there the Pussum's eyes, later to be called 'bottomless pools', betray 'an unfathomable hell of knowledge' (79, 65). Gerald himself, after his father's death, feels 'on the edge of an abyss . . . suspended on the edge of a void', a 'bottomless void, in which his heart swung perishing' (337), while Gudrun too, into whom he pours all his 'pent-up darkness', feels 'cast out into the outer darkness' (346). Birkin will later describe the evil Loerke as an 'obscene monster of the darkness', living like a rat 'in the river of corruption just where it falls over into the bottomless pit' (428), although Ursula imagines him continuing to make 'playful remarks as he wandered in hell' (468). *Women in Love*, in other words, positively teems with damned and desperate characters in a world veering out of control.

There is, of course, a positive side to the Book of Revelation, a vision of the New Jerusalem paved with pearls, a tree of life in the middle and 'a pure river of water of life, clear as crystal' (Rev. 22: 1–2). Birkin draws upon this positive imagery in the chapter entitled 'Water-Party', contrasting 'the dark river of dissolution' with 'the silver river of life, rolling on and quickening all the world to a brightness, on and on to heaven, flowing into a bright eternal sea, a heaven of angels thronging' (172). Marriage with Ursula, which he imagines as 'the Paradisal entry into pure, single being', conjures up further images from the Book of Revelation, with Beldover, lit up by the evening sun, taking on the appearance of 'Jerusalem to his fancy . . . all strange and transcendent' (254–5). This seems also to be the point of a later passage in which the two lovers drive towards Southwell Minster while 'the golden lights showed like slabs of revelation in the shop windows' and the Minster itself, in Birkin's words, 'looks like quartz crystals sticking up out of the dark hollow' (312). Quartz is not actually named among the 'precious stones' of the New Jerusalem but the water there is 'clear as crystal' (Rev. 22: 1), combining with the 'golden lights' and 'revelation' to provide what seems at least a glimpse of the New Jerusalem, a suggestion of its distant possibility.

Most of *Women in Love*, however, focuses on the dark, destructive side of the apocalypse. Not only Birkin, but many of the other characters spend much of their time speculating on the end of the world. Gudrun, who began the novel wanting the miners' wives who jeer at her stockings to be 'annihilated' (13), ends it cynically constructing alternative scenarios for the end of the world, either by 'a ridiculous catastrophe of man's invention' or by the freezing over of the whole globe (453). She is particularly dismissive of Birkin's belief in 'a new heaven and a new earth' (Rev. 21: 1). 'Go and find your new world, dear,' she says patronisingly, 'her voice clanging with false benignity' (*WL* 438). Having ended *The Rainbow* with a vision of renewed life symbolised by the sign given by God to Noah, she closes *Women in Love* questioning Birkin's dreams of 'eternal union with a man'. There are few signs that the renewal of their society, which has been Birkin's constant theme, is a realistic possibility. 'Whatever the mystery which has brought forth man and the universe,' Birkin concludes, in partial if pessimistic resolution of his religious quest, 'it is a non-human mystery, it has its own great ends, man is not the criterion' (478). He finds it in some ways 'consoling' that the 'mystery of creation' remains 'fathomless, infallible, inexhaustible forever' (479) but this is not much to set against the darkness and damnation of so much of the novel. If *Women in Love* can be said in some respects to rework the Book of Revelation, it does so in a mood of despair, emphasising the dark elements of the biblical apocalypse, the end of the world as we know it, with little confidence in the beginning of a better one.

The Lost Girl, which was published in the same month as *Women in Love*, plays with some of the same themes but in much lighter vein. Having had such difficulty getting *Women in Love* published, Lawrence appears deliberately to have set out to provide what readers and critics seemed to want. In this, of course, he can be said to some extent to have succeeded, this being the only novel of his ever to receive a prize (*LG* li). *The Lost Girl*, which began life in late 1912 as 'Elsa Culverwell', a twenty-page fragment reprinted in the Appendix to the new Cambridge edition, and continued as 'The Insurrection of Miss Houghton', written in 1913, was resurrected in the spring of 1920, the final draft being produced in a mere eight weeks. 'Elsa Culverwell' and the opening chapters of *The Lost Girl*, which overlap in many respects, both satirise the society based upon the Congregational Chapel. 'Everybody was religious', writes the first-person narrator of the early draft, even her mother imagining herself as 'a kind of bride of Christ' while her father too, as superintendent of the Sunday School, 'enjoyed religion' as 'a kind of delicious sensation' (348). He is also mocked in the final version of the novel, where his prayers are described as 'beautiful' (9). Biblical allusions underline the way his religion is tamed for bourgeois consumption. Noting, for example, the neatness with which he peels an apple, the narrator observes, 'the elegant Adam of commerce gave Eve her own back, nicely cored, and had no more to do with her'. His shop alone arouses his enthusiasm, causing him to dance before his stock 'like David before the ark' (3). Biblical allusion here functions as mock-heroic satire, the reference to David serving merely to contrast the absence of any genuine religious feeling on his part .

It is against this kind of religiosity, the respectable morality of the Congregational Chapel, that Alvina Houghton rebels and it is in terms of this narrow morality that she is labelled a 'lost girl'. When her emotions are awakened by a troupe of travelling performers for whom she plays the role of prisoner captured by Red Indians, the narrator describes their performance in terms of the opening chapters of the Book of Genesis:

It was a lovely sight, suggesting the world's morning, before Eve had bitten any white-fleshed apple, whilst she was still dusky, dark-eyed, and still. And then her stealthy sympathy with the white prisoner! Now indeed she was the dusky Eve tempted into knowledge. (161)

Alvina herself is tempted into a different, more carnal knowledge by one of the troupe, a moral lapse which brings upon her the judgement, 'You're a lost girl!' Alvina, however, rejects both the language of nonconformist guilt and the terminology of the fall; she insists, 'I like being lost' (217), and decides, as she snuggles in the bedclothes in which she has just enjoyed her lover, that 'She didn't care a bit, really, about her own downfall' (234). Her 'financial downfall' (238), the fact that her father's debts exceed the value of his legacy, means more to her than any supposed moral lapse.

The Lost Girl clearly undermines the whole concept of the fall as conventionally understood. Its Eve, rather than losing her life as a result of her sexual boldness, gains it, refusing to be bullied by moralists such as Dr Mitchell, who is portrayed yelling at errant patients who dare to drink alcohol like 'God-almighty . . . finding the core of an apple flung away among the dead-nettle of paradise' (253). Alvina decides not to marry him but her beloved Ciccio, who has the merit, in the manuscript version of the novel at least, of demonstrating his 'godliness' silently (393). They travel together to Italy, England and its 'corpse-grey cliffs' sinking behind them 'like a long, ash-grey coffin' (294). In Italy she remains 'quite, quite lost' (306), the conventional meaning of the word, as in Wilde, carelessly laughed away, along with the whole Christian framework of salvation. Lawrence picks up the jaded language of Christian orthodoxy and flings it back, like the Adam of his watercolour, 'Throwing Back the Apple'.

Mr Noon, written towards the end of 1920 but not finally published until 1984, tells a similar, more autobiographical, story of loss and gain, the loss of conventional faith being represented by the narrator as an emancipation. Part I is set like *The Lost Girl* within a community dominated by the Congregational chapel, while Part II draws on Lawrence's own escape with Frieda to Germany and Italy, drama-tising some of the ideas and attitudes expressed in *Twilight in Italy*. Again, as in much of his work of this period, *Mr Noon* presents internal religious conflicts in intertextual terms as a struggle between the beginning of Genesis and the beginning of John's Gospel, between a celebration of creation (especially of all flesh) and the misguided attempt to supplant the flesh with the Word, to sublate the body in the spirit. The narrator, in one of several disconcertingly direct Meredithian addresses to the reader, suggests that we have 'left off believing in positive evil . . . Adam no more delves than Eve spins, in our day' (*MN* 20). Gilbert Noon himself is soon presented defying both 'fathers and stone tablets' (26), a reference, of course, to the ten commandments so dramatically discarded by Lawrence as by Nietzsche. Forced to resign his schoolteaching post, he departs for Germany, where he is led into sexual freedom by the married Johanna, who refuses to play the role of 'a weeping Magdalen' (129) but exults in her sexual liberation, taking 'sex as a religion' and feeling 'bound to administer the cup of consolation' to any man in need (139). Picking up the reversal of the notion of original sin from *The Lost Girl*, the narrator teases his 'gentle reader' by suggesting that 'Magdalen had only *one* fall, and that was when she fell to feet-washing', abandoning her pride in self-abasement (141). The whole novel, like its predecessor, is written in overtly Nietzschean opposition to conventional Christian morality.

The intertextual conflict between Genesis and John in this novel becomes particularly evident in the mockery with which the narrator treats Johanna's vestigial religiosity, which leads her to enter Detsch cathedral with another of her lovers and to light a candle to the Virgin. Lawrence enjoys the obscene joke that it is only because her lover's 'brief passion was drooping and almost spent' that she wants 'to stick up a good stout candle of wax to burn on the altar of the Virgin' (155). He stresses the conflict between the two candles, the two kinds of love, the 'beautiful tall erect candle of chastened aspiration' and 'the dusky, crimson-burning torch of unhallowed passion' which the two lovers try unsuccessfully to deny. The flame consumes the 'mundane flesh' of the 'material wax' as it struggles 'to escape into the boundless eternity' just as the lovers long 'to escape from the limitations of this five-franc mould of a corpse' into an eternal, spiritual existence. Johanna meditates like John at the beginning of his gospel on the light shining in the darkness, watching the flame of the candle 'fighting for life . . . and yet . . . forced to leave the lovely warm place of presence, to be driven over the threshold of existence into the howling wilderness of infinite chaos, where the world is void and dark' (156). The narrator, however, makes it clear that he prefers the chaos of creation, the beginning of Genesis, to the Word of the opening of John's Gospel, 'the great spirit of Uplift' against which he launches a fierce tirade (156–7).

Lawrence's own preference for Genesis over John emerges all too clearly in a passage celebrating the 'tree of life' of Genesis, which is full of 'the dark sap of life', in contrast to Christ, whose desire to be 'a free, abstract spirit' led him to be 'crucified upon the tree of the eternal, primal sensual soul' (189–90). The narrator plays once more with the opening words of the gospel, turning them against their original meaning: 'If *In the beginning was the Word* – then sex is a word also. – And we know that the Word is one word for all of us. Therefore why not free sexual love, as free as human speech?' (193). The following paragraph supplies his answer:

Why not? Because the *a priori* are all wrong. In the beginning was *not* the Word, but something from which the Word merely proceeded later on. Let us stick to the first and greatest god, and let the Logos look after itself. The first, great, passionately generating God. (194)

As in the 'Foreword to *Sons and Lovers*', Lawrence here finds John's God much less impressive than that of Genesis. In fictionalising the journey across the Alps recounted earlier in *Twilight in Italy* Lawrence portrays Gilbert Noon as more irreverent to the Christs in the Tyrol than he himself had been. Gilbert shocks the convent-educated Johanna by inviting a Christus down from his cross and offering him a drink. 'A drop of Dunkels,' he explains, 'would do him good. He can't spend *all* the time up there. I don't begrudge him a century or two – but there's a time to hang on a cross, and there's a time to get down and go your ways' (202). Once again, the wisdom of the Old Testament, on this occasion the doctrine of the 'proper time' from Ecclesiastes 3, is preferred to the unnatural spirituality of the New. Gilbert Noon is also more critical of the Bavarian crucifixes than Lawrence had been in *Twilight in Italy*, finding in their lingering medieval piety 'an almost Russian, dark mysticism, a worship of cruelty and pain and torture and death: a dark death worship', a product of fear which he traces back to the 'northern, tree-dark gods' (249). He also anticipates Lawrence's later fiction by imagining what would have happened if Pilate had changed his mind and ordered Jesus to be taken down from the cross (254).

  Gilbert's real conversion, however, described in apocalyptic terms, occurs when he touches Johanna in bed. It is then, as a result of the 'sudden shock of new experience' of 'deep, sensual, silken bliss' that 'his soul broke like a dry rock that breaks and gushes into life'. The allusions here to Exodus 17: 6, Numbers 20: 11 and Isaiah 48: 21 are again blasphemously transferred from spiritual to sexual significance (333). The Book of Revelation comes in with the notion of a new world replacing the old as Gilbert finds in Johanna a replacement for his mother:

it needs a sort of cataclysm to get out of the old world into the new. It needs a very painful shedding of an old skin. It needs a fight with the matrix of the old era, a bitter struggle to the death with the old, warm, well-known mother of our days. Fight the old, enclosing mother of our days – fight her to the death – and defeat her – and then we shall burst out into a new heaven and a new earth, delicious. (290)

What Lawrence is describing here is not, of course, the emergence of 'a new heaven and a new earth' as a result of divine intervention, as in the Book of Revelation (Rev. 21: 1), but a change of ideology, of world-view, as well as a change of lovers, a turning from his mother to Frieda. The old set of beliefs is described as 'an ideal sky' which has 'withered and shown you a much vaster universe'. That 'ideal sky', however, turns out to be 'a horrible low ceiling under which we stifle to death', 'a painted ceiling' which 'doesn't fall all in one smash' but gradually begins to crack and to reveal a 'glimpse' of the 'infinite' (291). It is an image which captures a sense of the sacred similar to that of Derrida and Bataille as something that can only emerge once an outdated ideology, in this case the metaphysical economy of Christianity, is fractured, allowing whatever lies 'behind the veil' to appear (Derrida 1978: 251–61).

The manuscript of *Mr Noon* itself breaks off at this point with the arrival of some new clothes for Johanna, perhaps an indication of the Carlylean flavour of this passage in which the falseness of the old beliefs, the old clothes, becomes apparent. Again like Derrida, Lawrence cannot abandon the old language with the old metaphysics. He has no tools but those of his own culture, no language but that of the Bible within which to describe his discovery of its limitations. What he is able to do, however, is to bring out the contradictions within this biblical language, in particular the conflict between the celebration of the flesh to be found within the Book of Genesis and its attempted suppression within John. In terms of the oppositions dominant in Lawrence's thinking from the 'Foreword to *Sons and Lovers*' to 'The Crown', the masculine spirituality of John must learn to marry, or at least to cohabit with the feminine flesh of Genesis. This perhaps is why the heroine of this novel is called Johanna.

CHAPTER 9

Books of Exodus: 'Aaron's Rod', 'Kangaroo' and 'The Boy in the Bush'

Lawrence called *Aaron's Rod* 'the last of my serious English novels – the end of *The Rainbow, Women in Love* line' (*Letters* IV 92–3). It can also, however, be seen as the first of a new line of 'leadership novels' whose protagonists seek desperately for spiritual guidance. Both this and his two Australian novels, *Kangaroo* and *The Boy in the Bush*, retain apocalyptic elements from the old 'line', starting from the assumption that the old world and the old religion are doomed. What they introduce, in biblical terms, is a concentration upon the theme of Exodus: all the protagonists are portrayed as escaping slavery to tradition and travelling through the wilderness of alienation towards a promised land of new ideas. The novels are not, of course, quite as programmatic, as straightforwardly allegorical, as this. In the Australian novels, for example, the wilderness is literally the outback, the bush. But the underlying structure of all these novels owes a great deal to the Book of Exodus.

The writing of *Aaron's Rod*, like so many of Lawrence's novels, spanned a number of years. Begun towards the end of 1917, it continued 'very slowly and fitfully' through 1918 (III 216) with little hope of publication, since no publisher had been prepared to 'risk' *Women in Love* (III 280). Abandoned altogether in 1919, it was resumed in July 1920 only to be set aside that November before being finished in June 1921 and published the following year. The title, of course, draws attention to its biblical parallels. In the text itself, it has been claimed, allusions to the story of Moses and his brother Aaron 'are so skillfully interwoven into the central narrative of the novel that one can scarcely scan a single page of *Aaron's Rod* without encountering some reference, however oblique, to the biblical legend' (Baker 1983: 46). Typologically, the flowering rod of Aaron relates to the tree of Jesse, blossoming to herald the birth of Christ: Isaiah prophesies that 'a rod' shall spring 'out of the stem of Jesse, and a Branch shall grow out of his roots' (Isa. 11: 1), the Latin for rod (*virga*) being close to that for virgin (*virgo*). In frescoes such as those of Giotto, with which Lawrence was familiar, Joseph is presented with a rod which buds with lilies, suggesting the imminent (and immaculate) birth of Christ. The legend of Tannhauser, also known to Lawrence at least in its Wagnerian form, which portrays a medieval knight who 'cannot be forgiven his pagan liaison with Venus unless a clerical staff blooms', adds to the complex web of allusion in the novel (Hyde 1992: 119–21).

In the Book of Exodus God appears to Moses in a bush which 'burned with fire' but 'was not consumed', calling upon him to lead his people out of bondage in Egypt 'unto a land flowing with milk and honey' (Exod. 3: 2–8). Moses initially expresses reluctance to accept this mission, disclaiming all eloquence (4: 10), but is told by God that he should work with his brother Aaron, 'who can speak well' (4: 14). When they appear before Pharaoh in chapter 7, Aaron casts his rod on the ground, where it becomes a serpent, and when Pharaoh's magicians perform similar tricks, Aaron's rod swallows up theirs. Aaron subsequently uses his rod to bring the plagues upon Egypt, turning their water to blood and bringing down upon them frogs, lice and flies until the magicians exclaim, 'This *is* the finger of God' (8: 19). Aaron and his sons are to be consecrated priests, God tells Moses, by being anointed with oil (29: 7, 30: 30–32 and 40: 13). When their authority to acts as priests is challenged by Korah and others, who argue that 'all the congregation are holy' (Numbers 16: 3), God supports Aaron's claim first by bringing a plague upon the challengers and then by devising a test which shall prove whom He chooses: each of the tribes of Israel shall lay rods in the tabernacle and the one which blossoms (which turns out to be Aaron's) can claim God's favour (17: 6–8). Later, when the Israelites complain of thirst, Aaron and Moses are told by God, 'speak ye unto the rock before their eyes; and it shall give forth his water' (20: 8). What Moses does, however, is to smite the rock with his rod, a variation on this command which so angers God that, although He makes water come forth 'abundantly' out of the rock, He deprives them of the privilege of themselves leading their people into the promised land (20: 12). Moses is granted his Pisgah-vision of the land but dies before the Israelites enter it (Deut. 34: 4–5).

This biblical narrative, as Mara Kalnins explains in her editorial note to the title of the novel, provides Lawrence with 'a parallel to the state of England in his time; that is, a nation wandering in the wilderness, seeking for spiritual leadership', leadership which the novel suggests can be found among artists (*AR* 313). Aaron Sisson's rod, in this respect, becomes his flute while it is tempting to read it also as a phallic serpent, representing sexual liberation, an over-turning of the strict sexual taboos of the Pentateuch. Kalnins also suggests that Lawrence, as 'a keen botanist', would have been aware of the plant commonly called Aaron's Rod, which 'was reputed to have strong healing properties and to ward off evil' (313). That *Aaron's Rod* is about breaking with old religious traditions is apparent in the opening chapters: the first, 'The Blue Ball', makes much of Aaron's daughter accidentally breaking this Christmas decoration handed down for generations, whose shattered fragments Aaron subjects to close inspection (11). Chapter 3, 'The Lighted Tree', 'becomes a parody of the familiar biblical episode' of the burning bush, Julia's dancing around the tree mimicking the reverence paid to the biblical bush (Baker 1983: 47). The title of chapter 4, 'Pillar of Salt', gives biblical resonance to Aaron's decision to leave his wife Lottie, who has become an encumbrance to him. Aaron's leaving of his wife and home in this novel clearly signals that he, like Lot, will not allow family ties or nostalgia to keep him in a place in which he sees himself as enslaved.

Some of the biblical allusions in the novel, as Baker notes, are comic. Aaron's first encounter with the 'Moses' of the novel, Rawdon Lilly, for example, occurs 'in an "Egyptian" context: at a performance of *Aïda* at the Royal Opera House, Covent Garden', from which the audience, like the children of Israel, make a hasty exit (Baker 1983: 49). But the characters who comprise Lilly's artistic set are satirised quite savagely. Virginia Hyde detects one of several parodies of the eucharist in the way Jim Bricknell devours 'hunks of bread' and glasses of burgundy while pontificating about Christ's love and sacrifice, 'the finest thing time has ever produced' (*AR* 76–7; Hyde 1992: 129). Lilly, however, pronounces himself 'sick of Christianity' or at any rate 'this modern Christ-mongery' (78) and his response to Jim's preaching simply to laugh. This does not prevent him having 'a certain belief in himself as a saviour' (73), a belief which becomes evident in his anointing of his newest disciple Aaron with oil. It is more a massage, even perhaps a seduction, than an anointing, with Lilly rubbing 'every speck' of Aaron's lower body with oil but it is done 'in a sort of incantation' (96) and after it is over

Lilly ponders the way the people he saves go on to resent him: 'they all prefer to kick against the pricks' (97). The fact that Lilly uses Christ's words to Paul on the road to Damascus (Acts 9: 5) confirms the religious significance in Lilly's eyes of his relationship with Aaron, who, as suspected, is soon resisting the older man's assumption of spiritual leadership, his claim to be 'a God-Almighty' (*AR* 111). Baker even suggests that Aaron for a time takes on the role of Pharaoh to Lilly's Moses, stubbornly hardening his heart to the call for liberation (Baker 1983: 50–1). He is sufficiently receptive to Lilly, however, to join him in Italy, where, like Tannhauser, he is led astray for a time, his Venus being the Marchesa del Torre, whose name, according to Hyde, conjures up the image of the golden calf, falsely worshipped by the biblical Aaron in Exodus 32: 4–6 (V. Hyde 1992: 131). She is described as 'metallic', glistening 'as if she were dusted with dark gold-dust' (*AR* 249). He could also be seen as a David to her Bathsheba, for he goes directly from admiring Michelangelo's statue of the 'great naked David' (211) to admiring the Marchesa's 'full-bosomed beauty' (219). Not for the first time, the sheer density of biblical allusion in Lawrence threatens to engulf his characters in contradictory and overdetermined significance.

Aaron for a while enjoys wielding his phallic 'rod of power', his 'male godhead' (258), over the Marchesa, whose husband complains of her sexual voraciousness, her insatiable interest in the serpent, characteristic of Eve (243). Aaron himself conjures up an extraordinary biblical image to express his own sense that the Marchesa is simply using him as 'God and victim' in her own sacred rite. Looking at 'his own phallic God-and-victim self' lying with her 'curled on his breast' he feels detached from his own body: 'himself, he stood far off, like Moses's sister Miriam' (273). The reference here, according to Kalnins in her edition of the novel (329), is to Numbers 12, where Miriam, having rebelled with Aaron against Moses, is cursed with leprosy but then cured as a result of Moses' intercession, although she is still 'shut out from the camp seven days' (Num. 12: 15). The point of contact between the two passages seems to be the revulsion with which both Aarons regard the women. In the novel it is not exactly guilt, a sense of their sinfulness, so much as a resentment at being used, which causes Aaron to break with the Marchesa as a moral leper.

It is not until the last two chapters of the novel that Aaron hears Lilly's solution to the problems of their dying civilisation, whose ideals are described as a corpse beyond the reach of any resurrection: 'By this time he stinketh – and I'm sorry for any Christus who brings him to life again, to stink livingly for another thirty years: the beastly Lazarus of our idealism' (*AR* 281). There is another parody of the eucharist in the final chapter of the novel, when Aaron has an extraordinary cannibalistic dream of eating the naked body of a man 'stuffed tight with prepared meat, as the skin of a Bologna sausage' (286). As they drink wine in the Tuscan sunshine, Lilly attempts to extirpate the remnants of his friend's religious quest: 'Forget the very words religion, and God, and love', he urges, since 'the very words rivet us down and don't let us move' (291). Of the 'two great dynamic urges in *life*: love and power', identified in *Apocalypse* as Nietzsche's 'two divine things in life' (*A* 165), it is the latter Lilly advises Aaron to follow, leaving all 'love-whooshing' to the Buddhists and Christians (*AR* 293–4). He should reject everything external, relying entirely on 'the Holy Ghost which is inside you', which is the 'only Godhead' (296). It is at this point that Lilly uses the image of the Tree of Life and the budding rod, symbolic of a new religious development. Even Nietzsche, who clearly lies behind this attack upon the idealism of love, is found wanting, since his 'will-to-power', according to Lilly, is too conscious, too intellectual, submerging the 'power-urge' in the 'love-will' (297–8). What Lilly wants is 'a fathomless submission to the heroic soul in a greater man', a submission he accuses Aaron of continuing to resist. The novel ends irresolutely with Lilly once more throwing at Aaron the accusation of the risen Christ to the apostle Paul, that 'you kick against the pricks' (299). The suggestion may be that Aaron, like Paul, is on the verge of conversion but it is by no means clear that Lilly is the new leader for whom he is looking.

It is clear, however, in this final chapter, entitled 'Words', that for Lawrence at this stage of his career Christian doctrine is no longer worthy of credence. Lilly himself, like Lawrence, continues to use the language and imagery of the Bible. But he does so, one could argue, like Derrida, *sous rature* (under erasure), as an act of bricolage, no longer fitting them into the traditional metaphysical framework but building new possibilities from the ruins of the old. 'There's no God outside you', he tells Aaron (295), and proceeds on the following page to preach in biblical terms about the 'Godhead' within (296):

You are your own Tree of Life, roots and limbs and trunk. Somewhere within the wholeness of the tree lies the very self, the quick: its own innate Holy Ghost. And this Holy Ghost puts forth new buds, and pushes past old limits, and shakes off a whole body of dying leaves. And the old limits hate being empassed [sic], and the old leaves hate to fall. But they must, if the tree-soul says so . . . (296)

What Lawrence finds in *Aaron's Rod*, as in other novels of this period, is that he cannot altogether abandon the religious language and vision of his upbringing. What he can do is develop it, complicate it, and alter its significance by reinscribing it in new senses and in different contexts. The image of shaking off the dead leaves in order to put forth new buds encapsulates metaphorically the critical and yet creative process in which he is engaged. His pruning seems rather harsh, virtually stripping the old tree before grafting new meanings onto it. But there is, he insists, an element of continuity, going beyond the tradition by means of the tradition.

Lawrence's next novel was the product of the period he spent in Australia, from May to August 1922. The writing of the novel *Kangaroo*, a 'thinly disguised autobiography' (*K* xxiii), took up half of that period, from the beginning of June to mid-July, although, like so many of his novels, it was subject to heavy revision before its publication in September 1923. It too is deeply religious, sketching its hero's search for a credible faith, a quest for personal fulfilment which embraces new concepts of the divine, 'dark gods' beyond the moralistic monotheistic Judaeo-Christian tradition. What references there are to the Bible are for the most part pejorative, engaging critically with what Lawrence found unacceptable in Jewish and Christian morality. The Ten Commandments and the Sermon on the Mount in particular are subjected to a negative form of midrashic interrogation, weighed and found wanting as the protagonist continues his quest for more satisfying solutions to his religious quest.

The novel's protagonist Richard Somers, a writer clearly based upon Lawrence himself, is introduced shortly after leaving Europe, which he regards as 'finished' (13) for Australia, which he continues to see as a potential paradise, 'a sort of harmless Eden' for people to inhabit 'once they have settled the old Adam in themselves' (305). Even at the end of the novel, when he prepares to leave for America, Somers sees the bush itself as 'a corner of paradise' (355). Whatever difficulties men make for themselves in their social and political life, the country itself remains a symbol of the wonder and beauty of creation. It is with 'mankind' rather than with creation that he feels

he still has something to 'fight out' (68–9).The original manuscript
has Somers explaining more fully his preference for 'the dark-blood-
mystery of the old world' over 'Christian uplift' (421) although he
suffers from a sense that the two people who had really loved him,
his mother and his wife, had believed in him as an individual, a 'son
of man' with lower-case initial letters, rather than 'the impersonal
man, the man that would go beyond them' (98). He clearly has
elements of an upper-case Son of Man within him, wanting to bring
into the world 'a new religious inspiration, . . . a new religious idea'
which will not repeat the mistake of Christianity, 'a religion which
preaches the despising of the material world' (99).

The eponymous Kangaroo appeals to Somers because, as well as
displaying a 'Jehovah-like . . . kindliness', he too wants to establish 'a
kind of Church' with a 'profound reverence for life'. Kangaroo,
whose physical characteristics and religious intensity are said to
derive from two of Lawrence's Jewish friends, Samuel Koteliansky
and David Eder (375), expresses 'admiration for the Roman Catholic
Church as an institution' but rejects its creed, its insistence on 'sin
and repentance and redemption' and the 'salvation of souls'
(111–12). He dislikes the 'principle of permanency', the attempt to fix
everything in a final state, as in the Ten Commandments, which he
sees as 'millstones round our necks'. All such commandments, he
teaches, 'should fade as flowers do' and not 'immortalise themselves
into stone' (113). Somers is clearly impressed with this aspect of
Kangaroo's thinking and by his 'loveliness', his 'warm, wise heart'
(113). But he is also critical of Kangaroo, who reminds him of 'the
lamb of God grown into a sheep' (114), an image which captures the
difficulty of preserving the ideals of youthful Christianity along with
a mature realism tempered by the experience of two thousand years.

Harriet tells Kangaroo that he's too much like 'Abraham's bosom',
the biblical metaphor for heaven (Luke 16: 22), a label at which he
laughs uproariously but which suggests a certain sanctimoniousness,
a vestigial otherworldliness against which both Somers and his wife
eventually rebel. He too claims to be a 'son of man' seeking like-
minded 'sons of men'. 'Deep calls to deep', he announces, in solemn
echo of Psalm 42: 7. He cannot 'speculate about God,' he tells them,
but he believes that 'the fire that is in my heart is God' (*K* 121–2).
Somers defends Kangaroo to William James, a rather sceptical
follower, who calls him 'a funny sort of Saviour' without much
'crown of thorns about him', who would 'look funny on a cross'

(128), but objects to his continued preaching of love. Somers wants to go beyond the moralistic limits of liberal humanism, beyond the narrow concerns of individuals, outlining to Kangaroo in the manuscript his belief in awe and 'sacred fear', a Jewish sense of 'the divine unknown', as the basis of religion (429–30). The final text of this theological discussion places more emphasis on the physical, with Somers advocating 'a re-entry into us of the great God, who enters us from below, not from above', an image which, combined with references to 'the lower self, the dark self, the phallic self' (135), suggest a reaching of the sacred through the shattering of sexual taboos, a dark route to the sacred other well beyond the bounds of the Judaeo-Christian tradition reminiscent of Bataille (Wright 1999).

Breaking away from tradition, however, as the narrator explains at the beginning of the following chapter, is always difficult and dangerous. Pioneers can appear absurd, isolated, or mad in their pursuit of 'strange gods'. Having 'come to the end of his own tether', Somers wonders whether it is 'better to be savagely tugging at the end of your rope, or wander at random tetherless' (*K* 149). He is able to laugh at himself 'looking at the ends of the tether he presumed he had just broken' but turns his anger on traditionalists, who are 'immensely sniffy about the people who stray loose trailing the broken end of their old rope, and looking for a new way through the bush', even setting up 'inquisitions and every manner of torture chamber to compel people to refrain from breaking their tethers' (149–50). The 'new way through the bush', like that of the Israelites, involves uncertainty about the eventual goal. What Somers can say about his 'undefined and undefinable faith', however, continues to employ biblical phrases such as the 'peace like a river' of Isaiah. He also welcomes the sight of a rainbow because it 'was always a symbol to him – a good symbol: of this peace' (154–5). He cannot altogether rid himself of these fragments of the Bible, which remain attached to him, to employ his own metaphor, like the broken bits of his own former tether.

Somers continues to engage in prolonged theological discussions not only with Kangaroo and his followers but with Struthers, the labour leader, to whom he insists on the need for absolute values, for a belief in 'the God who is the source of all passion', 'the great dark God who alone will sustain us', without which 'the loving comrades would smash one another' (199). Struthers mocks the way the Psalms call perpetually and ineffectually upon God to save the people of

Israel. But although Somers is moved by Struthers' enthusiasm for the working-people and their ability to build 'Christ's democracy' on 'brother-love' he is disappointed at the limited, secular nature of the enterprise, hankering as he still does after 'the great dark God, the Nameless, of the first dark religions' (202). In the manuscript version of this discussion he waxes lyrical on the virtues of ancient Egypt, 'when the mysteries of the Gods and the temples and the divine kings stimulated all kinds of life-responses in the people, which we have lost'. Struthers, 'tin Moses that he is', merely laughs, not wanting to return to 'the plagues of mice and locusts', unwilling to offer up his 'first-born to a fatted calf or a golden serpent' (446–7). The Book of Exodus, instead of being a source of hope for the liberation of the people, becomes merely the butt of coarse, uncomprehending jokes. Finding his faith once more rejected, Somers is tempted to despair altogether of his sacred mission:

Love seemed to have gone out of him like a squib, and along with it, faith, hope, charity and all the whole bunch of keys . . . Now, lo, he'd lost his apostle's robe in the bush, and couldn't quite see himself. (447)

He can emulate neither Moses nor the apostles Peter, who is given 'the keys of the kingdom of heaven' in Matthew 16: 19, or Paul, preacher of faith, hope and charity in 1 Corinthians 13. *The Boy in the Bush* takes the possibility of being an apostle or a biblical patriarch in the modern world more seriously, as we shall see, but Somers is more concerned about breaking with the Judaeo-Christian tradition. He has another argument with Kangaroo in which he upholds the virtues of the Celts, who remembered 'older gods, older ideals, different gods: before the Jews invented a mental Jehovah, and a spiritual Christ' (206). The manuscript has even more anti-Jewish material, which Lawrence may have excised out of consideration for Seltzer, his Jewish publisher (xliii), in which Somers defends the Celts against 'fanatic monotheists like the Jews' (449). But he left in the text Somers' parting attack on the Australian as 'a Kangaroo of Judah', a debased form of the Lion of Judah celebrated in Genesis 49: 9 and Revelation 5: 5, a 'Jehovah with a great heavy tail and a belly pouch'. 'What's the good of men trying to be gods?' Somers asks: 'You're a Jew, and you must be Jehovah or nothing. We're Christians, all little christs walking without our crucifixes' (210). Both appear equally ridiculous.

It is the despair that follows this argument with Kangaroo which triggers in Somers the memory of his persecution during the war, closely based upon Lawrence's own experience. Hounded from medical to medical to be constantly re-graded for possible military service, Somers is depicted as a martyr, with the 'immobile face of a crucified Christ who makes no complaint', in the tradition of the suffering servant of Isaiah 53 (247). He is branded as an outsider, 'set apart from mankind, a Cain, or worse' (249), which helps to explain why he feels 'broken off from his fellow-men' and 'broken off from the England he had belonged to' (259). He retains a belief in God, not the 'ideal God' of an 'all-too-limitedly-human' consciousness derided by Nietzsche but the 'great living darkness which we represent by the glyph, God' (265–6). This God is more 'a new way of knowing' than an object of knowledge, more an 'anti-idea' than a concept. He is certainly 'not a God scribbling on tablets of stone or bronze. No everlasting decalogues. No sermons on mounts, either. The dark God, the forever unrevealed. The God who is many gods to many men: all things to all men.' Again, it is significant that Lawrence has to resort in this final phrase to the language of St Paul (1 Cor. 9: 22) even to go beyond Christianity.

That Lawrence means finally to slough off the Judaeo-Christian tradition, however, is evident from the onslaught that follows on the Ten Commandments and the Sermon on the Mount, which are both subjected to critical interrogation. 'Life makes no absolute statement', Somers is made to think, adducing the first commandment (Exod. 20: 3) and the injunction in Leviticus 19: 18 to 'love thy neighbour as thyself,' both of them taken up by Jesus in Mark 12:31 and Matthew 19: 19. He brings out the many difficulties surrounding this 'wildly problematic commandment' before moving on to the Beatitudes, which again he finds more complex than they are sometimes thought. He proceeds to go through Matthew 5 subjecting six of the Beatitudes to qualifications and objections before finally falling asleep. Somers' real grudge against Jesus, like Nietzsche's, appears to be that he got there first. Not being able to preach the Sermon on the Mount, he is left with the lesser alternative, the fate of all critics, merely to comment upon them.

As soon as he is awake, Somers returns to his biblical criticism, rejecting the 'spikenard' of sentimentality surrounding the figure of Jesus, the ointment poured over his feet by the woman at Bethany (Mark 14: 3 and Matt. 26: 7) and 'the sweet odour of the balm of human beatitudes' (*K* 280). He also subjects the words of Revelation, 'the beginning and the end, the alpha and the omega' (1: 8, 21: 6 and 22: 13), and of 1 Corinthians, both the celebration of love, 'Charity suffereth long' (13: 5) and Christ's institution of the Eucharist (12: 24), to significant, blasphemous, variations, advocating what appears to be cannibalism in what he calls 'the other communion. – "This is thy body which I take from thee and eat"' (*K* 281–3). Still not satisfied that he has finally killed off the Judaeo-Christian tradition, Somers returns to his interrogation of the Ten Commandments, subjecting God's claim to be 'a jealous God' of Exodus 20: 5 to revision and placing it in dialogue with the eucharistic promise of Revelation 3: 20: 'Behold, I stand at the door, and knock: if any man hear my voice, and open the door, I will come in to him, and will sup with him, and he with me.' It was Victorian science, he suggests, which shut the door in the first place, lighting up the enclosed 'compound so brilliantly with electric light, that really, there was no outside' (284–5). As in *The Rainbow*, Lawrence deplores the fact that there is no room for the sacred in the enclosed world of scientific enlightenment.

Somers returns to this image of 'the dark God knocking afresh at the door' in the following chapter, attacking the mass of people who are deaf to his call, reluctant to acknowledge anything they cannot understand (297). He calls on 'the Gods of the other world' to vindicate him against 'these liars', the masses who deny the mysterious (292). He rejects Kangaroo too, choosing 'the Lord Almighty' rather than 'Kangaroo as God Himself' (304). Kangaroo on his deathbed quotes Christ, hoping to 'draw all men unto me' (John 12: 32), echoing the language of Exodus and the Psalms as he pleads with Somers, 'Don't harden your heart. Don't stiffen your neck before your old Jewish Kangaroo' (cf. Psalms 95: 8 and 75: 5). He even uses the language of the first letter of John: 'Perfect love casteth out fear' (I John 4: 18). His voice still has some appeal for Somers, to whom it comes as an 'annunciation', while his face becomes 'beautiful again, like a transfiguration' (*K* 324). He nevertheless refuses to tell the dying Kangaroo, at this point representative of the dying Judaeo-Christian tradition, that he loves him.

The novel ends with Somers leaving Australia for another land temporarily imbued with more promise, America, but not before confirming his belief in this 'other' God, beyond representation, walking along the coast and admiring the strange creatures in the sea, visiting the zoo to wonder at the animals there, and making a final visit to the bush at twilight, 'when night fell so delicately yet with such soft mystery' (342). Lawrence is perhaps better at evoking a sense of the mysterious in describing precise moments such as this than in attempting to bludgeon his readers into abandoning traditional Judaeo-Christian beliefs. His continued wrestling with the Bible in this novel appears more of a personal battle, an attempt to convince himself as much as his readers that it is possible to go beyond the tradition by means of the tradition. The Bible is burned into his consciousness; he cannot escape it but is compelled to revise it in ways that illustrate what he still finds attractive within its pages.

Lawrence's other Australian novel, *The Boy in the Bush*, is the product of Lawrence's rewriting of an original manuscript called 'The House of Ellis' by Mollie Skinner, a nurse at the Leithdale guesthouse for convalescents near Perth, where Lawrence stayed on his arrival in Australia in May 1922. Just as Lawrence felt compelled to rewrite the Bible, so his reworking of Skinner's novel illustrates what Frederick Carter called his 'insistent desire to amend, enhance and colour anything that deeply moved his interest' (Carter 1932: 32). She apparently showed him her first novel, *Letters of a V.A.D.*, about her experiences as a nurse in the First World War, prompting him to suggest a possible subject for a second, based upon the terrors of the Australian bush. Her autobiography recalls him telling her how much the bush frightened him 'as if dark gods possessed the place. My very soul shakes with terror when I wander out there in the moonlight' (Skinner 1972: 112–13). When she sent the typescript to him in New York, where he read it on his return from Mexico in August 1923, he replied offering to 're-cast it' since there was 'real quality' but 'without form, like the world before creation' (*Letters* IV 495–6). Not waiting to receive her permission to play the role of God, to bring her formless material into order, Lawrence began rewriting at once, which suggests to Paul Eggert, editor of the Cambridge edition of the novel, that 'he had glimpsed a significantly new direction and new emphases' for it (*BB* xxvii). It was to become his 'major literary occupation' for the next three months as well as for January 1924 (xxiv).

Lawrence's accounts of the process of rewriting confirm the extent of his involvement in it. A note written on the back of two photographs of Mexico recalls his ambivalence towards an original typescript which was 'full of good stuff' but 'so confused that I wrote it all out again, altering freely' (373). In the 'Preface to *Black Swans*', another novel by Skinner, he employs yet another biblical image to describe his unwillingness to abandon the whole project, to follow Pilate and 'play the hand-washing part'. Instead, he recalls, 'I wrote the whole book over again, from start to finish', keeping the basic plot but 'putting in and leaving out' as he felt appropriate. Skinner's account of the rewriting confirms Lawrence's, as does the survival of the whole manuscript of *The Boy in the Bush* in his hand. He would hardly have written out 580 pages of a novel in which he had not become deeply involved. When he revised her later unpublished novel, 'Eve in the Land of Nod', in 1928, his role was much more limited, confined to handwritten additions to the typescript with occasional interleaved passages of his own (lii). But with *The Boy in the Bush*, according to Skinner, his contribution increased as the novel wore on, becoming especially evident in the last two-thirds. Even a line-count of the passages she marked as Lawrence's late in 1924 (at Edward Garnett's request) would assign more than a third to him (xxx).

It is tempting to attribute all the biblical material in *The Boy in the Bush* to Lawrence, but Mollie Skinner shared with him a fascination with the Bible and its language. Her autobiography, *The Fifth Sparrow*, takes its title from Luke 12: 6, which is quoted in the epigraph: 'Are not five sparrows sold for two farthings, and not one of them is forgotten before God?' It recalls a religious upbringing which left her, like Lawrence, with a lasting love of hymns, which 'soaked into [her] mind', becoming the source of prayer and soothing her 'in anxious night watches' (Skinner 1972: 16). Like Lawrence, she moved away from the church of her upbringing, which was Anglican, taking an interest in esoteric thought and theosophy, although unlike him she remained within the Christian fold, ending as a Quaker. She retained a powerful sense of providential guidance, referring to 'a Hand on my shoulder' at key moments of her life (19, 130). By the time she met Lawrence, she records, 'proper religion' in the sense of commitment to a particular church, had long since left her (129). Her brother Jack too, whom Lawrence suggested she make the hero of the novel, was a similarly independent character (17), sharing with the novelist what Lawrence, in a letter to Mollie on Jack's death, called 'a revolt against the fixed thing' in any aspect of life (158). They clearly shared a religious heterodoxy which made co-operation possible but which also makes it hard exactly to distinguish their separate contributions to the novel. One can only take the whole of the final version of *The Boy in the Bush* as it stands as a novel for which Lawrence was prepared to take joint responsibility.

The Boy in the Bush has been called 'an elaborate variation upon the Cain–Abel theme' (Tindall 1972: 18), one intertextual strand of which appears to have been mediated by Hermann Hesse's *Demian*, which Lawrence discussed with Mabel Luhan in February 1924. The first part of *Demian*, he recalled, in which the eponymous hero introduces the first-person narrator to a new way of reading the story of Cain, 'interested me', unlike the last part, in which the narrator falls in love with *Demian*'s mother, which he thought '*sau dumm*' (*Letters* IV 576). It is in the second chapter of the novel, entitled 'Cain', that *Demian* suggests to the narrator, Sinclair, that this story, like many in the Bible, can be seen 'from another angle' than the narrow orthodoxy of their religious teachers. *Demian* explains the 'sign' of Cain as 'something in his face that frightened other people', a mark of greater independence and intelligence. Cain, who has the strength to kill his brother, inspires 'other weaklings' with fear, which they justify in terms of the God-given mark (Hesse 1995: 32–3). In the course of the novel, Sinclair, who had earlier belonged entirely to the conventionally 'good' world of his parents, gradually transfers his allegiance to the 'other' world represented by Cain. He becomes part of a circle surrounding *Demian* and his mother who bear this 'sign' as a mark of their difference from the majority, their commitment to 'another kind of vision' (160). Their role, as *Demian* explains it, is precisely to shock the conventional into new religious awareness. The hero of *The Boy in the Bush*, I suggest, like that of Hesse's novel, can be seen to assume a similarly independent Cain-like role, leaving behind the values of his family, discovering the dark god of the bush, killing his 'brother' and returning to patriarchal practices (such as bigamy) which shock the more conventionally religious.

Another significant intertext for *The Boy in the Bush*, I would claim, is Jane Harrison's study of *Ancient Art and Ritual*. Among the examples Harrison takes for her chapter on 'Primitive Ritual: Pantomimic Dances' is not only the 'attitude of the Australian towards the Kangaroo', which, she explains, 'is one of affection tempered by deep religious awe', an attitude reflected in Lawrence's novel of that title (Harrison 1927: 45–46), but also a ritual involving a resurrection witnessed by some boys in the bush. Aboriginal rites marking the onset of spring, she acknowledges, may not appear ostensibly religious, consciously addressed to a theological construct, but they are a religious celebration of man's 'will to live' (64). She proceeds to describe in some detail how boys belonging to 'some tribes of Southeast Australia' cover up an old man with sticks and earth. The 'buried man holds in his hand a small bush which seems to be growing from the ground' and this bush 'begins to quiver' as the man himself starts up from the grave (107). Harrison compares this spring festival not only with the rites of Adonis and Indian bear dances but with our own 'Jack-in-the Green' (113). It seems too much for coincidence that Jack, the hero of *The Boy in the Bush*, should also rise from his lengthy illness as from the dead to fuller life. Both Hesse and Harrison, I suggest, contribute to Lawrence's reworking of the Bible in this novel.

The importance of the Bible for Lawrence's hero is apparent from the opening chapter, which records that the only prize Jack

had ever won at school was for scripture. The bible-language exerted a certain fascination over him, and in the background of his consciousness the bible images always hovered. When he was moved, it was scripture that came to his aid. So now he stood, silent with the shyness of youth, thinking over and over: 'There shall be a new heaven and a new earth.' (*BB* 8)

Australia clearly represents for Jack a new world with an opportunity of improving on his performance in the old. Having been expelled both from school and agricultural college in the old world, grievously disappointing his father, he sees himself as a worthy successor to the 'sinners' or convicts with which Australia was first populated; he too 'was a sinner, a Cain' (10). The significance of this identification on Jack's part with Cain is not at this stage apparent. Much is made, on the contrary, of his innocent appearance and of his being unaware either that he had 'sinned' or that he would in future (10). There are plenty of other biblical allusions in the early chapters, many of them from the Book of Exodus, recalling the pioneering journey of the children of Israel through the wilderness into the Promised Land. At Wandoo, the Ellises' farm, for example, young Lennie's tears come suddenly 'as if smitten from a rock' (63, cf. Exod. 17: 6) while Mary is compared with 'Moses' sister watching over events' (88, cf. Exod. 2: 4).

There is also biblical significance in the story that emerges first from Tom about the disputes between the different branches of the Ellis family, the children of Tom's father Jacob and the 'Reds', the family descended from Jacob's twin brother Easu, a corruption of the biblical Esau (68). Jacob was originally called Frank in the manuscript but his name was changed to Jacob, further emphasising the biblical analogy, in the typescript for the first English edition, which was revised by Lawrence (442). The story of brotherly rivalry between the Ellises follows the biblical narrative of Jacob and Esau fairly closely: as Tom explains to Jack, his grandfather died without leaving a will but his father inherited Wandoo, although he 'wandered' and 'was gone for years', being officially regarded as the older of the twins, a fact disputed by the Reds (64). The Reds, also bearing the surname Ellis, gained their nickname because of their appearance: Red Ellis, the eldest son, is described as 'a tall, sinewy, red-faced man with reddish hair and reddish beard' (65), the beard being an interlinear excrescence in the original manuscript, presumably added by Lawrence, who had a clear personal interest in red beards. Esau, as Eggert explains, is Hebrew for shaggy or hairy, a characteristic he has from birth (Gen. 25: 25). Rebekah in the biblical narrative, like Gran in the novel, prefers her smooth son and ensures he receives his father's blessing and property.

It is Jack, however, who has the most powerful claim to be a biblical patriarch. Immediately settling into Jacob's family, he experiences a fierce rivalry with young Easu, son of the disinherited twin, a rivalry that extends to cricket, riding and romance (they both court Monica) before reaching its climax in their two violent fights, in the second of which he shoots and kills Easu. Before all this happens, however, he develops a powerful, individual religious awareness, built upon the teaching of his mother, who tells him not to listen to 'the world's opinion' but to the 'glow inside you. That's the spirit of God inside you' (*BB* 22). Gran reinforces this advice, telling him 'God is y'rself' and 'y'rself is God', an unorthodox belief which she later rephrases, 'The best in yourself is God' (77–8). Jack learns to supplement this inward spirituality with an awareness of the otherness, the transcendence, of the God on whom he calls when tending the sick Herbert. His experience of the bush, 'a new paradise from which man had not been cast out' (92), further develops his sense of a God different from any conventional representation of Him, certainly far removed from 'his father's world and his father's gods' (94). As with Somers in *Kangaroo*, it is clear that he is moving towards a new religious understanding, 'a new way through the bush' (*K* 154).

That Jack's understanding of religion is both biblical and unorthodox emerges in his reaction to Sundays at Wandoo, with their solemn public readings from the family Bible. He is described, as at the opening of the novel, as knowing the Bible 'pretty well' and having 'no objection to it':

On the contrary, it supplied his imagination with a chief stock of images, his ear with the greatest solemn pleasure of words, and his soul with a queer heterogeneous ethic. He never really connected the bible with christianity proper, the christianity of aunts and clergymen. He had no use for christianity proper: just dismissed it. But the bible was perhaps the foundation of his consciousness. Do what seems good to you in the sight of the Lord. This was the moral he always drew from bible lore. And since the Lord, for him, was always the Lord Almighty, Almighty God, Maker of Heaven and Earth, Jesus being only a side issue; since the Lord was always Jehovah the great and dark, for him, one might do as David did, in the sight of the Lord, or as Jacob, or as Abraham or Moses or Joshua or Isaiah, in the sight of the Lord. The sight of the Lord was a vast strange scope of vision, in the semi-dark. (*BB* 141)

The hostility towards orthodox Christianity, 'christianity proper', that conventional interpretation of the Bible which attempts to fix its meaning, is significant here as is the fact that for Jack, as for Lawrence and Nietzsche, the Old Testament has greater resonance than the New. Jesus is relegated to 'a side issue' while David, dancing naked before the Lord (2 Sam. 6: 2), Jacob, wrestling with Him (Gen. 32), Abraham, entertaining Him to supper (Gen. 18), Moses, also encountering Him in the bush (Exodus 3), Joshua and Isaiah, similarly entering into direct relationship with Him, are the figures who excite Jack's imagination. His imagination, like Lawrence's, is also set alight by apocalyptic imagery in the Bible. He is vouchsafed a vision of two horsemen riding from the west in what 'seemed like a transfiguration', one of them 'as if he were coming, small and Daniel-like, out of the vast furnace-mouth of creation' (*BB* 147), a reference to Daniel 3: 14–25, where a fourth figure 'like a Son of God' is seen in the furnace together with the three men who refuse to worship Nebuchadnezzar's golden images. These horsemen, 'trotting in the glorified cloud of the earth, spuming a glory all round them . . . coming with a proclamation of doom', also have antecedents in the Book of Revelation. Their effect on Jack is to instil into him a sense both of 'doom' and 'splendour', an increased awareness that there 'were vaster, more unspeakable gods than the gods of his fathers' (147). It is their very 'unspeakability', their refusal to be grasped in terms of conventional Christian doctrine, which guarantees their transcendence, marking them out as 'other'.

Jack's religious development is charted in the novel by his progressive rejection or modification of traditional biblical teaching. He rebels violently against Jesus' injunction 'Love your enemies' (Matt. 5: 44), repeated to him by his pious aunts, preferring to 'get into communication, or communion, with his own Lord' than to partake of the eucharistic sacrament so dear to them: 'he knew he never wanted to taste that Body, nor drink that Blood' (*BB* 167). Sundays at Wandoo bring fresh biblical passages for him to interrogate as Jacob Ellis reads aloud from the family Bible. As in *The Rainbow*, the text of the novel intersperses biblical readings with Jack's commentary upon them. The first passage upon which he meditates is Psalm 24: 3–4, advocating 'clean hands and a pure heart' in those who would 'ascend into the hill of the Lord'. Looking at his own hands later in the day, he is reminded of his desire to make love to Monica and to kill Easu, desires he refuses to consider unclean: 'And he was not going to try to pluck them out', in explicit rejection of Jesus' command, 'if thine eye offend thee, pluck it out' (Matt. 18: 9). He continues to reject conventional Christian readings of this psalm, arguing that 'the hands must move in the darkest acts, if they are to remain really clean' (*BB* 172–3). Throughout the novel biblical texts are pummelled, pulled and stretched until they are made to mean something with which Jack can feel comfortable.

Jack is a little less violent with Psalm 21, a plea to God not to forsake the elderly, which he relates to Gran, herself at the point of death. It is when he moves on to the New Testament reading, from 1 Corinthians 15: 40–4, that his challenge to conventional Christianity becomes more evident. His memory of the passage, to begin with, is not complete, although the omissions are indicated by dashes: 'There is one glory of the sun, and another glory of the moon, and another glory of the stars – There is a natural body and a spiritual body –.' Jack no sooner quotes these Pauline phrases, however, than he takes issue with them, disputing the idea that there is only 'one glory of the sun' (173–4). He then repeats the words of St Paul with his own additional commentary, seeing the 'glory of the moon' in terms of his own nocturnal ramblings in the bush. This, of course, was precisely the experience which sparked Lawrence's initial suggestion of the subject for the whole novel.

Jack continues to give his personal gloss on the words of St Paul, although his language assumes a more critical tone when the apostle attempts to distinguish between the 'natural' and 'the spiritual body' (1 Cor. 15: 44). He realises how much he had always hated this 'spiritual body' as worshipped by his aunts and by a somewhat absurd list of hated 'spiritual' people headed by the poet Shelley and including all vegetarians and socialists. More important than these arbitrary prejudices, however, is his attachment to the Old Testament as solidly grounded in the body, the flesh (*BB* 175). He continues to appropriate St Paul's language, celebrating his new-found awareness of the glories of the sun and the moon in a new sacrament, a new Lord's Supper combining body and spirit. He gives a savage twist to Paul's account of the institution of the Eucharist in 1 Corinthians 11: 24–27, turning it into something much more physical, more explicitly sexual:

This glowing, intoxicated body, drunk with the sun and the moon, drunk from the cup in the hand of the Lord, this was his spiritual body.

And when the flame came up in him, tearing from his bowels, in the sudden new desire for Monica, this was his spiritual body, the body transfigured with fire. (176)

Even his desire to kill Easu, who 'seemed to him like the Antichrist', is seen by Jack to be part of this 'spiritual body' which Easu, dominating his horse and degrading Monica, wants to subjugate.

Jack's meditation upon these biblical passages, placing them in the context of his own particular concerns, degenerates for a time into complaints against all those close to him. He alone, it would seem, is open like Moses to the glory of the burning bush, allowing the fire of the Lord to burn and drinking from 'the cup of the fierce glory of the Lord' (176–7). As elsewhere in Lawrence, a traditional Christian concept, in this case the sacrament of the eucharist, is transformed into a much fiercer, more 'primitive', Old Testament mentality. When he returns finally to 1 Corinthians 15: 41–44, he either misremembers or deliberately misquotes it, curiously substituting 'quiet' for 'glory', perhaps recalling Paul's advice to the Thessalonians 'that ye study to be quiet' (1 Thess. 4: 11):

There is a quiet of the sun and another quiet of the moon, and another quiet of the stars; for one star differs from another in quiet. So also is the resurrection of the dead. It is sown a natural body; it is raised a spiritual body.

'Was that Scripture? Or wasn't it?', he proceeds to ask, as well he might, having given such a garbled version of the biblical text. He begins to meditate once more on the significance of the 'natural body' before even he runs out of stamina (*BB* 178). As with Ursula's midrashic speculation upon Genesis and her interrogation of the Sermon on the Mount, which Lawrence had the sense to omit from the final text of *The Rainbow*, it seems at times almost an automatic reflex for him (and his characters) to fall into this mode of critical dialogue with the Bible. At this point in *The Boy in the Bush* the novel is in danger of turning into a particularly tendentious form of biblical commentary.

The remainder of the novel portrays Jack's development into an outsider, a Hessian Cain, burning with a deep inner conviction. He becomes increasingly aware of his anger towards Easu, an 'invisible fire' makes him feel 'as if he belonged to a race apart . . . like the race of Cain'. He sympathises with other outsiders such as the aborigines and is welcomed on the road as '*The Stranger within our gates!*' (202), a phrase deriving from Exodus 20: 10. The God he discovers in the bush has the same terrifying qualities as the landscape: 'in the wild bush, God seemed another God, . . . vaster, more calm and more deeply, sensually potent' (227–8). When he returns to Wandoo, he seems to the biblically illiterate Lennie like 'the angel that stood in Jacob's doorway an' looked like a man' (276). He is himself more accurate in expressing his wish 'to go like Abraham under the wild sky, speaking to a fierce wild Lord, and having angels stand in his doorway' (333).

This sacred otherness becomes most apparent after Jack's killing of Easu, an act of self-defence which, like Cain's, both marks him as different and appears to bring him into God's protection. He is carried away into the bush by his horse, who presses forward 'as if directed by God'. He mutters, 'I have dipped my hand in blood!', after Psalm 68: 23, which allows for the dipping of feet 'in the blood of thine enemies' (283). He calls himself 'a lord of death', an implicit rejection, according to Eggert, of the God of the New Testament, who 'is not a God of the dead, but of the living' (Luke 20: 38). Eggert also finds possible references here to Osiris, ' "Universal Lord" . . . of the world of the dead' and Mictlantecuhtli, the Aztec lord of the dead who mixes blood and bone to forge a new humanity (*BB* 425–6). But Jack addresses his 'mysterious Lord' in language which clearly alludes to the sacrament on whose institution in 1 Corinthians he had earlier dwelt in such detail, offering him his 'hand in blood' as 'a sort of pledge or baptism, or a sacrifice' (284). He recognises that this represents something of a departure from orthodox Christianity but supposes that his Lord 'meant me to be like this'. He cannot imagine himself in a more conventional role as a lawyer or politician, 'Or anything that goes to church and sings hymns and has supper after church on the best linen table-cloth.' Only 'a big, fat, reesty sort of God,' he concludes, could enjoy such worship. His own God is not so easily satisfied or so transparent: He 'is dark and you can't see him . . . And he doesn't know himself what he thinks' (285).

Jack's recovery from the wounds inflicted by Easu continues to be accompanied by echoes from the Bible, in particular from John 3: 7, 'Ye must be born again' (291). He recognises an obligation to recover since he was 'dark-anointed . . . with the dark unction between his brows' (292), a reference to the Old Testament rite of royal anointing. He continues to see himself in Old Testament terms as 'a man forged by the Lord of Hosts' (296). Although he marries Monica and fathers children by her, he remains an 'eternal stranger' who can never finally be known or possessed (301), evincing an inaccessibility whose religious dimension is even more apparent in the original manuscript, which stresses his refusal to 'give final intimacy to any human being whatsoever. He had given his ultimate intimacy to his own male God' (482). Returning to Perth, he confronts the conventional Mary and her even more conventional Aunt Matilda with his new religious ideas. The manuscript even has him compare himself to St Paul: 'if Paul went to Damascus, I went to Kalgoorlie. Why should I not have seen my own god?' (486). It is, however, to the untamed figures of the Old Testament that he turns in the final text for models for his own siding with the 'uncanny' Ellises against Aunt Matilda and 'the dead-certain people of this world':

Let there be another, deeper, fiercer, untamed sort of goodness, like in the days of Abraham and Samson and Saul. If Jack was to be good he would be good with these great old men, the heroic fathers, not with the Saints. The Christian goodness had gone bad, decayed almost into poison. It needed again the old heroic goodness of untamed men, with the wild great God who was for ever too unknown to be a paragon. (319)

Abraham's example also gives Jack the courage to contemplate having two wives, Mary as well as Monica. He proposes to Mary that she sleep with him in the stable, priding himself on his refusal to 'play the mild Saint Joseph' (331), a deliberately provocative re-working of the details of Christ's nativity.

The last two chapters of the novel portray Jack struggling to hold on to his biblical vision in a society which he feels hates him. It is not just his father and aunts, always representative of the old beliefs, but even his mother and his friends who hate him. 'They would all like to kill the non-conforming one' (335). Because he stands out against their conventional values, they persecute him: 'Daniel in the den of lions was a comfortable man in comparison' (337). But he is prepared to stand alone in what he calls 'spontaneous royalty . . . like Abraham or Saul' (380). He rides out of Perth (on his horse Adam), resolving no longer 'to play at being really pleasant and ordinary' but to 'have the courage to turn his face right away from mankind' (341), to accept his prophetic role in the words of Joshua on which he ponders: 'Be strong and of a good courage; be not afraid, neither be thou dismayed: for the Lord thy God is with thee withersoever thou goest' (Josh. 1: 9). A final encounter with the unconventional Hilda Blessington, who expresses willingness to be 'a man's second or third wife' (*BB* 346) and promises to visit him, gives him unexpected encouragement, sending him off laughing and chuckling into 'the silent grey bush, in which he had once been lost' (347). These are the final words of the novel, hardly a vision of Paradise Regained, but a glimpse of a future which could be different. Lawrence has not only rewritten Mollie Skinner's original manuscript but the Bible itself, recreating in Western Australia the religious intensity, the closeness to God and the obliviousness to conventional morality of a biblical patriarch.

None of these novels reach positive conclusions, leaving their protagonists still committed to an ongoing search for religious truth, still wandering in the wilderness and well short of the promised land. This, of course, reflects Lawrence's own position at this time, also travelling from place to place in search of a fully satisfying home. Perhaps the point of these novels is that there can be no rest, no fixed solution to man's religious needs. Whatever answers are propounded, including those suggested by the Bible as read by its more orthodox interpreters, need continually to be reread, revised and rewritten in order to continue to have relevance to Lawrence and his protagonists.

CHAPTER 10

Prose 'Sketches', 'Evangelistic Beasts', and stories with biblical 'overtones'

Lawrence's continuing search for new sources of the sacred, new 'answers' to the old religious quest, drove him in the last decade of his life into a pattern of almost perpetual movement: from England to Italy, from there to Australia via Ceylon, then on to the United States, from which he visited Mexico before returning to Europe to spend his last years in Italy and France. His anger at the failure of Christianity to adapt to new conditions of living, its refusal to abandon the Greek metaphysics in which its official doctrine had been framed, often spills over in the writing of these years into blasphemy, parody and explicit critique of the Bible. Much of this writing could be called Nietzschean both in form and content, reaching towards a joyful wisdom, a gay science, through the parodic reworking of scripture. The retelling of the fall, re-accented by Lawrence not as a fall *into* sin and sensuality, of course, but *out of* sensual awareness and into repression, requiring a further quest to regain the paradisal state of ancient civilisations, is particularly prominent in Lawrence's prose of the 1920s, which ranges from travel writing to history and psychology, including a number of essays explicitly on religion. His poetry of this period, *Birds, Beasts and Flowers*, also engages subversively with key biblical texts, most obviously in the series entitled 'Evangelistic Beasts', which satirises the gospels. The four volumes of short stories published in this period also contain much parodic reworking of biblical material. This is Lawrence at his most critical of conventional Christianity, most radical in his revision of the Bible.

Much of the travel writing centres upon Italy, the product of two periods in which first Sicily (1919–22) and then Tuscany (1926–8) became his home. *Sea and Sardinia*, written after a trip to that island in 1921, has little sustained discussion of religion, although at one Cagliari is compared to Jerusalem or some other biblical town in a 'monkish, illuminated missal' (*SS* 53). At another, Lawrence mocks the notion of an immaculate conception, laughing at the description of Joseph in the Cathedral there as 'the true potential father of Our Lord': 'What can it profit a man,' he wonders, in the manner of Matthew 16: 26, 'to be the potential father of anybody' (59). He is glad that the Sardinians don't go in for 'the grovelling Madonna-worship' characteristic of other parts of Italy (67). Instead, altogether uncontaminated by the command to love their neighbours (88), they seem more like pagans worshipping 'the far, mysterious gods of the early Mediterranean' (116). There is more of the sacred, as far as he is concerned, in the 'transfiguration' of the almond trees in the 'sea-glare' which 'whitened all the air as with a sort of God-presence' (148), than in 'this dreary Christianity of ours' (121). The whole point of the book is to celebrate the island's natural elements in contrast with its superimposed religious beliefs.

Christianity is more central to the account of his visit in 1920 to the Benedictine monastery of Montecassino in his 'Introduction to the *Memoirs of the Foreign Legion*' by Maurice Magnus, which becomes for a while an Arnoldian lament for the passing of a lost world of faith and a critique of soulless modernity. Looking down from the summit of its mountain on to the 'barren' world beneath, the steel lines of the railway leading into 'another world', Lawrence, like Arnold in 'Stanzas from the Grande Chartreuse', feels out of place in 'both worlds'. He also produces a paragraph in the style of *The Golden Bough*, capturing Frazer's characteristic mixture of rationalism and nostalgia for this 'sacred grove' and hill, which 'must have been one of man's intense sacred places for three thousand years' (*Phoenix* II 325–6). He accuses Magnus himself of being 'worldly' (324), of being a 'modern rogue' with his 'modern creed' of making money out of everything (333, 338), even a Judas, 'betraying with a kiss . . . selling the good feeling he had tried to arouse, and had aroused, for any handful of silver he could get' (354). But he cannot honestly maintain the role of Jesus, agonising on his mountain, for long; he quickly leaves the monastery and appears more comfortable in the train back to Sicily 'among the fat Neapolitans eating their macaroni, with the big glass windows steamed opaque and the rain beating outside' (327). There is in this introduction a delicate balance between sacred and secular both in himself and in the outside world.

Lawrence returned to Italy in November 1925, embarking on

what Earl Brewster called 'our Etruscan pilgrimage' in March 1926 (Brewster 1934: 122), visiting the tombs and other remains of a civilisation he felt had succeeded in combining the sacred and the sensual. His letters of this period celebrate Etruscan art as just as 'sacred' as 'the ideal of the Greeks and Germans' (*Letters* V 464–5). His *Sketches of Etruscan Places*, written in the winter of 1927–8 although not published until 1932, sustain this contrast between their 'phallic consciousness' and the 'mental and spiritual consciousness we are accustomed to' (*EP* 17), again deconstructing the Greco-Christian tendency to separate the two, to privilege matter over over spirit, mind over body. He even suggests that the Etruscans may have contributed to the some of the more positive elements in the Jewish tradition, imagining ships sailing to Etruria 'in the days of Solomon', even perhaps in 'the days of Abraham' (28), when the Etruscan 'religious seers' were 'leaders in the sacred mysteries' (37). Their cosmic awareness, he suggests, 'was even, half-transmitted, at the back of David's mind, and voiced in the Psalms' although David personified 'the living cosmos' as a 'personal god' (58). *Etruscan Places* repeatedly contrasts the profound cosmic awareness of the ancient Etruscans with the Judaeo-Christian worship of the word, the Logos.

Lawrence's continuing religious quest is apparent in all his extensive non-fiction of this period, even in *Movements in European History*, a school textbook originally commissioned in 1918 and published under the pseudonym Lawrence H. Davison in 1921. The 'Epilogue' to the second edition of 1925 proved too religious, ironically, for Charles Williams, one of two readers asked to comment on it (*MEH*a: xiii). *Movements* certainly paints a rosy picture of pagan religion, which involved 'no preaching, no praying, no talk about sin or salvation, no service at all' but was 'part of the active, actual, everyday, normal life' (*MEH*b 25–6). Lawrence explains to his young audience that the Greeks and Romans, unlike the Jews, were not 'jealous of strange gods' (a clear challenge to the God of Exodus 20: 5, who describes himself as 'a jealous God') but simply worshipped 'everything that was wonderful' (26–7). Christianity is seen to have appealed mainly to the poor and oppressed, offering them an escape into an eternity of happiness. Expanding upon similar suggestions in Gibbon (Gibbon I 454), his main source for the origins of Christianity, he interprets the visions of the Book of Revelation as the product of an oppressed people whose images of majesty would necessarily have been couched in terms derived from secular power. He draws a vivid picture of early Christian slaves longing for revenge against their masters, imagining how they would have felt 'as they saw the Roman ladies borne through the streets in golden litters', swearing revenge and dreaming of a time when the roles would be reversed, the Romans 'cast down into eternal punishment' and the Christians 'walking the bright streets of glass, in the New Jerusalem' (*MEHb* 32). This portrait of the early Church will find more sustained expression in *Apocalypse*.

Religion returns to prominence in the chapters on the Crusades and the Reformation. Lawrence is sympathetic towards the sense of wonder characteristic of medieval Christians, though he is critical of the Church for its attitude towards the Bible:

a mysterious holy book which the common people never saw, and which they could never read if they did see it, for it was written in Latin. Sometimes the priests read them little pieces: about the heavens opening, or about the stones rolling back from the Sepulchre as Jesus rose from the dead. And it seemed terrible and wonderful. It seemed to the people as if the priests knew great, deep mysteries, of which only a fragment was revealed to ordinary men. The ordinary Christians read nothing and knew nothing by themselves. (144)

The Reformation, of course, changed all this. Following R. B. Mowat's account in *The Later Middle Ages*, Lawrence celebrates the work of biblical scholars such as John Reuchlin, who 'studied Hebrew so that he could get at the true meaning of the Old Testament' and even tried to 'save the Jewish writings', midrashic and kabbalistic material, 'from the flames of the Inquisitors' (173). John Colet's work on the original Greek of Paul's letters is held up for similar approval as pioneering more appropriate ways of reading them as 'human documents, not just mysterious religious utterances' (174). The uncritical faith of the Middle Ages thus gave way to the informed but no less passionate faith of the Reformers based upon a relationship with God 'so near and personal that it is unspeakable' (175). Lawrence credits Luther with being 'the first to make religion truly human and nearer' (175), propounding a religion centred in the heart (181). The remainder of the book has less to say about religion, apart from the epilogue, which urges his readers to begin the necessary process of post-war religious renewal. The whole book is heavily reliant upon secondary sources (Crumpton 1985) but Lawrence still manages to impose his own beliefs upon them.

All Lawrence's writing of this period in fact, whatever its ostensible subject, could be said to be religious. The original typescript pages of the first version of *Fantasia of the Unconscious*, begun in June 1921, comprise 'a new Lawrencian version of the Gospel according to St John' (Kinkead-Weekes 1996: 659). The final version, published in America in 1922 and in England the following year, although primarily concerned to expound Lawrence's views on Freud, sexuality and human relations, repeatedly returns to the religious question. The 'Foreword', for example, ends with a recognition of the need for religious 'vision' but insists that it should not be tied to an outdated metaphysic, which is 'wearing woefully thin'. If we want to renew our lives and our vision, Lawrence insists, with a vivid biblical image drawn from the gospel accounts of the crucifixion, 'We've got to rip the old veil of a vision across, and find what the heart really believes in, after all' (*Fant.* 15–16). The opening chapter of *Fantasia* suggests 'the essentially religious or creative motive is the first motive for all human activity', however much that is denied by Freud and other scientists (18). Lawrence himself rejects impractical idealistic visions from 'Pisgah', exhorting his readers to bring their religion down to earth: 'Downhill to the land of milk and honey' (19). The second chapter, provocatively entitled 'The Holy Family', celebrates the individuality that made Jesus respect 'his own Holy Ghost' and deny his mother (43). As in *Studies in Classic American Literature*, however, Lawrence is soon retelling the opening chapters of Genesis, expounding his own version of an original fall from instinctive to cerebral knowledge:

Why were we driven out of Paradise? Why did we fall into this gnawing disease of unappeasable dissatisfaction? Not because we sinned. Ah, no. All the animals in Paradise enjoyed the sensual passion of coition. Not because we sinned, but because we got our sex into our head.

When Eve ate that particular apple, she became aware of her own womanhood, mentally. And mentally she began to experiment with it. She has been experimenting ever since. So has man. To the rage and horror of both of them. (85)

The snake is seen to be guilty of perverting woman 'into mentality' (188) leaving Adam with the recourse of battering Eve out of 'her own self-conscious preoccupation with herself'. He should, Lawrence suggests, rip off her clothes, 'Reduce her once more to a naked Eve, and send the apple flying' (191). Not for the last time, Lawrence reworks the familiar story, retaining its basic ingredients (the characters and the plot) but totally reversing its significance.

Fantasia of the Unconscious repeats some of Lawrence's perennial complaints, such as the absurdity of the male claim that Eve was created from his spare rib (98). More provocatively, it mocks Jesus' claim not to need domesticity, the feminine 'world of love, of emotion, of sympathy'. Even He, according to Lawrence, should have learnt to be 'man enough . . . to come home at tea-time and put his slippers on', thus avoiding becoming one of the world's 'failures' (100–1). This passage, when it appeared in an excerpt from the book in Murry's magazine, the *Adelphi*, provoked a storm of protest from readers and a massive drop in circulation (Ellis 1998: 135). Lawrence plays similarly provocative games with St Paul, parodying his exhortation to Ephesian wives to submit to their husbands (*Fant.* 147; cf. Eph. 5: 22, 25). His continual recourse to pastiche of the Bible, it must be admitted, would try the patience of the most indulgent reader.

Psychoanalysis and the Unconscious, originally written and published earlier than *Fantasia* (in 1920) but printed after it in the Phoenix and subsequent editions as a more tentative exploration of similar themes (10), returns to Lawrence's two key biblical passages, the beginning of Genesis and the beginning of John's Gospel. It is when the mind *knows* what should be the province of the heart, Lawrence insists,

that sin enters. Adam and Eve fell, not because they had sex, or even because they committed the sexual act, but because they became aware of their sex and of the possibility of the act. When sex became to them a mental object – that is, when they discovered that they could deliberately enter upon and even provoke sexual activity in themselves, then they were cursed and cast out of Eden. (206)

The opening of John's Gospel, in contrast, is taken as a paradigmatic case of the attempted suppression of the body by the mind. Lawrence first quotes and then immediately rebels against the claims embodied in the opening words of the gospel, which are seen as another example of the arrogant claim to be able to explain life, an accusation also brought against science in general and Freud in particular. Lawrence urges his readers rather to embrace 'the old religious faculty' (216), retaining a respect and reverence for all authentic forms of life.

Another group of essays Lawrence wrote during this period, many of which revert sooner or later to the subject of religion, was collected in the volume entitled *Reflections on the Death of a Porcupine*,

first published in 1925. These form a less coherent group than those
on American literature but continue some of their themes. An essay
on 'Democracy', for example, which grew out of his work on
Whitman, vents Lawrence's anger against a materialism which has
no interest in religion. Also under attack are all logocentric discourses, all theological systems which are simply examples of man
inventing a set of ideas and then proceeding 'to worship his
fabrication, and himself as the mouthpiece of the Logos' (*Ref.* 69).
Lawrence, like Blake, repeatedly contrasts one model of God, which
regards Him as 'a great Mind' who 'floats in space . . . drawing with
a pair of compasses and making everything to scale', with his own
emphasis on the 'actual living quick itself' which 'is alone the
creative reality' (77). Another essay in the Cambridge edition of
Reflections, 'Education of the People', written in Sicily in 1920 but not
published before it appeared posthumously in *Phoenix*, insists along
Old Testament lines, 'Our God is the Unnamed, the Veiled, and any
attempt to give names, or remove veils, is just a mental impertinence'
(108). Lawrence's theology is consistently more Jewish than Greek, as
are his images of 'the fleshpots of the old fat peace' (115) and of
children being '*led* into the Canaan of their promise', a reference to
the promise made by God to Abraham in Genesis 17: 8 (116).

Lawrence's opposition to Christian orthodoxy emerges strongly in
an essay first published in Middleton Murry's newly founded *Adelphi*
in December 1923, 'The Proper Study', which insists, in Wildean
vein, that all commandments are there to be broken (170). He takes
up the early Christian imagery of Jesus as the fish and offers his own,
playful explanation of its origin: 'Because he fell . . . into the Great
Ocean that is outside the shore' of common human knowledge (171).
He proceeds to write of a new kind of literature that will emulate
St Paul's engagement with the sacred and mysterious in his 'true
novel' (173). The use of the word 'novel' to refer to the Bible here, as
in the essays considered earlier in relation to *The Rainbow,* points to
the modern novel as the new Bible to which Lawrence looks for a re-
awakening of religious feeling.

Lawrence wrote a number of articles on explicitly religious
subjects for the *Adelphi.* 'On Being Religious' launches straight into a
discussion of the word 'God', refusing to stipulate precisely what this
'queer little word means' (187). Rather than enter into monological
discourse on the subject, he launches into a dialogue between
himself and a series of supposed believers in God which illustrates

the difficulties inherent in all theological language. Lawrence at one point assumes the role of the angel at the tomb after the resurrection, with a disturbingly different, irreverent message:

The Almighty has vacated the throne, abdicated, climbed down. It's no good your looking up into the sky. It's empty. Where the Most High used to sit listening to woes, supplications and repentances, there's nothing but a great gap in the empyrean. You can still go on praying to that gap if you like. The Most High has gone out. (189)

He also plays with the biblical account of Jacob's ladder (Gen. 28: 12), suggesting that it is God who has 'climbed down. He has just calmly stepped down the ladder of the angels, and is standing behind you, grinning' (*Ref.* 189). Lawrence clearly enjoys rewriting biblical episodes in this satirical vein, insisting that 'this isn't a deliberate piece of blasphemy' but an attempt to illustrate the inadequacy of all language about God. He even plays with the metaphors in the claim of the Johannine Jesus, 'I am the way, the truth, and the life' (John 14: 6), making of it something less absolute than conventional Christian doctrine. Jesus is presented as one among several 'other saviours, in other lands, at other times, with other messages', all of whom as 'Sons of God' offer 'Different Ways of Salvation' (190–3).

Another essay in this series, 'On Human Destiny', mixes familiar biblical metaphors, not wanting the 'Old tablets of stone', the commandments, to become 'a mill-stone round our necks', distinguishing like later postmodern theologians between God, who is eternal, and 'my idea of Him', which is 'perishable' (209). 'On Being a Man' returns once more to the story of the fall, deploring the fear of sex that undermines many marriages. Lawrence's fundamental argument is that men and women had lost touch with their deeper unconscious selves, 'the real Adam and Eve' within (218). The war, however, had provided a new insight into these deep elemental passions:

It was an alarming apple we pulled from the Tree of Life that time. With a weird, new flavour of experience.

But we spat it out. We spat out the apple of a tremendous experience, and glibly announced ourselves unchanged. *We are not changed, Oh no!* Instead of knowing, like Adam, a new nakedness of ourselves, waking to a new knowledge altogether, we simply wallowed in dead, wet fig-leaves, till we were plastered all over with platitudes.

Now in the evening cool, the Lord is walking in the garden and looking with amazement on our glib, platitudinously over-plastered imbecility. And

all kinds of serpents are waking from a winter sleep and smiling to
themselves as they yawn, along our paths. (222)

Here, as elsewhere, Lawrence displays an astonishing capacity to
find new meanings in this old tale, developing the image of the
fig-leaf into an example of the power of ideology (in this case the
platitudes of the institutional churches) to conceal the naked (and
unpleasant) truth, its failure to offer real protection against the
renewed power of evil represented by these refreshed serpents.

Two other essays intended for this *Adelphi* series, which were
going to be called 'On Writing a Book' and 'On Reading a Book'
(*Letters* IV 549) but eventually appeared for the first time as a single
essay in *Phoenix* entitled 'Books', present Christianity as having
outlived its usefulness. Had he lived in the year 400, Lawrence
claims, he would have been 'a true and passionate Christian'. As he
lives in 1924, however, when 'the Christian venture is done', he
believes 'We must start on a new venture towards God' (*Ref.* 200).
Two further essays written at this time and reprinted in the
Cambridge edition of *Reflections* repeat the view that Christianity has
had its day. The first, 'Climbing Down Pisgah', satirises the
materialism which sees the 'Promised Land' as Pittsburgh with
Canaan full of kerosene (226). The second, entitled 'Resurrection',
provoked by a reading of Tolstoy's novel of that title, probes the
extent to which he can still believe in the Christian doctrine of the
resurrection. Lawrence presents the First World War as 'the Calvary
of all real Christian men' since when 'the world has been without a
Lord'. Three days have passed, however, 'and it is time to roll away
the stone. It is time for the Lord in us to arise' (233). The
resurrection he sees not as a particular historical event in the life of
one individual but as an existential experience open to all, urging
his readers to rise 'and push back the stone', to become 'lords with
the Lord' (235). Throughout these essays Lawrence shows little
respect for the original historical meaning of the biblical texts to
which he repeatedly turns. What interests him is what they can
mean now.

This is also true of Lawrence's poetry of the early 1920s, collected
in *Birds, Beasts and Flowers* (1923), which he regarded as his 'best book
of poems', the title encapsulating its parodic intent, mocking as it
does a phrase in the Reverend S. Baring-Gould's pious 'Evening
Hymn' in which, 'as darkness gathers' and

Stars begin to peep,
Birds and beasts and flowers
Soon will be asleep. (*CP* 1012)

None of the creatures celebrated in this volume is either this tame or
this docile, preserving as they do a fierce pride in their bestiality, a
Nietzschean joy in their bodies. These poems, however, are deeply
religious in the sense Lawrence admired in the ancient Etruscans:
the amount of '*true*, sincere, religious concentration' they bring upon
their objects (*EP* 92). But they are subversively religious, providing
what Sandra Gilbert has called 'a revisionary synthesis of myths'
from the Bible and ancient Greece, a 'sophisticated and subversive
engagement with Christian mythology' (Gilbert 1990: 329–31). They
subject Greek–Christian logocentrism to a decidedly Jewish deconstruction, undermining the binary opposition between body and
spirit in which the latter is constantly privileged above the former.
Lawrence presents himself, according to Gilbert, as 'a diabolical
poet, a Blakeian prophet of hell' (322), reversing orthodox Christian
attitudes towards good and evil, retelling the fall as a willing
enjoyment of the fruits of the earth, and celebrating the descent into
hell as a regeneration of energy.

The myth of the fall, that evil came into the world because of the
greed, sensuality and disobedience of one woman, appears in the very
first item of the volume, entitled 'Fruits', the first of a series of prose
prefaces to the various sections of the volume which were first
included in the illustrated edition of *Birds, Beasts and Flowers* in 1930.
Many of these prefaces (but not this one) have been traced to John
Burnet's *Early Greek Philosophy*, which alerted Lawrence to an earlier,
less logocentric way of thinking even in Greece. This preface is
printed as a quotation but seems to stem from Lawrence himself,
celebrating all fruits as female, from the fig, 'a catchword for the
female fissure', to the pomegranate, 'the apple of love', and, of
course, the apple of Eden, which he labels 'Eve's fruit. To her it
belonged, and she offered it to the man. Even the apples of knowledge
are Eve's fruit, the woman's' (*P* 277). The significant difference
Lawrence again brings to the biblical narrative is in his celebrating
rather than condemning Eve for bringing such knowledge.

The first poems in the volume celebrate the sensuous qualities of
these fruits, their 'hellish' wonder and the 'perfect drunkenness' and
'intoxication' to which they can lead (280–1). 'Figs', as well as
symbolising the female part, are seen to partake of its mystery,

prompting a return to the theme of Eve, whose downfall was her consciousness of her nakedness:

When Eve once knew *in her mind* that she was naked
She quickly sewed fig-leaves, and sewed the same for the man.
She'd been naked all her days before,
But till then, till that apple of knowledge, she hadn't had the fact on her mind.

Lawrence develops the exchange between God and Eve (and through her, all women) in midrashic manner, making his women more openly mocking and rebellious towards God, whose indignation at their burgeoning sexuality only makes them laugh:

> *What then, good Lord!* cry the women.
> *We have kept our secret long enough.*
> *We are a ripe fig.*
> *Let us burst into affirmation.*   (284)

Lawrence does not appear to side entirely with the women, reminding them that 'ripe figs won't keep' and remaining doubtful about female 'self-assertion'. What they forget, he suggests, is the beauty of secrecy. The following poem, 'Grapes', celebrates the beauty of the world before 'Noah's flood . . . before eyes saw too much' although in Lawrence's retelling of Genesis 9 it is not Noah's nakedness and intoxication which are deplored so much as the loss of an innocent world when all were 'in naked communion communicating as now our clothed vision can never communicate' (286).

Biblical myth is also reworked in 'The Revolutionary', which celebrates a figure never actually named but who calls himself 'a blind Samson' and shares some of the characteristics of the Samson celebrated by Milton, Handel and Blake (V. Hyde 1992: 68–9). Again, the biblical text is significantly altered: the pillars which this hero wishes to bring crashing down are not those of the Philistines, as in the Book of Judges, but those of his society, the self-appointed guardians of bourgeois morality. Lawrence's revolutionary, who feels imprisoned rather than liberated by this religion of stone tablets, with its narrow morality and pallid spirituality, looks to replace it with a more full-blooded religion: 'See if I am not Lord of the dark and moving hosts / Before I die' (*CP* 287–9). The section on 'Fruits' ends with a poem entitled 'Peace', whose persona also waits for the apocalyptic destruction of his society.

The following sections on 'Trees' and 'Flowers' maintain a focus on the downfall of civilisations, deploring the decline of the Etruscans, 'whom Rome thought vicious' (297–8). 'Almond Blossom' attributes to trees a similar history to that of Israel:

> Trees suffer, like races, down the long ages.
> They wander and are exiled, they live in exile through long ages
> Like drawn blades never sheathed, hacked and gone black,
> The alien trees in alien lands . . .   (304–5)

The echo in these last words of what Jethro says to Moses in Exodus 18: 3 simply confirms how saturated Lawrence is in biblical language. In this poem the almond tree is made to bear the symbolic weight not only of the resurrection (its traditional signification) but of the crucifixion before becoming the tree of life itself (Gen. 2: 9). In 'Purple Anemones' it is made clear that the religious significance of flowers cannot be tied to one tradition: it is not *'The white God'* who gave us flowers, nor is it Jesus who is *'the god of flowers'* but rather Pluto, making 'Little hells of colour' open at the feet of Persephone (*CP* 307–9).

That Lawrence is 'subversively revising Christian mythology' in this volume (Gilbert 1990: 344) becomes even clearer in the following section entitled 'The Evangelistic Beasts', written in October 1920. The problem with the animal symbolism traditionally associated with the authors of the four gospels, according to Lawrence, is that they have become so spiritualised as to lose all invigorating animality. 'They are not all beasts' anyway, as the opening poem, 'St Matthew' begins. Matthew himself is traditionally represented as a man, unlike Mark the lion, Luke the bull and John the eagle. Lawrence's Matthew prides himself on being a full-blooded male, unlike Jesus, who

> was not quite a man.
> He was the Son of Man
> *Filius Meus*, O remorseless logic
> Out of his own mouth.   (*CP* 320)

Lawrence's attack on the logocentric Greek philosophy behind John's Gospel is furthered here by the Jewish Matthew, who quotes John's Jesus claiming, 'And I, if I be lifted up, will draw all men unto me' (John 12: 32). Matthew, 'being a man / Cannot be lifted up', although he is drawn to Jesus and hopes after death to become 'a soul in bliss, an angel'. He appears at best ambivalent about this, however, asking Jesus to let him continue at least for the moment to enjoy the things of this earth:

> Before my heart stops beating . . .
> Put me down again on the earth, Jesus, on the brown soil

> Where flowers sprout in the acrid humus, and fade into
>   humus again.
> Where beasts drop their unlicked young, and pasture, and
>   drop their droppings among the turf.   (*CP* 321)

Unlike Jesus, the initial letters of whose Greek titles (*Iesus Christos Huios Theou Soter*) spell out ICHTHUS or fish, Matthew's spiritual journeys always return to earth 'like a fish seeking the bottom', plunging down through seaweed

> Into the fathomless, bottomless pit
> Where my soul falls in the last throes of bottomless convulsion,
>   and is fallen
> Utterly beyond Thee, Dove of the Spirit;
> Beyond everything, except itself.   (322)

Lawrence's Matthew not only casts doubt on the notion of this 'fall' as a decline but retells John's account in Revelation of the casting of Satan into the bottomless pit as a Nietzschean journey 'beyond' bourgeois standards of morality, affirming 'bestial' physical vitality above the feeble spirituality of the dove. This Matthew points out that even the Son of Man cannot 'quaff out the dregs of terrestrial manhood', which 'fall back' and 'burn into drops of blood' which fill the wings on which he flies upward. The imagery here seems to point towards a physical arousal, a phallic rather than a spiritual resurrection.

What this poem celebrates, in other words, is the dual nature of man, a duality supposedly affirmed at Chalcedon but in practice denied by the conventional Christian privileging of the spirit over the body. 'Listen, Paraclete,' urges Lawrence's Matthew, deliberately using the Greek theological term for the Comforter, or Holy Spirit, the third person of that highly logocentric concept of the Trinity,

> I can no more deny the bat-wings of my fathom-flickering
>   spirit of darkness
> Than the wings of the Morning and Thee, Thou Glorified. (323)

'Wings of the morning' is a characteristically Jewish phrase from Psalm 139, an intensely physical celebration of the immanence of God in His creation. The whole point of the psalm is that God is to be found everywhere, not just in heaven but also at the heart of creation. Matthew, in other words, brings the Jewish tradition to bear against later Greek theological concepts which are in danger of suppressing the physical altogether.

'St Mark' also conflates a number of biblical passages, beginning with the image of the lion of Judah from Genesis 49:

> There was a lion in Judah
> Which whelped and was Mark. (323)

In the Book of Revelation 'the Lion of the tribe of Juda' is the beast who opens the book with seven seals, traditionally identified as Mark (Rev. 5: 5). All four beasts around the throne of the Lamb are said to have six wings (4: 7–8), which provokes Lawrence into wondering how a 'lion of the spirit' differs from other lions. He draws a strong contrast between the lion as he once was, lashing his tail and thinking of blood, and the lion as he becomes in Judaeo-Christian symbolism from Isaiah's prophecy of a time when he will lie down with the lamb. This regenerate symbolic lion, as depicted in Carpaccio's painting of the lion of St Mark in Venice, seems more of 'a curly sheep-dog' than a savage beast, although he may still be sharpening his teeth on the wolves and even give some of his sheep 'a real nip here and there' (*CP* 323–5).

'St Luke' plays with the same unlikelihood of the bull, with his mighty chest and horns, whose black blood once served as a burnt offering, submitting to the Lamb or agreeing to serve the Son of Man. The end of this poem, has the 'bull of the proletariat' throw off the yoke of two thousand years and recover its natural strength and independence. Lawrence's hostility towards orthodox Christian doctrine becomes even more apparent in 'St John', the eagle whose intellectual arrogance is seen to be responsible for the most fully logocentric theology. Jesus himself had been 'innocent' of philosophy, 'one of Nature's phenomena', a dove, but his significance, according to John, required 'the mind-soaring eagle of an Evangelist' to bring out, 'an eagle staring down on the Sun' from a position of assumed intellectual superiority. The capitalised 'Word', 'The Logos', is thus presented as the 'offspring of the almighty Johannine mind'. Lawrence, however, refuses to take this eagle at its own high estimate and resolves irreverently to put salt on its tail and shoo it off to Patmos, where he finds it 'looking rather shabby and island-bound', combining the theosophic image of the 'mundane egg' hatching 'a new chick' with his own favourite symbol of rebirth 'from the ashes' to suggest a remoulding of the Word in less metaphysical form (328–9).

'The Evangelistic Beasts' serve both to clarify Lawrence's theological aim in this whole volume and to act 'as a kind of bridge'

between his encounter with the vegetable kingdom and the world of
animals:

these subversive redefinitions of Biblical symbols prepare us, finally, for
even more outrageous reappraisals to come: the snake who is poisonous but
lordly, the ass who was foolish *because* he carried Jesus into Jerusalem, the
demonic turkeycock who should replace the ethereal peacock, the
mountain lion who is more valuable than a million people, the bulldog who
ought to 'learn' pagan loyalty rather than Christian loving, and the tortoise
whose inchoate orgasmic scream is a kind of anti-Platonic paradigm for
human speech. (Gilbert 1990: 345)

The anti-logocentric purpose of these poems is less immediately
apparent, which is perhaps one of the reasons why they have become
more popular, certainly more anthologised, than Lawrence's more
recondite wrestlings with theology. The animals themselves, rather
than their symbolic significance, become the focus of attention as
Lawrence moves on from the critique of logocentrism to a celebration of the physical. The section entitled 'Creatures' celebrates the
'otherness' (both their difference from man and their transcendence)
of such unglamorous creatures as 'The Mosquito', 'Fish' and 'Bats',
poems which evoke an explicitly religious response but in terms very
different from Christian orthodoxy. Fish, for example, who were
'Born before God was love', provide evidence of 'Other Gods /
Beyond my range . . . gods beyond my God' (*CP* 338). Lawrence also
pokes fund at his own need to be so 'religious' about everything. The
comic poem, 'Man and Bat', for example, which recounts an attempt
to eject a bat from a hotel bedroom, finally draws the line at bats:

> I admit a God in every crevice,
> But not bats in my room;
> Nor the God of bats . . .   (346)

This is one creature even Lawrence refuses to worship.

The section on 'Reptiles' returns to a sense of the symbolic
significance of some of these creatures, especially the serpent
referred to in the preface, who, as a result of God's curse in Genesis
3: 14, 'must go with his belly on the ground' (348). The difference in
Lawrence's 'Snake', of course, is that although the man is culturally
conditioned into thinking of it as evil ('The voice of my education
said to me / He must be killed'), he is also able for a time to
recognise its grandeur, the way it 'looked around like a god'. In the

end he reverts to conventional fear, hurling a log at it, but has the grace to regret this:

> And so, I missed my chance with one of the lords
> Of life.
> And I have something to expiate;
> A pettiness. (349–51)

'Snake' works as a poem on a number of different levels: read literally, it describes a particularly vivid encounter with a particular creature. But it can also be read as a midrashic development of the Book of Genesis, expanding upon the serpent in the Garden of Eden, who serves, according to Ross Murfin,

> not as a living example of the earth Lawrence wants to come to know in all its mysterious otherness, but rather as an analogy for that past that led up to and made Lawrence what he is . . . The snake signifies the world view Lawrence inherits, the tree of tradition, history, religion, literature, and other forms of human 'knowledge' that are always tempting him to be unoriginal . . . (Murfin 1983: 108)

Murfin finds echoes not only of Genesis but of Milton, Dante, Keats and Coleridge (whose Ancient Mariner first fears but then learns to bless the water snakes) in Lawrence's poem, which enacts that struggle with both the biblical and the literary canon which Bloom would see as the subject of all poetry (109–16).

The sequence of poems about tortoises which follows 'Snake' also operates on several levels. They are full of detailed, accurate description but they also make bold comparisons between these humble creatures and Christ. 'Tortoise Shell' notices how the marks on the back of the baby tortoise resemble the cross as if 'The Lord wrote it all down on the little slate / Of the baby tortoise' (*CP* 356). 'Tortoise Family Connections', however, establishes the creature's difference from Christ as it calmly ignores its mother:

> He does not even trouble to answer: 'Woman, what have I to do
>   with thee?'
> He wearily looks the other way. . . (357)

Later in the poem, Lawrence plays with the absurdity of an original Edenic myth centering upon a tortoise-Adam 'in a garden of inert clods' and even a tortoise-God 'in the dark-creation morning . . . Ringing the soundless bell of his presence in chaos' (358). In 'Lui et Elle' the adolescent tortoise finds himself 'crucified into sex' (361), a phrase repeated in 'Tortoise Shout', which compares the coital cry of the tortoise not only with the disciples 'screaming in Pentecost, receiving the ghost' (365) but with Christ giving up the ghost on the cross:

> The same cry from the tortoise as from Christ, the Osiris-cry
>   of abandonment,
> That which is whole, torn asunder,
> That which is in part, finding its whole again throughout
>   the universe.   (367)

The violence of this poem, which is 'obscene blasphemy to the orthodox', may have 'parallels in Nietzsche and Yeats when they treat the Passion' (Bloom 1961: 365). But it is perhaps only in Lawrence (and possibly Bataille) that the opening of the individual to the other in sex is a sacred act quite seriously comparable to the crucifixion (Wright 1999: 60). As Deleuze and Guattari observe, 'Lawrence's becoming tortoise has nothing to do with a sentimental or domestic relation', everything to do with a sacred conception of animal life (Deleuze 1988: 244).

The following two sections of *Beasts* celebrate a range first of 'Birds' then of 'Animals', mostly observed in New Mexico, all of them displaying something of the divine. Those animals who retain their natural qualities, such as the 'He-Goat', who 'turns with a start, to fight, to challenge, to suddenly butt', are admired more ('then you see the God that he is' (*CP* 381)) than those, like 'The Ass', who allow themselves to be imposed upon, taken for a ride first by Joseph and Mary and then by Jesus (377–80). In a poem first entitled 'Taos' Lawrence himself is given an animal identity, 'The Red Wolf', by the Indian he encounters in the New Mexican desert at the end of the day, a day which comes to represent the end of Western civilisation, of 'white mythology'. The Indian mocks, '*Where's your God, you white one? / Where's your white God?*', to receive the somewhat crestfallen reply,

> He fell to dust as the twilight fell,
> Was fume as I trod
> The last step out of the east.

Having abandoned his own religious tradition, Lawrence presents himself as a 'hungry stray', prepared to wait for the Indian 'to come back with a new story' (403–5). The final section of the volume, 'Ghosts', as well as exorcising a few spectres from the past, such as his mother, includes her among the 'Spirits Summoned West' to begin a new life (410–12). At this stage in his religious development Lawrence is clearly looking elsewhere than Christianity for the fulfilment of what remain deeply religious needs.

Lawrence's religious quest is also evident in the many short stories he published in the 1920s, of which there were four volumes: *England, My England* (1922), *The Ladybird, The Fox, The Captain's Doll* (1923), *St Mawr together with The Princess* (1925) and *The Woman Who Rode Away and Other Stories* (1928). Many had been written earlier, of course, and were often extensively revised for publication in these collections. To claim, as Widmer does, that these stories are not only his 'central writings' but must in many cases be read as 'exercises in the religious life' (Widmer 1962: viii, 167) is perhaps to overstate the case. Like the novels of this period, however, they can often be seen aggressively to appropriate the Bible, employing biblical images against the grain of their conventional Christian interpretation.

The story that gave its title to the volume *England, My England*, first written in 1915, draws upon several elements in Genesis in order to examine English attitudes towards the war, the whole mentality of sacrifice and the sense of exclusion suffered by those not caught up in jingoistic fervour. It begins with a man working in an ancient garden on the edge of a snake-infested common, although it is not a snake which triggers his downfall but a sickle he has left lying in the grass, which cripples 'his first-born child whom he loved so much' (*EE* 18). The link with Abraham's sacrifice of his son is clear from an earlier reference to the dominating grandfather, an archetypal patriarch who exudes 'paternal godhead', in which 'fatherhood had even the right to sacrifice the child to God, like Isaac' (16). The accident leaves the father very much an outsider, 'like Ishmael', although even he is swallowed up by 'the whole great law of sacrifice' (26), for the story ends with him signing up and being killed in action. Like Wilfred Owen's 'Parable of the Old Man and the Young' (1917), which follows the details of Genesis 22 even more closely before violently twisting the end of the story, 'England, My England' satirises a country which has built a sterile religion of sacrifice upon biblical foundations.

Some of the other stories in this volume have biblically resonant titles. 'Samson and Delilah', for instance, first written in Cornwall in 1916 with a New Testament title, 'The Prodigal Husband', was 're-christened' for publication in the *English Review* the following year (*Letters* III 34). Both biblical narratives to which these titles refer are significantly modified in the retelling: the prodigal returns to less than a festive welcome (being bound and imprisoned) while it is Samson rather than Delilah who is portrayed as the traitor. There are additional allusions to the violence of Cain in 'Monkey Nuts' (*EE* 73–4) and the nostalgic conservatism of Lot's wife in 'The Last Straw', in which the passionate lady's maid Fanny feels herself above the man to whom she is betrothed, who drops aitches from the Book of Revelation (158). None of these biblical allusions, it should be said, are of great interpretive significance.

It is only in 'The Ladybird', the third of the stories that comprise *The Fox, The Captain's Doll, The Ladybird* that religion could be said to re-emerge as a central issue. First written in 1915 as 'The Thimble', it was envisaged as a story about 'resurrection' (*Letters* II 418, 420). The Ladybird is *Marienkäfer* in German, of course, which is why the Czech Count Dionys calls it a 'Mary-beetle' (*Fox* 173). The opening words of the final version of the story, 'How many swords had Lady Beveridge in her pierced heart!' (157), also refer to Mary, warned by Simeon that the suffering of her son will be 'a sword' her soul (Luke 2: 34–5). Lady Beveridge, who loses her sons in the war, continues to obey Christ's injunction of Matthew 5: 44 to 'love her enemies' (*Fox* 157). It is while visiting a hospital for the enemy wounded that she recognises Count Dionys, who had been a guest in her house before the war, when he had given her daughter a thimble decorated with the family crest: 'a gold snake at the bottom, and a Mary-beetle of green stone at the top' (173). These symbols, as the Count himself explains, have esoteric significance, the snake being associated with Dionysus, God of wine, while the 'beetle of our Lady' is 'a descendant of the Egyptian scarabeus' (209), described by Madame Blavatsky in *The Secret Doctrine* as an emblem of ongoing human life and of reincarnation (270).

There is also, of course, a Nietzschean dimension to Dionysus, who represents the unconscious forces of darkness and rapture in opposition to the Apollonian principle of light, order and reason. *The Will to Power* contrasts '*Dionysus and the Crucified*', the former representing 'the religious affirmation of life, life whole and not denied in part' while the latter stands for 'suffering . . . as an objection to this life, as a formula for its condemnation' (*WP* 542–3). Count Dionys in this story is similarly opposed to Christian morality, liberating Lady Beveridge's daughter Daphne from her bondage to Christian morality, the 'tablets of stone' that must be broken 'piece by piece' (*Fox* 181). Her husband Basil returns from the war shrinking like Christ from all forms of touch (192). In a reversal of the post-resurrection encounter with Magdalen in the gospels, he kneels before Daphne, kissing her feet and worshipping her (193). She, however, prefers to play Magdalen to Dionys, not only bathing his feet with tears but also touching and arousing him (215–16). The story ends with husband and wife remaining together, although he can offer her only 'pure love' (218–9), while the Count knows that she will always in her 'heart of hearts' be 'the wife of the ladybird' (220). As in the later novella *The Escaped Cock*, Lawrence here gives the story of the resurrection a deliberately provocative Nietzschean twist.

Lawrence's increasing impatience with orthodox Christianity is also evident in *St Mawr and Other Stories*, especially 'The Overtone', the most explicit in its turning of the Bible against Christianity. His 'use of the Great God Pan . . . as a counterforce to Christ', as Brian Finney argues, is one of a number of similar references made in 1924, including his 'London Letter' to Willard Johnson, which also recounts the legend that 'When Jesus was born, the spirits wailed round the Mediterranean: Pan is dead' (*StM* xxii). His essay on 'Pan in America' begins with a similar assertion, presenting Pan as an 'outlaw, even in the early days of the gods. A sort of Ishmael among the bushes', a 'nympholept' whose passion had been turned into lust by centuries of Judaeo-Christian disapproval (*Phoenix* 22–3). 'The Last Laugh', collected in *The Woman Who Rode Away and Other Stories*, brings Pan back to life, luring its hero into sexual promiscuity, desecrating a church and finally punishing those who repress their Pantheistic emotions. Pan also makes significant appearances in *St Mawr* itself and in *The Plumed Serpent*, which supports the traditional dating of 1924 for 'The Overtone' although a much earlier date has been suggested (Kinkead-Weekes 1993: 75–80).

In 'The Overtone' a middle-aged nympholept named Renshaw confesses to a young woman only too eager to be seized that 'Pan is dead', which she interprets as an admission of sexual inactivity on his part (*StM* 13). Renshaw blames his loss of desire on his wife's frigidity, excluding him from 'the promised land that was justly his' (9). He continues to dwell on this event in biblical terms: this was 'his real charge against her on the Judgment Day' (10). Ironically, the biblical allusion here is to the day of judgment (2 Peter 2: 9–10), which threatens 'them that walk after the flesh in the lust of uncleanness'. Renshaw claims, on the contrary, that his was 'a holy desire on his part . . . almost like taking off his shoes before God', as in Exodus 3: 5. It is 'as if she could not trust herself so near the Burning Bush' (10).The manuscript at this point writes of 'her denial of him', her refusal to 'partake of this Mystery' as 'her one sin against him' (230). She, however, blames him for the death of their love, comparing his denial of her conjugal rights with St Peter's denial of Christ in an extraordinary 'bitter psalm' which combines the gospel narratives of St Peter's denial with ironic references to the erotic Song of Solomon.

In the Song of Solomon the poet represents his beloved as a fertile vineyard, enumerating the separate marvels of her body, her eyes, her hair, her teeth, her lips and temples, her neck, her breasts and all other parts of her body. He gives particular emphasis to her animal qualities, likening her teeth to sheep and her breasts to roes. Chapter 4 likens her lips to a honeycomb while claiming, of course, that she is also chaste: 'a spring shut up, a fountain sealed'. He must therefore plead for permission to enter 'his garden, and eat his pleasant fruits' (Song 4: 10–16). Chapter 5 celebrates the fact that his beloved has allowed him to enjoy these fruits: 'I have gathered my myrrh with my spice; I have eaten my honeycomb with my honey; I have drunk my wine with my milk' (5: 1). Mrs Renshaw's problem, however, is that her husband has done none of these things, which is why her 'psalm' is so bitter, full of distorted vegetation and stunted growth, 'little abortions of flowers'. Even when she broke her 'comb' and put it to his lips, she complains, 'you turned your mouth aside and said "You have made my face unclean, and smeared my mouth." . . . the bowl was thrown from my hands, and broke in pieces at my feet' (*StM* 12). She also incorporates details of the cock crowing and the betrayer weeping from Mark 14 and Matthew 26 into her own narrative of rejected love.

The girl's reaction on hearing this lament of the scorned wife, like that of Peter in the gospels, is to go out 'into the garden, timidly, beginning to cry' (13). It is at this point that she discusses Pan and Christ, coming to the conclusion that if 'the faun of the young Jesus had run free, seen one white nymph's brief breast, he would not have been content to die on a cross' (15). She proceeds to sing her own song of running 'wild on the hills with Dionysos' with her lover lowering his nets into her water (15–16). Christ's post-resurrection fishing instructions to his disciples are here transformed provocatively into sexual symbolism. The fact that Christ eats fish and bread after his resurrection, of course, signifies that he is truly risen in the flesh, although for Lawrence, as will become even more apparent in *The Escaped Cock*, he is not properly risen until he enjoys the flesh of a woman. The girl in this story, it could be argued, has the best of both worlds, escaping into the woods at night for sensual pleasure and returning to the crucifix in daytime.

Many of the themes in 'The Overtone' recur in *St Mawr* itself, a more fully developed account of a dissatisfied wife, which also employs biblical parody to satirise the society in which she lives and which she finally leaves. Lou Witt quite literally worships her magnificent stallion St Mawr, ironically named after an obscure sixth-century founder of an abbey (although 'Mawr' is also the Welsh for 'big' or 'great'). She finds him 'uncanny', a 'splendid demon', 'like a god looking at her terribly out of the everlasting dark', in marked contrast to her 'self-controlled' and 'powerless' husband (31), who plans to have the horse gelded. She and her mother are presented as Eves, gazing forlornly out of a window at 'the wet, close, hedged-and-fenced English landscape' and reflecting how far they are from paradise:

The very apples on the trees looked so shut in, it was impossible to imagine any speck of 'Knowledge' lurking inside them. Good to eat, good to cook, good even for show. But the wild sap of untameable and inexhaustible knowledge – no! Bred out of them. Geldings, even the apples. (97)

When her husband is sent a ring with an intaglio of the well-endowed god of fertility and gardens, Priapus, under an apple bough, Lou develops this parodic vision of the Garden of Eden still further, seeing the young women who admire his '*stunningly* naughty' painted apples as further evidence that 'there's nothing so artificial as sinning nowadays' (114). In yet more biblical pastiche, her mother imagines pouring tea into the hat sported by the Dean's wife, which looks like a crumpled cup and saucer, while the Dean responds, in a parody of the 23rd Psalm, '*My head is covered with cream, my cup runneth over*' (89). In all these examples, of course, the Bible is not the target of Lawrence's satire but its vehicle, serving to ridicule the society which pretends to live by its values.

It is while having dinner with the Dean and other friends of her husband's, at whom Mrs Witt glowers 'as if she were dropping them down the bottomless pit' (64), that Lou hears from the painter

Cartwright, modelled on Lawrence's friend and co-worker on the Apocalypse, Frederick Carter, about Pan, 'the God that is hidden in everything' and 'visible only to the third eye of occult philosophy' (65). Lou continues to ponder the pervasiveness of evil and when Rico the groom falls under St Mawr, who is startled by a snake (the origin of all evil), she has a vision of him as Judas, 'the last of the gods of our era' (78–80). She and her mother continue to search for some kind of religious truth, a quest eventually takes them to a ranch in Texas, the harsh conditions of which confirm their 'cynical certainty, *that there was no merciful God in the heavens . . . no Almighty loving God*' but a deity both shaggier and more horrible, '*more awful and more splendid*' (147–8). The mysterious 'spirit' that she feels on the ranch has no interest in her personal salvation but finds her sex 'deep and sacred, deeper than I am' (155).

One of Lou's most positive experiences in *St Mawr* is the voyage across the Atlantic, when the porpoises and flying fish seen in the Gulf of Mexico bring home to her the 'marvellous beauty and fascination of natural wild things' in contrast with the 'horror of man's unnatural life' (129). The protagonist of 'The Flying Fish', an unfinished story begun in 1925 and published as an Appendix to the Cambridge edition of *St Mawr and Other Stories*, experiences similar pleasure from these fish. Gethin is the last of a long line of Days going back to the sixteenth century Sir Gilbert Day, author of an illuminated manuscript, an Elizabethan Book of Hours which he knows by heart. Gethin rejects his ancestor's 'symbolism and mysticism' but recognises the 'joy of life' evident in 'these fleshy, warm-bodied fish' (221). He resolves to return to Daybrook but never arrives, the manuscript breaking off three days out of Havana. Lawrence later told the Brewsters that the last part of the story would present 'regenerate man, a real life in this Garden of Eden' (xxxv), but never actually wrote it.

The Woman Who Rode Away and Other Stories takes up from *St Mawr* the theme of a woman dissatisfied with western civilisation and searching for something different. The unnamed woman tells the Indians she encounters that she's 'tired of the white man's god' and wants to know theirs, failing to appreciate the literalness of their question, 'do you bring your heart to the god of the Chilchui?' (*WRA* 52–4). As she watches the Indian women dance, however, the religious power of their culture challenges her own liberal humanist assumptions about herself, a moment of revaluation which is likened to that of Belshazzar seeing the writing on the wall in the Book of Daniel 5: 25–7 (60). She is told that the point of her sacrifice is to fulfil the Indian legend that 'when a white woman gives herself to our gods, then our gods will begin to make the world again, and the white man's gods will fall to pieces' (61). In the ceremonial leading up to the sacrifice, which involves being 'fumigated' with incense and sprinkled with water by 'gorgeous, terrifying priests in yellow and scarlet and black', she loses her 'commonplace consciousness', her 'ordinary personal consciousness', entering instead 'that other state of passional cosmic consciousness like one who is drugged' (63–4). She also becomes a 'mystic object' to the Indians. It is difficult to feel entirely at ease with a narrative that requires a woman's involuntary submission to sacrifice. Lawrence clearly expects his readers, however, to open their minds to a religious otherness beyond the comprehension of their own civilisation.

Other stories in this volume use biblical allusion for ironic effects, comic rather than cosmic purposes. The woman in 'Sun', for example, has only to sacrifice her clothing to achieve cosmic consciousness while 'Jimmy and the Desperate Woman' satirises the combination of arrogance and insecurity behind the protagonist's desire to be 'a sort of Solomon of wisdom, beauty, and wealth' to some woman (101). In 'Glad Ghosts', begun in December 1925 for publication in a collection of ghost stories the following year, the thought of being a disembodied spirit brings home to Lord Lathkill a heightened sense of the value of the flesh. He feels that he has become a living corpse, a risen and untouchable Jesus, even a copy of the Bible itself. Lady Lathkill's reaction to her husband's plea inspires in the first-person narrator a bitter reflection on the significance of the crucifixion for the women in Christ's life:

So slack, so broken she sat, it occurred to me that in this Crucifixion business, the crucified does not put himself alone on the cross. The woman is nailed even more inexorably up, and crucified in the body even more cruelly.

It is a monstrous thought. But the deed is even more monstrous. Oh Jesus! didn't you know that you couldn't be crucified alone? That the two thieves crucified along with you were the two women, your wife and your mother? You called them two thieves! But what would they call you, who had put their women's bodies on the cross? The abominable trinity on Calvary! (201)

The crucifixion narratives are here given a violent twist, with the onlooking women, Mary Magdalene, Mary the mother of James, and in John's account, Mary the mother of Jesus, who commits her into John's care (John 19: 25–7), being transformed into the crucified thieves. If it is a form of parody, it is an extremely serious, angry form of that genre, bringing out the horror and violence of the original too often obscured by familiarity.

Other biblical allusions in this volume are lighter, such as the remark of the jealous wife in 'Two Blue Birds' that she cannot be expected to become celibate overnight: 'It takes years for a woman like me to turn into a pillar of salt. At least I hope so!' (*WRA* 6). This story also portrays the Bible as misogynistic, wanting to control women, set them in their place and punish any disobedience on their part. But it does so lightly, through mockery rather than indignation, as does the reference to the wife hearing her husband's 'voice in the distance, dictating away' to his secretary 'like the voice of God to Samuel, alone and monotonous' (15). The satire here is partly directed against Compton Mackenzie, the model for the author-husband, but also towards the God he worshipped. Mackenzie also saw himself as a target of satire in 'The Man Who Loved Islands', written in 1926 and published in the *Dial* the following July, although it was omitted from the English edition of *The Woman Who Rode Away and Other Stories* when Mackenzie threatened legal action (xxxviii). The joke throughout is that the man who buys islands does so in a futile attempt to regain paradise. This is made explicit at various places in both versions of the story. In the first manuscript version he is depicted gloating over his first island: 'Why should it not itself be the final Happy Isle, . . . a world of pure perfection, a tiny Paradise-Regained?' (321–2). The final version is more down to earth, recording that 'He began, as we begin all attempts to regain Paradise, by spending money' (153). In spite of accidents and setbacks, there are still some occasions when the island would appear 'lovely as a morning in Paradise' (159). Other references to the Book of Genesis, however, are more sinister, such as the remark by a farm-hand that 'this island is surely one of the lean kine of Egypt' (159). That the whole venture is doomed seems clear from the narrator's comment about the 99–year lease being 'as good as everlasting. Since, if you are like Abraham, and want your offspring to be numberless as the sands of the sea-shore, you don't choose an island to start breeding on' (150). The point is that the island-lover is looking backwards rather than forwards, attempting to recreate a paradise born of hatred rather than love.

'The Lovely Lady', written in 1927 for a volume of murder stories compiled by Cynthia Asquith, and revised for eventual publication in 1933 in a volume to which it gave the title, is also ironic not only about its eponymous heroine, Pauline Attenborough, but also about the supposed paradise she builds for her son Robert whom she attempts to protect from her niece Cecilia. Robert has little enthusiasm for a paradise 'where the serpent won't let one get within a mile of an apple tree. A paradise where there is never a chance of a fall! A paradise with no temptation' (260). He prefers voluntarily to banish himself, as 'Adam ought to have said to the Lord, under the circumstances: "Thank you, Sir; but we prefer to go"' (261).

The biblical references in many of these stories could be said to be incidental rather than central to them. The quest for paradise continues to be a dominant theme, however, and there is renewed interest in the resurrection, prompted by Lawrence's own recovery from severe illness in Mexico in February 1925. This will find more sustained expression in the novella *The Escaped Cock* and in the later versions of *Lady Chatterley's Lover*. Before considering these, however, I want to turn to the prophetic voices to be found in the other products of Lawrence's period in Mexico, the two versions of *The Plumed Serpent* and his biblical drama *David*.

CHAPTER 11

Prophetic voices and 'red' mythology: 'The Plumed Serpent' and 'David'

Critics tend to write rather patronisingly about Lawrence's Mexican novel, the first draft of which, written in 1923, has now been published under its original title, *Quetzalcoatl*. The title under which it first appeared in a much-revised form early in 1926, *The Plumed Serpent*, a literal translation of the name of the Mexican God, suggested by its American publisher Knopf, struck Lawrence himself as 'rather millinery' (*Letters* V 254). Secker, its English publisher, recognised that it was 'a book to which Lawrence himself attaches great importance' (*PS* xli), a comment confirmed by Lawrence's correspondence (*Letters* IV 446, 455). Some of the early reviewers welcomed both the novel's Nietzschean critique of Christianity and its biblical aspirations, its reproduction of 'the flashing color and austere passions of the books of the Hebrew prophets' (*PS* xliii–iv). Modern readers, according to David Ellis, struggle with the 'extravagance' of Lawrence's new religion, turning with relief to descriptions of the landscape 'after yet another Quetzalcoatl hymn, or one more detailed description of the ceremonies' (Ellis 1998: 107–8). These aspects of the novel, however, are central to its whole conception, as a brief consideration of the changes in Lawrence's thinking on religion at this time will illustrate.

Lawrence saw himself as having been 'changed . . . for ever' by his encounters with Native American religion in New Mexico, which 'shattered the essential Christianity on which my character was established'. He particularly valued Native American revelling in 'red mythology', a term I want to coin for their full-blooded acceptance of religious symbolism, in contrast to 'white mythology', to use Derrida's term for the self-deluding claim of western philosophy to have rid itself of all figural 'taint', to express the unvarnished 'truth' (Derrida 1982: 207–71). Native Americans remained for Lawrence 'the most deeply religious race still living', preserving 'a living tradition going back far beyond the birth of Christ, beyond the pyramids, beyond Moses' (*Phoenix* 144–5). Lawrence seems here to align himself with the theosophical belief in an ancient wisdom much older than the Bible, a wisdom almost covered over by centuries of rationalising Judaeo-Christian interpretation. Crossing the border into Mexico itself, he noticed how powerful their mythology remained, how their gods 'bit', especially those depicted in the Temple of Quetzalcoatl, in clear contrast to the United States, where 'the gods have had their teeth pulled, and their claws cut, and their tails docked, till they seem real mild lambs' (105–6). Mexican theology was full-blooded, red in tooth and claw, in contrast to the anaemic theology of the west.

Mornings in Mexico, written in Oaxaca around Christmas 1924, develops the contrast between red and white mythology, comparing the uncompromising violence of the Aztec myths with the sentimentality which surrounds Christian celebration of the birth of their saviour. The Aztec goddess of love, 'a goddess of dirt and prostitution . . . without a touch of tenderness', produces not a nice little baby but 'a razor-edged knife of blackish-green flint . . . with which the priest makes a gash in his victim's breast, before he tears out the heart, to hold it smoking to the sun' (*MM* 32–3). Having established the contrast between the gentle Jesus who is the focus of Christian carolling and the fierce object of Aztec worship, Lawrence proceeds to emphasise the absence in Indian religion of the conceptual distinctions, the binary oppositions characteristic of Christianity. For them there is no subject versus object, Creator versus creature, spirit versus matter: 'The Indian does not consider himself as created, and therefore external to God, or the creature of God'. He makes no 'distinction between God and God's creation, or between Spirit and Matter' (61). There is 'no Ideal God . . . no Onlooker, no Mind' (62). This is a theme to which Lawrence returns in his meditation upon 'The Hopi Snake Dance', contrasting 'our religion', which 'says the cosmos is Matter, to be conquered by the Spirit of Man', and the Indian religion, which makes no division between God and His creation (74–5). The Hopi recognise the co-existence of good and evil in their snakes as in the world, whose 'origins are dark and dual', in contrast with western myths of origin, which involve a Godhead that was 'perfect to start with', a God who 'was in the beginning' along with Paradise and a Golden Age that has been lost (89).

These comparisons between Indian and Christian religion

indicate at least some of the ways in which Lawrence's encounter with earlier faiths forced him into a reconsideration of his own 'essential Christianity', a deconstruction of its binary oppositions and a recovery of the raw passions and red mythology it had mistakenly attempted to erase. A passage from his Mexican Notebook of late 1923 stresses his continuing commitment to many aspects of Christianity, including an 'all-overshadowing God', Jesus as 'one of the Sons of God' and the need for a church with 'an initiated priesthood' (*Ref.* 385). His insistence that 'on religious fundamentals' there was 'no breach' between his own position and that of the Catholic Church (385) may underestimate the extent both of his own radical break with western metaphysics and of the way in which that institution would continue to cling to its Greek metaphysical inheritance. But the religion he develops in his Mexican novel will be found to contain a number of genuinely Catholic features at a symbolic if not at a philosophical level.

Lawrence's reading in anthropology and theosophy can be seen to have contributed to his re-appraisal of Christianity at this time. One of the books he re-read in 1922 was *The Golden Bough* (Sagar 1982: 95), which has much to say about Mexico, for instance in the chapter entitled 'Eating the God', which celebrates the similarities between Aztec and Christian sacramentalism. Frazer finds in the sixteenth-century Jesuit historian Acosta a detailed description of the ceremonial eating of a dough image of the god Huitzilopochtli, which was cut, distributed and eaten 'in manner of a communion', which shows that 'the ancient Mexicans, even before the arrival of Christian missionaries, were fully acquainted with the theological doctrine of transubstantiation' (Frazer 1994: 506–7). The point of his irony here is to portray all religions as tarnished with the same superstitious brush, but Lawrence reads such similarities as evidence of a single source of all religious wisdom not only anthropologically, in terms of deep-seated human needs, but historically, in terms of past links between the Aztecs and the Jews.

Even more important for Lawrence's Mexican novel is the chapter of *The Golden Bough* entitled 'Killing the God in Mexico', which also celebrates the discovery by Spaniards in the sixteenth century of 'a barbarous and cruel religion which presented many curious points of analogy to the doctrine of their own church' (607). Frazer clearly enjoys recounting the gory details of Aztec sacrifices in which the human victim was taken to 'a small and lonely temple' on a mountain, held down by priests, 'cut open and decored' before the removed heart was offered to the sun (609). He proceeds to describe a similar sacrifice to 'a god named Quetzalcoatl' whose 'image, set upon a richly decorated altar or pedestal in a spacious temple, had the body of a man but the head of a bird' (611–12). Much of Lawrence's Mexican novel, as we shall see, is given to the description of similar ceremonies in honour of Quetzalcoatl.

Another element in Lawrence's enthusiasm for Mexican religion which was to feed strongly into both versions of his Mexican novel was his interest in theosophy, reactivated by Frederick Carter, with whom he began to correspond at the end of 1922. In March 1923 Carter sent Lawrence a copy of his manuscript 'The Dragon of the Alchemists', which they discussed both in letters and in person, when Lawrence visited Carter in Shropshire in December (*Letters* IV 547), a visit which resulted in a range of ambitious plans for joint publications on symbolism, the soul and 'the problem of the last end of the world' (Carter 1932: 5). These plans were eventually abandoned, although Carter published parts of the original manuscript in two short books, *The Dragon of the Alchemists* in 1926 and *The Dragon of Revelation* in 1931, the latter being prefaced by a rather hurt note deploring the fact that Lawrence's own *Apocalypse*, originally designed as an introduction to Carter's work, had been published without acknowledgement either of Carter's influence or of the origin of the book in a planned collaboration (Carter 1931: 7). In the absence of the original manuscript of 'The Dragon of the Apocalypse' it is worth looking briefly at the two books Carter succeeded in publishing, which give at least some indication of what was in the original manuscript read by Lawrence in 1923.

The Dragon of the Alchemists begins by stressing the importance of the Bible (especially its apocalyptic books) to alchemists and astrologers (Carter 1926: 10–12). Such powerful ancient symbols of religion as the dragon and the serpent, Carter argues, were 'the product of the psyche – of the imagination of man', expressing his relationship to the cosmos in figurative form (20). The dragon testifies to the glory once enjoyed by the 'Greater Man', the Lord of the Cosmos, represented by the kabbalistic Adam Kadmon (39). It is a 'familiar figure of wonder and of the marvellous' in myths and stories 'told by all the races of mankind'. This dragon, who 'rides in glory' in the centre of the Zodiac, is the 'good serpent', the 'winged serpent' who hatched the egg of the world, as opposed to his counterpart, the 'bad serpent' responsible for the fall. The 'flying dragon', Carter proceeds to explain, is the 'creeping serpent' of Genesis, transformed through a descent into the deep as described in the Book of Revelation, where its casting into the lake of fire (Rev 20: 10) symbolises the recovery or renewal of vital energy (symbolism which will be found to play an important part in The Plumed Serpent).

The Dragon of Revelation also focuses on the Book of Revelation, which it describes as 'great poetry . . . a storehouse of marvellous poetic imagery' (Carter 1931: 12), although Carter reads the whole Bible as an account of this process, from the loss of paradise in Genesis to the vision of its recovery in the Book of Revelation. This apocalyptic vision of the recovery of paradise, a significant element in earlier novels such as The Rainbow and Women in Love, plays an increasingly important role in Lawrence's later work, although it is as likely that Lawrence contributed to Carter's understanding of the relation between Genesis and Revelation expressed here in 1931 as it is that Lawrence drew on the earlier version of Carter's 'Dragon' which he read in Mexico in 1923. It should also be recognised that Carter and Lawrence disagreed over the relative significance of the body and the spirit. For Carter, as for other theosophists, it is the spirit which eventually conquers matter, leading 'the new man, the regenerate Adam' to escape the confines of the material world (90).

Lawrence acknowledged in 1929, however, 'There was something in that Dragon of the Cosmos lying across the heavens that has never left me' (Letters VII 456). He found Carter's style problematic and his accompanying drawings 'bullying and unreal', a 'vulgar' version of Blake, recommending he turn to pagan models, Mycenean, Cretan or Etruscan, which captured 'that queer otherness' of the natural world stripped of 'that boring Greek "beauty"' and 'that Jewish nasal ethics' (508, 519). He was later to explain that he rejected the theosophical version of the fall as much as the Christian: 'This "fall" into Matter (matter wasn't even conceived in 600 B.C. – no such idea) this "entombment" in the "envelope of flesh" is a new and pernicious idea arising about 500 B.C.' (544–5). Here, Lawrence can again be found to anticipate later deconstruction of the dualist division of matter and spirit, even making the same French pun on 'falling' and 'tomb' as Derrida in Glas (Derrida 1986: 22a). Carter acknowledged this difference between them, writing in D. H. Lawrence and the Body Mystical of their disagreements over St John, whom Lawrence saw as a 'usurper' who had 'spoiled' a great pagan document with his 'moralisations' (Carter 1932: 57; Woodman 1986: 48). This emerges even more clearly in *Apocalypse*, but it feeds in various complex ways into Lawrence's Mexican novel.

A Mexican connection with biblical symbolism can also be found in Blavatsky, who discusses 'QuetzoCohuatl', the 'serpent deity of the Mexicans', finding a number of similarities between 'the sun and serpent-worship of the Mexicans' and 'the religious writings of the . . . Mosaic Israelites'. The wand of the Mexican magician bearing the name of Quetzalcoatl, she claims, 'must be closely related to the traditional sapphic-stick of Moses' while a Mexican creation myth in which the Gods breathe a cloud of fire over the four ancestors of the human race 'so that they might see a certain distance only, and not be *like the gods themselves*', echoes the jealousy of Yahweh towards mankind at the end of Genesis 3. These links between ancient Mexico and ancient Israel, she argues, confirm legends about the earlier civilisation of Atlantis destroyed by flood, from which their shared wisdom could have descended (*SD* I 554–60). It was an argument echoed by the more orthodox if equally eccentric Lord Kingsborough, whose ten-volume study of the *Antiquities of Mexico* published from 1830 to 1848 also claimed that there had been a Jewish migration to Mexico which explained the Aztecs' apparent familiarity with biblical notions. Lawrence had read about Atlantis in Thomas Belt and Lewis Spence (*Plays* lxv) and recommended to Carter articles on the subject in *The Occult Review* (Sagar 1982: 95). He even makes Kate Leslie, the heroine of *The Plumed Serpent*, meditate upon the mysterious people of ancient Mexico at the time when 'countries rose above the oceans, like Atlantis and the lost continents of Polynesia' (*PS* 414, 477). There were possible historical as well as anthropological grounds, in other words, for the similarities between Christianity and Mexican religion.

It is, of course, a crucial aspect of both versions of Lawrence's Mexican novel that the attempt by Ramon and his co-religionists to resurrect the old Aztec religion is observed and assessed by their central consciousness, the middle-aged and sceptical Kate, the product of a western, Christian upbringing. Louis Martz claims that this is even more the case in the first draft, *Quetzalcoatl*, in which she 'watches with a mixture of fascination, revulsion and sympathy as this religious movement takes shape', never finally agreeing to do the three things to which she accedes at the end of *The Plumed Serpent*: to marry General Viedma, to become the avatar of the rain-goddess

Malintzi, and to stay in Mexico (*Q* 13). But, as we shall see, Kate remains critical even in her agreement to these three things in the final version of the novel, as did Lawrence himself, making significant changes to its last chapter to make this more apparent. In both versions of the novel, as in so much of Lawrence's fiction, the central female consciousness is the filter, in narrative terms the focaliser, through which all the events are seen. It is she who judges both the strengths and weaknesses of the new religion, assessing its capacity to meet modern requirements, in particular the spiritual void from which she is presented as suffering at the beginning of both novels. We should not assume that the new religion described in the novel is supposed to be the 'answer' to Lawrence's own religious quest.

Both versions of the novel begin in Mexico City with the sordid, degraded festival of the bull-fight, with which Kate is so disgusted that she leaves early, having lost all reverence for 'the great Mithraic beast' from whose sacrifice life was supposed to have begun (*PS* 17, 448). Mithraism, incidentally, is discussed by Frazer in relation to similar Christian and Aztec killing and eating of God (Frazer 1994: 360). Kate finds Mexico City altogether repulsive, with 'an underlying ugliness, a sort of squalid evil' (*PS* 21). She senses there, in the dominant metaphor of the book, something 'heavy' and 'oppressive', like the folds of some huge serpent that seems as if it could hardly raise itself' (24). Part of this heaviness, she admits to her American cousin Owen, lies in herself, but it is exacerbated by the rest of the human species, which she finds increasingly 'loathsome' (25–6). It will be a major task to revive any religious faith in her although she does find 'something . . . mysterious' in the scholarly Mexican Ramon Carrasco, whom she meets at a tea-party in the second chapter of both novels (*Q* 19–20). He forces her to recognise the void in herself as well as others, the 'bottomless pit of hollowness where the soul should be', a void not filled by the Catholic churches, which remain 'meaningless' to most Mexicans (44–6).

The apocalyptic dimension in Kate's gloomy vision of this 'bottomless pit' is given particular emphasis in the later version of the novel, in which Kate dwells on the way the white man, attempting to save the souls of the Indians, had succeeded only in losing his own soul. The original manuscript of this version has a long section, omitted from the final text, attacking the irreligion of her cousin Owen, a 'parlour socialist' who 'hated religion in any form' and suffers from what Kate, modifying Nietzsche, calls a 'will-to-emptiness'. She conjures up additional phrases from the Book of Revelation as she dwells on the 'god-spark' being 'cast out', as Satan is 'cast out into the earth' (Rev. 12: 9), leaving sensation 'clawing and scraping at the inner walls of the emptiness . . . The bottomless pit!' (20: 3). This, she feels, is the condition of the white man in the modern world, 'the god-power, the god-authority betrayed with Judas kisses'. It is in comparison with this gloomy vision of the west's betrayal not only of its own God but of all possibility of Godhead that even 'those old Aztecs, with their horrible religion and their unnatural, nauseating religious festivals' (*PS* 498–9), hold more in the way of hope for Lawrence's heroine than traditional Christianity.

It is in this melancholy state that Kate reads an account in the paper of a man emerging from Lake Chapala claiming to have spoken with the god Quetzalcoatl. *The Plumed Serpent* includes a much longer report of this incident as well as a more positive reaction on her part. In the first version she has to consult her guidebook to discover who he was, but now she recalls him as 'a sort of fair-faced, bearded god; the wind, the breath of life, the eyes that see and are unseen, like the stars by day' (58), details which incorporate a number of biblical themes: Genesis has much to say about 'the breath of life' (2: 7) while Psalm 136 celebrates the God who made the heavens, 'The sun to rule by day . . . The moon and stars to rule by night' (vv 8–9). Kate's recollections of Aztec religion in the final version of the novel are necessarily mediated by her own tradition, but she prefers this 'confusion of contradictory gleams of meaning' to any pretended clarity about religion:

Her Irish spirit was weary to death of definite meanings, and a god of one fixed purport: Gods should be iridescent, like the rainbow in the storm. Man creates a god in his own image, and the god grows old along with the men that made him . . . But the god-stuff roars eternally, like the sea, with too vast a sound to be heard . . . Ye must be born again. Even the gods must be born again. We must be born again. (*PS* 58–9)

Jesus' instruction to Nicodemus (John 3: 7), it is implied, is particularly appropriate to the religion based on his own teaching, which should recognise the limits as well as the power of its own symbols, their need to be renewed. This is a view reinforced by the young Mexican Mirabal, a character absent from the original version of the novel, who tells Kate that her own names for God have become tired:

Think of *Jahveh! Jehovah!* Think of *Jesus Christ!* How thin and poor they sound! Or *Jesucristo!* They are dead names, all the life withered out of them. Ah, it is time now for Jesus to go back to the place of the death of the gods, and take the long bath of being made young again. (*PS* 62)

Ramon quotes Jesus himself on the danger of putting new wine into old bottles (74–5; Matt 11: 7).

That Christianity as conventionally understood in the west is dead is also made apparent in the history of Cipriano, who fascinates Kate at the party by his 'semi-savage' power, as if he had the 'blood of reptiles in his veins, . . . the dragon of Mexico' (67). Cipriano, who had owed his English education in *Quetzalcoatl* to a rich English-woman, has a Catholic bishop to thank in *The Plumed Serpent* for the dubious privilege of an Oxford education during which he discovers that in England 'Even God was different, and the Blessed Mary.' His English education destroys everything that had seemed 'strange and mysterious, when I was a child, in Mexico', teaching him 'the laws of life, and . . . science' (69). Kate herself, however, who looks 'like an Ossianic goddess' (60), an ancient Celtic deity, re-awakens in him some of the 'wonder, the mystery' that he used to feel kneeling in front of 'the Santa Maria de la Soledad' (69).

Both versions of the novel portray Kate on arrival in Chapala being impressed by the 'mysterious quality in the atmosphere', which conveys 'a barbaric sacredness' (*Q* 60; cf. *PS* 93). As so often in his work, Lawrence here resorts to the language of the Bible in order to represent Kate's religious yearning. He presents her praying in the form of the Psalms, complete with poetic parallelism (the repetition of the same idea in slightly altered form): '*Give me the mystery and let the world live again for me!* Kate cried to her own soul. *And deliver me from man's automatism*' (*PS* 104–5). She also introduces theosophical terms into her biblical pastiche, 'addressing the silent life-breath which hung unrevealed in the atmosphere' with the closing invocation of the Book of Revelation, 'Come then!' (106). This breath, later endowed with initial capital letters as the 'Great Breath' (108), as William Tindall complained, emanates all too obviously from Blavatsky (Tindall 1972: 147).

As 'a white woman born of Christianity' (*Q* 96), it is only to be expected that Kate (like her creator) should think in biblical terms, filtering her understanding of Mexican religion through western images. Virginia Hyde claims that *Quetzalcoatl* 'refers more openly to the Bible than does *The Plumed Serpent*' (Hyde 1992: 177). The landscape around Chapala as described in the first version of the novel certainly fits the image of ancient Israel as Kate had imagined it, recalling 'her old visions of Israelites in deserts, and Abraham seeking water: remote pictures having an inward Jewish dreariness, which remained to her from the Old Testament'. Even the 'big, hairy pigs . . . seemed like the Bible' (*Q* 134). But *The Plumed Serpent* also gives the same lake and mountains a biblical setting. When Kate shares her picnic with the fishermen in their boat, luxuriating in their gratitude, that they 'can receive the gift of grace, and we can share it like a communion', it is difficult not to be reminded of Jesus and his disciples, especially when, like Peter at the transfiguration (Mark 9: 2, Matt. 17: 2), she says 'it is good to be here' and, like the Johannine Jesus (cf. John 15), 'This is the fulness of the vine' (*PS* 107). In the novel, of course, the scene is entirely natural, although for Kate it is no less wonderful and mysterious.

What Kate realises as she dwells in *Quetzalcoatl* on the cultural differences between herself and the Mexican family in whose house she lodges, is that the Christianity in its fully developed western form which had been imposed upon them by the Spaniards is not at all natural for them. The prophet of the new religion, Ramon, whose background, like Cipriano's, involves a western education, attending 'lectures in history and philosophy at Harvard' and travelling for two years in the United States (*Q* 109), reinforces this impression. He is supposed to have spent a decade studying the history of his own land, during which he turned against the Christianity exemplified by his wife, a devout Catholic full of 'love' for God and men but 'hostile to life' (109). Ramon has clearly read his Nietzsche: he respects Christianity as 'a great religion' but comes to see it as 'the religion of aliens' not of Mexicans (116), already 'collapsing' even in the west, lacking sufficient vitality to oppose 'the great Anti-christ of mechanism and materialism' (117). The more Ramon denounces 'the whited sepulchres of the pale faces' (100), however, the more he resembles an Old Testament prophet, in which tradition, of course, Christ himself used the same damning phrases of the Pharisees (Matt. 23: 27).

A similar irony surrounds Kate's revised meditations on the Christianity of the Mexicans in the family where she lodges, as they are presented in *The Plumed Serpent*. She comes to the same conclusion as in the earlier version of the novel, that 'Jesus is no Saviour to the Mexicans' but expresses this view in imagery derived from the gospels: 'He is a dead god in their tomb' while 'they find themselves at last shut in the tomb along with their dead god', desperately in need of 'some Saviour, some redeemer to drive a new way out, to the sun' (*PS* 136). Given the history of Mexico and the supposed background of Kate and of Ramon, it is not unrealistic to portray them as finding it difficult to disentangle the discourse of Christianity from that of the new religion. Also, given Lawrence's belief that all religion derives from a common source, it is hardly surprising that the symbols and images of Christianity continue to haunt the teaching and liturgy of Ramon and his followers even while they mount a sustained critique of its doctrine.

In the first version of the novel, Cipriano is initially suspicious of Ramon's emphasis on a religious basis for the changes Mexico requires, associating religion with 'sentimentality'. If they are to have a religion, he insists, it must be 'a religion of *men*, not of monks and women' (*Q* 120). When Ramon reveals his plan to replace Jesus, 'the white man's god', with the ancient gods of Mexico, Cipriano at first fears that this may be simply 'antiquarian' (125). Ramon, however, explains that Christianity is irredeemably coloured with a 'whiteness of the mind and the spirit' which needs replacing 'out of the dark of the blood of men'. The whole intellectual structure of Christianity, he explains, is built upon the repression of this dark element, the privileging of mind over matter, spirit over body. Ramon, who blesses Cipriano 'in the name of the unspeakable gods', causing a 'dark fountain of life' to rise up from his inner 'depths' to cast off the 'hard white shell' of his English education (126), clearly believes that white mythology must give way to red.

One of the differences between western and Indian ways of thinking, as Cipriano explains to Kate, is that in the west, everything from the parks to the fabrics to the people themselves are complete, finished, tidy. Indians, in contrast, have less confidence in their capacity to put everything in order, to tell the whole story, to represent the world exactly as it is. 'Indian women,' he tells her, 'when they weave blankets, weave their souls into them. So at the end they leave a place, some threads coming down to the edge, some loose place where their souls can come out.' Western women, by contrast, 'have no threads into the beyond' (162–3). The mythology of the new Mexican religion remains similarly open, less enclosed within a particular metaphysical system, making no claims to absolute truth. It is both traditional, in continuity with ancient religious forms, and proto-postmodern, eclectic in its selection of images and symbols, none of which are granted the status of ultimate truth. The white mythology which the Spaniards brought to Mexico, by contrast, although clearly 'invented by foreigners from Europe', as Ramon tells the Catholic bishop in their extended theological discussion in chapter 11 of *Quetzalcoatl*, makes a spurious claim to universality (174–5).

It is at this point, in response to the bishop's warnings against starting another heresy, that Lawrence gives Ramon the sentiments expressed in his own name in the Mexican Notebook of 1923, acknowledging a belief in Jesus as *a* Son of God, although 'the Most High has other divine Sons than Jesus' and 'even divine Daughters' (175). What seemed surprising in Lawrence's own claims to an affinity with Catholicism gains a little in credibility in the mouth of a Mexican. In the equivalent scene in the final version of the novel, Ramon explains to the Bishop that the Indians cannot understand the fully elaborated theology of 'high Christianity' because it is 'a religion of the spirit', requiring intellectual understanding. The Mexicans, he insists, must be spoken to in their own language, not that of a Roman but a broader Catholicism. The Catholic Church could claim to have 'become really the Universal Church', according to Ramon, only if it incorporated the insights of Mohammed, Buddha and Quetzalcoatl as well as Jesus. Then perhaps it could be labelled 'a church of all the religions', a truly 'Catholic Church of All the Sons of Men . . . the Sons of the One God' (*PS* 264–5). Ramon is here made to plead for a theological relativism which would respect cultural differences as geographically and historically contingent expressions of a deeper, ungraspable truth.

Both versions of the novel embody a powerful critique of orthodox Christianity. *The Plumed Serpent* continues with Ramon delivering a Nietzschean assault on the servile ethics of the Sermon on the Mount, deploring the fulfilment of Christ's prophecy that the meek should inherit the earth (*PS* 187, cf. Matt. 5:5), which draws from Carlotta a Pauline condemnation of 'the sin of pride. Men wise in their own conceit' (189, cf. Rom. 12: 16). He sees her loyalty to 'her Christ and her Blessed Virgin' as a matter of 'will' and 'charity', a refusal to remain open to the 'spontaneous flow, . . . the unforeseen comings and goings of the Holy Ghost' (207). He continues, however, to take Jesus as a model even for his rejection of conventional religion. Just as the Johannine Jesus rejects his mother's demands upon him at the wedding feast in Cana, saying 'Woman, what have I to do with thee?' (John 2: 4), so Ramon turns his back on his wife, rejecting her weak, over-charitable spirit: 'What have I to do with it!' (*PS* 210). He rejects her desire for oneness with God in terms which undermine the white mythology, the logocentric metaphysics, of the institution of the Eucharist as recorded in Matthew's Gospel (Matt. 12: 31–2): 'Even though I eat the body and drink the blood of Christ,' he exclaims, 'Christ is Christ and I am I, and the gulf is impassable' (*PS* 252). There is no essential transubstantiation for him, no fusing of essences either in the elements themselves or in their recipients.

Carlotta cannot accept her husband's supplanting of Jesus but Kate becomes increasingly sympathetic towards it, especially in *The Plumed Serpent*, in which she appears fully to accept his Nietzschean critique of Christianity. Watching some Indians leave their church, she resents the way Catholicism, instead of encouraging them to be independent, 'pushes them more and more into a soft, emotional helplessness' so that they consider themselves 'victims'. She even echoes the sardonic parody of the Sermon on the Mount of her mentor: 'Cursed are the falsely meek, for they are inheriting the earth' (*PS* 276, cf. Matt. 5: 5). As Carlotta lies dying before her, demanding the last rites, Kate conjures up a satiric vision of the crucifixion in which one of the thieves alongside Jesus is male while the other is female: 'the much more subtle, cold, sly, charitable thief of the woman in *her* own rights, forever chanting her beggar's whine about the love of God and the God of pity' (347). As Clark points out in a footnote to this passage in the Cambridge edition of the novel, Lawrence 'struck out some paragraphs which had prepared for these images' in the typescript, which has Cipriano denounce the dying Carlotta in mock-biblical terms, accusing her of bearing 'the fatherless children of your own denial', of giving 'your unnourishing body as a wafer, the oil and the wine held back' and stealing 'the oil and wine of a man' (529). It is, of course, the essence both of Jewish and Christian religion to help the fatherless (cf. Deut. 14: 29, James 1: 27) while 'unleavened wafers anointed with oil' were part of the sacrifice recommended in Leviticus (2: 4; 7: 12). The 'best of the oil, and all the best of the wine' are also recommended in Numbers 18: 12 before being taken up in the Book of Revelation, with its instruction to 'hurt not the oil and the wine' (6: 6). Cipriano turns all these biblical images against Christianity while Ramon also mocks Christian suppression of the body, sarcastically encouraging his sons, who remain loyal to their mother's religion, to forget their father altogether and to claim an 'immaculate conception' (*PS* 356).

The same bitterness, the same ambivalent combination of love and hatred towards the 'parent' religion, Christianity, a similar parodic use of the Bible to go beyond it, emerges in the liturgy Ramon devises for the worship of Quetzalcoatl. As Martz shows in his introduction to *Quetzalcoatl*, this is introduced more 'naturally' in the first version of the novel, which portrays Kate having to overcome an initial suspicion and dislike of all things Mexican (*Q* xiii–xvi). Chapter IX opens with her overhearing without fully understanding a duet sung by two cousins of the family in whose house she lodges, one taking the role of Quetzalcoatl and the other of Jesus. The first, taking the part of Quetzalcoatl, records having 'embraced the god Jesus' when he first came to Mexico, agreeing to make way for this alien god and his 'strange' teaching (145–6). The second cousin, assuming the role of Jesus, complains to his father that the Mexicans are too angry to hear of love, prompting the Father to call him home and send Quetzalcoatl in his place (151–2). In *Quetzalcoatl* this is just a song sung by two individuals. The new religion in the first version of the novel is altogether less formal than it becomes in *The Plumed Serpent*, more a matter of private emotion, poetry and song, opening gently onto a larger sense of life, than of public doctrine and pompous ceremonial.

In the later version of the novel, however, the same opening hymn is introduced as one of 'The Written Hymns of Quetzalcoatl' (the title of chapter XV), part of an official liturgy being circulated throughout the country. The leaflets on which the hymns are written bear at the top an official stamp, 'a rough print of an eagle within the ring of a serpent that had its tail in its mouth', the emblem also suggesting an eye, which combines genuinely Mexican with theosophical symbols (*PS* 118). The men carry banners depicting a yellow sun with a black centre, also traditionally Mexican (462), playing flutes and drums which remind Kate of the music accompanying Red Indian dances in New Mexico (117). But there are also Christian elements, biblical references both in the narrative voice and in what the men of Quetzalcoatl have to say. Kate, for example, is seen to be 'fascinated by the silent, half-naked ring of men in the torchlight' (121), reminiscent of the 'torchlight red on sweaty faces' of the disciples at Gethsemane as described in the opening of the final section of *The Waste Land* (published in 1922 under similarly Frazerian influence). As in Eliot's poem about the need for resurrection, the prophets Isaiah and Ezekiel play a significant part in what the men of Quetzalcoatl say. The 'man with the banner of the sun', like Isaiah (55: 1), offers his audience 'sweet water' (*PS* 123) and asks, like Ezekiel (37: 4), 'Are your bones not dry enough?' Quetzalcoatl himself claims, 'in the palm of my hand is the water of life' (*PS* 123), a conflation of phrases to be found throughout the Psalms and the Book of Revelation. The new religion draws much of its material from the Bible, partly as an act of postmodern bricolage, employing the tools that lie to hand, partly to indicate the common source of all religion, and partly (one cannot help suspecting) because Lawrence himself is so saturated with the language of the Bible as not always to be aware how much his own writing echoes it.

Biblical echoes certainly saturate the new liturgy in *The Plumed Serpent*. Just as the Johannine Jesus promises his disciples at the Last Supper, 'I will pray the Father, and he shall give you another Comforter . . . I will not leave you comfortless' (John 14: 12–18), so Ramon announces, 'the Father will not leave us alone' (*PS* 125). The Aztec Father is significantly different; for a start, he has a womb, being both male and female (125, 463). But when Kate joins the men of Quetzalcoatl dancing in the Plaza there are clear echoes of Genesis as she feels 'the waters over the earth wheeling upon the waters under the earth' and male fingers 'stooping over the face of the waters' (Gen. 1: 2–7). Unlike the angel in the Book of Revelation, whose 'face was as it were the sun' (10: 1), a face in the crowd 'was the face of dark heaven' (*PS* 131). In chapter XI a man sings 'in a small voice,' presumably like that which followed the earthquake and the fire in 1 Kings 19: 12, of 'The Lord of the Morning Star' (177), the star celebrated in Revelation 2: 28 and 22: 16. Ramon proceeds to preach his own unservile Sermon on the Mount, instructing his followers to consider the Mexican equivalent of the lilies of the field: 'Think neither to give nor to receive, only let the jasmine flower' (179). He also combines the Song of Solomon with the words of St Paul to the Romans (9: 25): 'And listen to thy love saying: Beloved' (180). Lawrence tests both the biblical knowledge and the patience of his readers as Ramon mixes these half-remembered passages of scripture with Aztec mythology and theosophic phrases about snakes, plasm and breath. That Lawrence is drawing upon his own memories of childhood is apparent in one of the hymns sung by the men of Quetzalcoatl, which is clearly based upon an old Sankey favourite, 'Shall you? Shall I?' (195) He was to celebrate the sense of wonder induced by such hymns in an essay of 1928 on 'Hymns in a Man's Life' (*Phoenix* II 599). I would suggest therefore that he has his Mexican celebrants sing a version of Sankey not in parody, but in deadly earnest, expressing the feelings of wonder common to all religion.

That Ramon is deliberately conflating Mexican and Christian religion is apparent in the way he speaks of Quetzalcoatl having 'risen and pushed the stone from the mouth of the tomb' (*PS* 200). The 'Second Hymn' of the new religion also celebrates Quetzalcoatl's resurrection while Jesus sings of his 'mother the moon' being dark, the Virgin of Guadalupe being represented like the woman of Revelation 12: 1 with the 'moon under her feet'. The Third Hymn, 'Quetzalcoatl Looks Down on Mexico', as well as commanding all images of Jesus, Mary and the saints to be removed, calls, like the angry deity of Genesis 6, 'Let us make an end / Of these ill-smelling tribes of men' (242). The Fourth, in both versions of the novel, protests against 'the greedy ones' who have exploited the natural resources of Mexico. The point in these last two hymns is that Christianity has failed to prevent the commercial exploitation of Mexico. *The Plumed Serpent* adds a prophecy about 'the dragon of thunder', who will 'curdle your blood like milk', like the God of whom Job complains (260, cf. Job 10: 10). The Mexican deity, these allusions suggest, is at least as quick to anger as that of the Old Testament prophets. He has not been watered down by Christian compassion and mercy.

Ramon himself possesses many of the characteristics of an Old Testament prophet. When he prays, naked in a dark room with his fists raised above his head, he experiences, like the eponymous hero of Lawrence's play *David*, an 'inhuman tension' (169). Kate recognises that she looks upon him with the same yearning as Salome upon John the Baptist (182, 184). But it is Jesus that he most resembles, especially when, like Peter in the gospels announcing the identity of the Messiah, Cipriano recognises him as 'the living Quetzalcoatl' (cf. Mark 8; Matt. 16). There are also resemblances to Jesus in his railing, like Matthew's angry protagonist, against the hypocrites who 'like washing the outside of the egg, to make it clean' (191). This Jesus, however, claims less knowledge of the Father, aggressively modifying his predecessor's Johannine confidence: 'No man knows my Father, and I know him not' (339, cf. John 10: 15). He also echoes St Paul: 'For save the Unknown God pours His Spirit over my head and His fire into my heart, . . . I am not. I am nothing. I am a dead gourd' (341). Ramon here conflates a phrase from the Acts of the Apostles (2: 17–18) with the well-known passage in which St Paul likens himself to a 'sounding brass' if he lacks charity (1 Cor. 13: 1–3). The gourd, incidentally, seems to have crept in from the Book of Jonah (4: 6–7). Most significantly of all, Ramon, unlike Jesus, does not offer *himself* as a sacrifice for the sin of the world but the prisoners taken in an attempt on his life. At the end of their ceremonial execution, however, Cipriano, in a provocative re-accenting of the central Christian sacrifice, utters the words of Christ on the cross, 'It is finished' (*PS* 382; John 19: 30).

Other aspects of Ramon's liturgy are also modelled upon Christian originals. In *Quetzalcoatl*, for example, the followers of the new movement symbolise their protest against wealthy capitalists exploiting the country by substituting the images of Jesus in several churches with grotesque models of Judas as 'a fat Mexican with a sticking-out stomach and tight trousers and turned-up moustaches' (*Q* 179). The removal of Christian images from the churches is incorporated into an elaborate, emotional liturgy in which the people sing 'Farewell' while Jesus explains, 'I am Jesus, going home. And my mother, the most pure Mary, with me goes too.' The young priest kneels in front of Ramon and, like Jesus to Peter, offers him 'the great key of the church' (186–7). There is even a Nietzschean ceremony of the death of God during which various images of Christ, the Virgin and a variety of saints are reverently removed from the Church, taken in solemn procession to the lake, ferried across to the Isle of Scorpions and burned, leaving Chapala for the moment 'empty of God' (190). The reconsecration of the church at Chapala is equally indebted to Nietzsche, this time to his prophet Zarathustra. Ramon appears to the sound of violins, guitars and violas, announcing his deity and acknowledging, 'In my Father's house are many mansions' (cf. John 14: 2). But it is the statue of Quetzalcoatl, standing in the niche where the Saviour had stood, which most clearly combines the traditional features of the Mexican God with a resemblance to Zarathustra, bedecked with the same symbols of an eagle with a serpent coiled around it (*TSZ* 52–3). Kate certainly recognises the Nietzschean significance of these symbols and of the imitative posture of the men, standing erect with their right arms high and palms facing upward, as if supporting an eagle, 'seeing how the new religion was to arise from the splendid animal virility of the people, instead of from humility' (*Q* 233). So does Carlotta, beseeching Jesus to forgive her husband before collapsing in fatal convulsions.

Ramon continues to see no contradiction between all this and Catholicism, calling himself 'a Catholic of the Catholics' and even sending a delegation to Rome confident that they will receive a warm welcome. Cipriano explains to a meeting of the Knights of Columbus (a reactionary Church group) that they should encourage their workers to join them rather than the 'bolshevist agitators'. There are, however, significant differences between the religion of Quetzalcoatl and Christianity, especially in the area of sexual ethics: Ramon explains that he does not want 'celibate priests' but proper 'men': 'My priests will be men, entire, and not eunuchs' (252–3). In pursuit of this full-blooded sexuality, he urges Cipriano, having assumed the mantle of the war-god Huitzilopochtli, to take Kate as his goddess-wife Malintzi.

The new religion of *Quetzalcoatl* also incorporates a number of esoteric elements, presumably a result of Lawrence's reading of Carter. Ramon refers to 'the mysteries', the hermetic tradition of Adam Kadmon, 'the redeemed Adam' (298). He proceeds to baffle her with talk of the Rosy Cross, the lance that 'makes no wound', the Tau, 'the Life-Loop', and 'the language of the old symbols' (299). He delivers a long theosophical discourse on the Great Creation, the gradual descent of the soul into matter. Only whereas Blavatsky and the other theosophists saw this as a descent, a degeneration, for Ramon (as for Lawrence) the soul can only benefit from 'wooing Matter and becoming flesh'. The soul, in Ramon's anti-theosophical reworking of the Book of Genesis, recaptures 'the pride of her flesh' embodied in 'the perfect Adam, and the perfect Eve'. It is 'the tragedy of the serpent, that great dragon', that as 'his soul climbed slowly down the stair of stars, through the seven spheres, towards the great accomplishment of incarnation, he failed in one of the stages' through cowardice and envy. Seeing 'Adam and Eve in the Garden, accomplished and perfect in the flesh, perfect in incarnation like pearls of the greatest price, and perfect in forgetting, like gods of the flesh', he encouraged them 'to eat of the Tree of Memory', causing them to feel guilt at what they should have celebrated. This is the 'bruise' inflicted by the serpent, a bruise deepened by God, who tells Adam and Eve to find their own way back to heaven: 'Climb back into bodilessness, as you climbed down' (303). Ramon also expounds the Book of Revelation in terms clearly indebted to Carter as a conquest over the flesh, a journey to the New Jerusalem which involves killing 'the passion of the body' and 'the mystery of the thighs', a 'triumph of the spirit' over the body and 'of Mind over Matter'. This, he proclaims bitterly, is 'the Little Creation of the Logos, the reversed creation, of the spirit seeking its own bodilessness. You have triumphed, you Galileans' (303–4). Ramon, in other words, appropriates theosophical symbolism but repudiates its replication of the traditional Christian privileging of spirit over matter.

Ramon ends this lengthy anti-Christian, counter-theosophical sermon by enjoining Kate to engage in a eucharistic initiation ceremony in terms which combine the symbolism of the horsemen of the Apocalypse with the language of the Psalms (24: 7, 9):

The rider on the white [horse] has passed by down the road of tombs, and the rider on the black horse is knocking with thunder at the gate. 'Lift up your heads, O ye gates!' (*Q* 306)

When Kate dares to question what drinking the 'vortex of the Dragon in the Cup' might mean, he denounces her as an 'insatiable Eve', intones Christ-like, 'This is your blood . . . This is my blood' over their wine glasses, and pontificates at length about desire as 'the Serpent in the Wilderness' (306–7). Given Lawrence's tendency to omit unintelligible theosophical material from the final version of his texts, it is probably fair to assume that he would have omitted some of these references from *Quetzalcoatl* if he had ever decided to publish the early version of what became *The Plumed Serpent*. He certainly cut similar material to be found in the manuscript of the final chapter of the final version of the novel, in which Ramon urges Kate to pass a lengthy message to the people of Europe, including more on 'the great Breath' and on the 'First Cause . . . like a dragon coiled at the centre of all the cosmos'. She continues to display a resistance to this, but he only gives her more messages for Europe, including yet another theosophical version of Genesis 3, in which the cross becomes a tree whose fruit they may now eat while 'the snake coils in peace round the ankles of Eve, and she no longer tries to bruise his head'. Kate quite reasonably objects, 'I shall never remember', but Ramon is not to be halted (*PS* 541–2): not, that is, until Lawrence decided to cut this material from the final version of the novel.

The Plumed Serpent, however, has Kate become much more fully committed to Ramon's new religion than she was in *Quetzalcoatl*, which ended indeterminately with her packing for the journey to Europe. In the final version of the novel she not only marries Cipriano but even agrees to become the goddess Malintzi in an exotic ceremony which involves embracing Cipriano naked on a rug of jaguar skins in front of the statue of Huitzilopochtli in the old parish church of Chapala. She recognises finally how far she has come from her Christian origins, that 'There are more ways than one of becoming like a little child' (392–3), but feels that she has recaptured some of the magic of 'aboriginal America', the wisdom of Atlantis, of the 'old pre-Flood world', 'the way of the world before the Flood, before the mental-spiritual world came into being', the days of Genesis 6 when the daughters of men mated with 'the old giants' (415). She assures Ramon that there is no danger of back-sliding, like 'Lot's wife' (426). The final version of the novel ends not with her packing but with her telling Cipriano that she does not want to leave Mexico, even if this is because he won't let her (444).

Both versions of Lawrence's Mexican novel will be regarded as readable only by those with an element of sympathy for his religious position, his belief that traditional Christianity had had its day and that the fundamental truths it had embodied in the mythological and symbolic forms of its time could be given new life in different forms. Even for readers sympathetic towards his understanding of Christianity as originally 'red' but overlaid with centuries of 'white' mythology, the constant biblical echoes are likely to become wearing. It is much easier to accept constant citation of the Bible from a genuine biblical prophet, as in the play *David*, than from a fictional Mexican, re-accenting the familiar language of the King James Bible through Nietzsche and Carter.

Lawrence had begun planning a religious play, to be 'either Aztec or Jewish', perhaps about 'King David or Moses' (*Letters* V 174), in November 1924, but it was not until the following March, while recuperating from illness, that he begun working on two biblical plays, one about Noah and the other about David, the latter possibly prompted by Frieda's questions about the 'puzzling figure' of David in the Books of Samuel which she was re-reading in German (Ellis 1998: 244; *Plays* lx). Only a fragment of 'Noah's Flood' survives, although his comments about it to the actress Ida Rauh, for whom he was writing the roles both of Japhet and Michal, give a clear indication of its basic aim: to contrast the religious 'demi-gods', Noah and his family, with the 'jeering-jazzing sort of people' in the decadent world, 'the wives wavering between the two: and the ark gradually rising among the jeering' (*Letters* V 217). The surviving fragment has three of the 'sons of men' complaining about 'the sons of God', the 'demi-gods', from whom, like Prometheus, they want to wrest the gift of fire (*Plays* 559). The fact that Noah and his sons are made to wear robes of the same colours as the celebrants of the new religion in *The Plumed Serpent* has been seen to link this play with the myth of Atlantis, 'the way of the world before the Flood' as envisaged in that novel, before the advent of what Lawrence's deleted introduction to the play refers to as 'modern humanists' (lxv–vi). There are also Miltonic echoes in their attempted rebellion against God (Sklar 1975: 221); their revolt represents a decline in religious wonder, the men scorning 'the Great White Bird' for moping at their lack of response to him (*Plays* 561). The men in the first manuscript version of the play attribute the superiority of the demi-gods solely to their possession of 'the red bird' of fire; 'with it,' they claim, 'we are greater than they, for they are stupid and vague' (823). The satire in these scenes seems mainly to be directed at the rise of irreligious modernity, the claim rationally to explain every-thing, and the consequent decline of genuine religious awe.

David charts a similar decline in religious sensibility, David himself representing the growth of undesirable rationality. Lawrence's attitude to the King of Israel after whom he was named, as we have seen, had undergone a number of changes. In *Study of Thomas Hardy*, he had been a very positive figure, representing the approach of God, his dance before the ark a model of sensual worship *before* the separation of mind from body. The first version of 'The Crown' of 1915 had also presented him as a sensual lion as opposed to a spiritual unicorn (Hyde 1992: 57). Lawrence's revisions to 'The Crown' for publication ten years later, however, criticise him as the 'small man slaying the great', killing Goliath and 'overthrowing the heroic Saul', thereby ushering in an age of 'petty egoism' (*Ref.* 268). *Etruscan Places*, which has been seen to clarify some of the play's obscurities (*Plays* lxx), also presents David as responsible for a decline in the sense of the sacred, his psalms celebrating a personal God rather than a wonderful cosmos (*EP* 57–8). An essay of 1919 on

'David', included in the Cambridge edition of *Etruscan Places*, occupies a mid-way point between these extremes, taking Michelangelo's famous statue in Florence as a combination of the best of both worlds, lion and unicorn, the physical and the spiritual. Lawrence finds Nietzsche's opposite principles held in perfect balance in this great achievement of the Renaissance: 'for one moment Dionysus touched the hand of the Crucified' (188). Christ, of course, in biblical genealogy, is the Son of David, descended from the tree of Jesse, David's father. David himself therefore faces both ways, looking back to the more 'primitive' sensual worship of his predecessors while anticipating elements of less desirable (and desiring) Christian spirituality. The play focuses on this pivotal moment in Israel's religious development. In Nietzschean terms, it illustrates 'the movement away from a Dionysian, primitive, passionate religious impulse . . . to a more Appollonian era under David' (Gamache 1982: 240). In terms of the anthropology of *The Golden Bough*, it illustrates the necessity of what Frazer (in the chapter 'Killing the God', which describes Christ replacing Pan) sees as the necessary slaying of the old representative of God: 'The man-god must be killed as soon as he shews symptoms that his powers are beginning to fail', to be succeeded by 'a vigorous successor' (Frazer 1994: 228). Saul inevitably bows to David once his powers begin to decline.

The action of the play follows fairly faithfully the plot of 1 Samuel 15–20, from Saul's refusal to slay Agag, King of the Amalekites, which first loses him Samuel's support, through the election of David as the next King of Israel and his defeat of Goliath to his having to hide from the enraged and jealous Saul. It begins with Merab and Michal, the daughters of Saul, celebrating his victory over the Amalekites. The mood soon changes, however, once Samuel learns that Saul has disobeyed the divine command not to spare either Agag or his cattle. In the biblical narrative, Samuel 'hewed Agag in pieces before the Lord' (1 Sam. 15: 33). Lawrence, who had written to the original director of the need to 'get that feeling of primitive religious passion across to a London audience' (*Letters* V 557), panders to that audience's sensibilities by presenting this slaughter '*behind a wall*' (*Plays* 441).

It is, however, the language of the play which is most striking. Lawrence has his prophet use an astonishing array of synonyms for what Abner calls 'the God of the Unknown Name', the God of Israel whose name was considered too sacred to pronounce (438; cf. 657).

In less than two pages Samuel refers to 'the Deep', 'the Breather of the skies', 'the Living Breath', 'the Voice of the Beyond', 'the living Wrath', 'the Nameless', 'the Thunder', 'the Wind of Strength', and 'the great Wish' (438–9). Some of these epithets were substituted for the more conventional title 'God' or 'Lord' in Lawrence's revisions to the first proof in what the Cambridge editors interpret as a gesture towards 'the animist religions of the North American Indians' (lxxi). But a significant number, they also notice, are genuinely biblical: 'the Deep' is a phrase which recurs frequently in the Psalms (107: 24, 42: 7), the 'Living Breath' may have gained theosophical overtones but it has its origins in God's breathing of life into Adam (Gen. 2: 7), while the Lord is said to have 'thundered with a great thunder' in 1 Samuel 7: 10 as well as in the Psalms (18: 13, 77: 18, 81: 7).

The play in fact reproduces so much of the King James Bible that it is inconceivable that Lawrence did not have a copy beside him while writing. Around these authentic passages of Samuel, however, he weaves a 'prose so often endowed with the cadences' of the King James version 'that it is impossible – without checking – to tell precisely where quotation stops and pastiche begins' (*Plays* lxix).

Lawrence's ability to reproduce the rhythm and syntax of the Authorized Version is particularly evident in Samuel's long speech in scene 2, built upon a single phrase in the biblical narrative: 'nevertheless Samuel mourned for Saul' (1 Sam. 15: 35; Sklar 1975: 233). Samuel calls on God, 'Speak to me out of the whirlwind . . . My bowels are twisted in a knot of grief, in a knot of anguish for my son, for him whom I anointed beneath the firmament of might' (*Plays* 442). The whirlwind here can be traced to the Book of Job (38: 1, 40: 6), the bowels to Lamentations (1: 20), the firmament to Genesis (1: 6–8), the might to 1 Chronicles (29: 12). But Lawrence does more than simply weave together a cluster of biblical phrases, writing as it were by Numbers. He reproduces stylistic features, such as poetic parallelism (repeating an idea raised in the first half of the sentence with amplification), investing it with his own theology. He thus has Samuel proclaim, 'Like waters He moves through the world, like a fish I swim in the flood of God himself.' It is also possible to detect familar imagery from *Birds, Beasts and Flowers* in Samuel's lament that 'Saul has fallen off, as a ripe fig falls and bursts' (*Plays* 442). The language of the King James Bible, in Bakhtin's terms, is made to carry a Lawrencian accent even in these convincing passages of biblical pastiche.

Scene III switches to Bethlehem, where Jesse, awaiting the arrival of Samuel, encapsulates Lawrence's belief in openness to the other, the sacred, celebrating the way the prophet comes 'with the other vision in his eyes' and 'uncovers the secret path of the Lord' (445). When the election falls on David, Eliab is made ironically to complain of a divine characteristic later to be celebrated in Mary's song of praise, 'He hath filled the hungry with good things; and the rich he hath sent empty away' (Luke 1: 53): 'He has anointed the youngest, and the oldest he has passed over' (*Plays* 450). Lawrence follows the account in 1 Samuel of Saul losing the blessing of God, the love of David and Jonathan, who are made to strip somewhat daringly down to leather loin-straps, and the defeat of Goliath, which necessarily occurs offstage. Lawrence at one point has a man '*singing loud and manly, from Psalm 8*' (450) and at another incorporates much of Psalm 5 unacknowledged in David's long speech in scene 13 (501). These lengthy quotations from the Bible, however, are relatively rare; the rest is a combination of short quotation and pastiche, often recognisably Lawrencian in theme, as in Saul's envy of David's youthful vigour: 'Blitheness in a man is the Lord in his body' (471). Lawrence also incorporates some of his favourite images from the Song of Solomon into the love-scenes between David and Michael, whom he encounters by a well more in the manner of Genesis than Samuel (Gen. 24: 11–16; 39: 1–13). David has much to say about the fruit of the pomegranate and 'the rose of Sharon' (*Plays*, 498; cf. Song 2: 1 and 4–6). He laments the way the threat of Saul prevents his heart singing 'between thy breasts' as the wellbeloved in the Song of Solomon 'shall be all night betwixt my breasts' (1: 13). He also pleads to 'sleep among the lilies' (*Plays* 505) just as the wellbeloved 'feedeth among the lilies' in that most erotic of biblical texts (Song 2: 16).

Lawrence's David, however, gradually loses both his sensuality and his role at the centre of the play, which is usurped by Saul. Lawrence discarded the original versions of scenes 15 and 16, in which Saul is conventionally jealous of David, giving greater substance to Saul's complaints about the kind of religion his successor represents. This is already apparent in the first version of the ending of scene 16, when Saul claims, 'There is but one sin, to deny the <bright> flame of God its rushing leap in my body, as Jonathan denies it', allowing 'the foxy son of Jesse' to 'steal his life'. The house of David, Saul predicts, will succeed in masking this flame for a

while before its 'masks will at last melt into ash', Saul himself looking
forward to being part of 'the flame that consumes his house' (*Plays*
584–5). It becomes increasingly clear in the final ending of the play,
however, that David represents a loss of cosmic energy, a decline
from an era of generous openness to the sacred to one in which God
is tamed and rationalised. A soldier predicts at the end of scene 15
that 'when the seed of David have put the Lord inside a house, the
glory will be gone, and men will walk with no transfiguration' (520).
The final scene ends with Jonathan predicting greatness for David,
but regretting that 'thy wisdom is the wisdom of the subtle, and
behind thy wisdom lies prudence' (524). In Frieda's German translation of the scene Lawrence added further accusations of ambition
and self-will, '*Ehrsucht und Eigenwille*' (687). Jonathan, like Saul in the
earlier version, looks forward to a time when 'the day of David at
last shall be finished, and wisdom no more be fox-faced, and the
blood gets back its flame' (524–5).

The 'day of David', of course, refers to the Christian era, the play
itself, as Virginia Hyde notices (Hyde 1992: 60–1), pointing up some
of the parallels between David and Jesus himself, even having David
say 'My day is not yet come' (*Plays* 450, cf. John 2: 4: 'Mine hour is
not yet come'). The Son of Man is 'lifted up' on the cross, in
typological fulfilment of Moses and the serpent (John 3: 14), which
explains why David asks, 'who am I to be suddenly lifted up' (476). A
herdsman is made to prophesy great things of the tree of Jesse,
planting his stick in the ground and saying, 'Stick may thou flourish!
May thou bud and blossom and be a great tree' (495). As usual,
Lawrence somewhat twists conventional Christian typology,
deploring as he does many of the developments of the mainstream
Judaeo-Christian tradition.

It is also typical of Lawrence that he makes few allowances for his
audience, resenting any suggestion that the play was difficult to
follow and dismissing unsympathetic reviewers as 'eunuchs' with 'no
balls' (*Letters* VI 62). The first edition, in fact, had been well received,
praised for its 'emotional solemnity' and poetry (*Plays* lxxix). But the
much-postponed first production at the Regent Theatre in London
in May 1927 was a disaster, widely attacked for its lack of dramatic
development. The actor playing Saul kept on forgetting his lines,
while many of the supposedly solemn scenes succeeded only in
appearing unintentionally comic (lxxxvii). Lawrence had, incidentally, written his own music for the play, based upon the songs sung

to him by Kot in the days of Rananim (*Letters* V 557; *Plays* 587–601). Kot tried to comfort Lawrence, suggesting that 'in the hands of a first rate producer, with real good actors . . . the play could be extremely good' (*Letters* VI 66). But this has yet to be proved.

David Ellis is probably right to say that the play could hardly have been 'comprehensible without some familiarity with Lawrence's private myths of the history of human culture' (Ellis and Mills 1998: 247). Its episodic structure had also been more effective in his 'leadership' novels, from *Aaron's Rod* to *The Plumed Serpent*, than it was on stage (Laird 1988: 206). Read sympathetically within these contexts, it can be said to capture a powerful sense of the sacred and to portray a key moment in the decline of religious sensibility (as Lawrence understood it) from red mythology, alive to the grandeur of the cosmos, to the tamer theology of Christianity, more rational and less open to the transcendent.

CHAPTER 12

The Risen Lord: 'The Escaped Cock', 'Lady Chatterley's Lover' and the paintings

Christ, of course, was the most prominent figure in Lawrence's religious thinking. The image of the crucified Christ loomed understandably large in the war years although even a poem such as 'Eloi, Eloi, Lama Sabachthani?' (1914) is followed in *The Complete Poems* by 'Resurrection', written about a year later, which charts the consciousness of the recovering Christ along with signs of a resurrection in nature. 'Resurrection of the Flesh', written earlier in 1915, violently overturns the command of Jesus to Mary Magdalen not to touch him. The Jesus of this poem, like the fictional Christs in Lawrence's later work, wants to remove all 'heavy books of stone! / Kill off the Word, that's had so much to say!' and celebrate his risen flesh (*CP* 737–8). Lawrence's letters of these early war years display a similar turn from the crucifixion to the resurrection. He told Lady Cynthia Asquith in January 1915, for example, that although his soul had been 'in the tomb . . . with the flat stone over it . . . All the time I knew I should have to rise again' (*Letters* II 268–9). In November he described to her how his heart had been 'smashed into a thousand fragments . . . like Osiris' but that 'these Gethsemane Calvary and Sepulchre stages must be over now: there must be a resurrection' (II 454). He told other friends and sympathisers that the suffering of Jesus may be 'very beautiful', like the rest of the Christian story: 'But Christianity should teach us now, that after our Crucifixion, and the darkness of the tomb, we shall rise again in the flesh . . . resurrected in the bodies' (II 248–50; cf. II 347–8). It was in 1915 that he picked up the symbol of the phoenix from Katharine Jenner's book on *Christian Symbolism*, where it is seen to represent 'the resurrection of the dead and its triumph over death . . . a recognised emblem of the Resurrection of Christ' (Jenner 1910: 150; *Letters* II 252). His fiction of this period, notably *The Rainbow* and 'The Thimble', as we have seen, also contains significantly revised references to the

214

resurrection, attempting to reverse conventional Christian fear of the body.

Resurrection returns as a dominant theme of Lawrence's writing in the last five years of his life, after his remarkable recovery from illness in Mexico in February 1925, a recovery we have seen reflected in a number of the stories dating from this period. His most extended treatment of resurrection, however, came in *The Escaped Cock*, inspired by a children's toy model of a white rooster escaping from an egg, which he and Earl Brewster saw in a shop window on their Etruscan pilgrimage. It was Brewster, apparently, who suggested it would make a good title: 'The Escaped Cock – A Story of the Resurrection' (Ellis 1998: 356). The original short story, when it first appeared in *The Forum*, had its title changed to 'Resurrection' on the front cover (though not in the table of contents), presumably to prevent its readers seeing a crude phallic pun in the title, although there was 'public uproar over the story' anyway (*EC* 146; Ellis 1998: 681). *The Man Who Died*, the title under which it was published posthumously in 1931, appears to have no authorial sanction apart from the frequency with which the phrase 'the man who had died' occurs in the novella itself, a phrase which avoids openly identifying the protagonist as Jesus himself.

Whether or not Lawrence was familiar with the bronze icon 'The Saviour of the World' in the Vatican Museum, a figure in which an erect phallus replaces the beak of a cock's head, which itself sits on a man's head and shoulders (Hinz and Teunissen 1976: 295–6), it is clear that the cock plays a central part in the story, partly as a Nietzschean symbol of vitality and partly as the animal associated with that pagan type of Christ, Asclepius, the God of Healing. Nietzsche makes his problematic Socrates, wearied of life and sick of the flesh, offer a rooster to Asclepius in *Twilight of the Idols* (*TI* 281–2). There are a number of other literary analogues for the basic plot of the *The Escaped Cock*, of which the novel Lawrence is most likely to have encountered, given his familiarity with much of George Moore's work, is *The Brook Kerith*, published in 1916, in which Christ is nursed back to health by Joseph of Arimathea before returning to his Essene community convinced of the need for a broader religious celebration of life. In Moore's novel too the convalescent Jesus asks if he may feed the chickens, an early sign of his 'awakening to physical life and beauty' (Thompson 1975: 224–6).

Nietzsche, however, I would suggest, is the single most important thinker behind *The Escaped Cock*. In *Thus Spoke Zarathustra*, as we saw, Nietzsche has his prophet explain that Jesus, had he lived longer, 'would have learned to live and learned to love the earth – and laughter as well' (*TSZ* 98). *Twilight of the Idols* presents the Sermon on the Mount as part of a 'war on passion' , an impulse towards the 'castration' of all desire, and a general hostility to life characteristic of Christianity (*TI* 52). *The Anti-Christ* blames not Jesus but his followers for the '*anti-natural* castration of a God into a God of the merely good' (138) while *The Will to Power* places the responsibility for 'the loss of an organ' and for the whole '*emasculation* of a man's character', the 'extirpation' of the passions involved in the belief that 'only the castrated man is a good man', upon Christianity (*WP* 207).

The best summary of the plot of *The Escaped Cock* is probably the one Lawrence himself gave Brewster in a letter of May 1927. It is

a story of the Resurrection, where Jesus gets up and feels very sick about everything, and can't stand the old crowd any more – so cuts out – and as he heals up, he begins to find what an astonishing place the world is, far more marvellous than any salvation or heaven – and thanks his stars he needn't have a 'mission' any more. (*Letters* VI 50)

It begins with the man who had died awaking 'from a long sleep', bandaged, cold and in pain, in a carved hole in the rock at the same 'hour before dawn' as the eponymous cock escapes from its peasant owner (*EC* 14). He helps recapture the bird, assuring the astonished peasant, who stares at his 'dead-white face' with understandable horror, 'I am not dead. They took me down too soon. So I have risen up' (23). This rising is completely natural, not at all miraculous, a matter of recovering and deciding to get up, although the man continues to feel a 'great void nausea of utter disillusion' (25). He recovers a renewed sense of life, however, when he hears the cock crowing 'the necessity to live, and even to cry out the triumph of life' (33–4), a Nietzschean vitality also evident in 'the unsteady, rocking vibration of the bent bird' as it pounces on its favourite hen (36). He resolves no longer to interfere with people's souls, repeating to Madeleine in the garden the *Noli me tangere* of John's Gospel, although he says, 'I am not yet healed and in touch with men' (40), significantly altered from Jesus's claim to be 'not yet ascended unto the Father' (John 20: 17). Madeleine, in Lawrence's revised account of the resurrection, cannot accept this all-too-human Jesus, initiating the orthodox belief that 'the Master was risen . . . but not as man; as pure God, who should not be touched by flesh' (*EC* 49–50). The man, however, continues to brood over the Nietzschean lesson he has learned, 'that the body, too, has its . . . life' (53–4) while Lawrence continues to play with details from the gospel resurrection narratives: the man says his farewells from the three women 'at dawn on the third morning' and even makes an appearance on the Emmaus Road, trying gently to correct his disciples' excitement over his imminent ascension. The *Forum* version ends with the man questioning the whole concept of salvation: 'From what, and to what, could this infinite whirl be saved?' (120).

Part Two of *The Escaped Cock*, written more than a year after Part One while Lawrence was convalescing in Switzerland, develops the portrayal of the healing process by which the man is reconciled to the world and to his body. Following Frazer in *The Golden Bough*, Lawrence links the account of Christ's resurrection with the myth of the Egyptian God Osiris, the husband of Isis, whose body was cut into pieces by his jealous brother Set (LeDoux 1972: 134–5). Isis, in the original myth, manages to find all the parts except for the genitals, which had been eaten by fish and which she replaces with an image of her own before Ra, the sun-god arranges to have the reassembled and complete Osiris arise from the dead (*EC* 124–5). Lawrence's manuscript names 'the genitals' (167) as the most important part of the dismembered body which Osiris gradually reassembles. It is clear even from the published text, however, that this is 'the last reality, the final clue to him, that alone could bring him really back to her' (86–7).

As in Part One of the story, it is the sight of others making love (in this case two slaves) which encourages both the priestess of Isis and the man who had died to believe that their prayers have been answered. The man, to begin with, is frightened of the priestess and her perfumed shrine, begging her not to touch him. Having been 'tortured . . . to death' with the 'touch' of men, he remains wary even of 'the tender touch of life' (110–11). The priestess, however, gradually heals his scars, bringing his wounded body back to life. In the scene which provided the subject of Lawrence's watercolour for the first edition of *The Escaped Cock* she is described stooping over his wound, the manuscript again naming the 'slain penis' which the publishers of the first edition removed. There is a crude and blasphemous *double entendre* in the man's finally crying out, 'I am risen!' (144), followed, in continuing subversion of traditional

Christian theology, by the claim, 'This is the great atonement, the being in touch' (148).

It is, even without the words omitted from the manuscript in the first edition, an astonishingly bold and transgressive rewriting of the gospel accounts of the resurrection, embodying all of Lawrence's Nietzschean critique of conventional Christianity and its fear of the body. It is important, however, to recognise that Lawrence remained quite orthodox in some aspects of his understanding of the resurrection. In 1929, for example, in an essay on 'The Risen Lord' for a series published by the magazine *Everyman* on 'A Religion for the Young', he corrects what he sees as an error on the part of the churches of his day, who preach 'Christ crucified' at the expense of the Risen Christ. This, he explains, is only 'half the truth', an unbalanced focus upon suffering produced by the war, when the image of the sheltering mother, the Madonna, had been replaced by 'the image of Christ crucified . . . Christ tortured on the cross'. Now he argues, over a decade after the end of the war, it is no longer appropriate to linger in 'the closed grey disillusion of Christ Crucified, dead and buried'. Now is the time to follow the Catholic Church and the countries of the mediterranean in celebrating 'Christ risen in the flesh! . . . and if with hands and feet, then with lips and stomach and genitals of a man. Christ risen, and risen in the whole of His flesh, not with some left out'. In continuation of the theme of *The Escaped Cock*, he concludes:

If Jesus rose from the dead in triumph, a man on earth triumphant in renewed flesh, triumphant over the mechanical anti-life convention of Jewish priests, Roman despotism, and universal money-lust . . . .a man at last full and free in flesh and soul . . . If Jesus rose as a full man, in full flesh and soul, then He rose to take a woman to Himself, to live with her, and to know the tenderness and blossoming of the twoness with her . . . (*Phoenix* 571–5).

This is also the subject of the painting entitled 'Resurrection', completed in May 1927, immediately after Lawrence had written Part One of *The Escaped Cock*. Lawrence's own description of the painting has 'Jesus stepping up, rather grey in the face, from the tomb, with his old ma helping him from behind, and Mary Magdalen easing him up towards her bosom' (*Letters* VI 72). The Lawrencian Christ-figure it depicts may be 'rather grey', only beginning to recover from his ordeal, his arms hanging rather feebly at his side, but his face, with its clipped Lawrencian beard, makes him a stronger, more masculine figure than many earlier medieval and Renaissance Christs. Leo Steinberg, of course, has shown the extent to which Christ's sexuality was by no means ignored in Renaissance art (Steinberg 1996). But in this painting, as in the fictional accounts of Christ's recovery from crucifixion, Lawrence seems to be attempting to 'remasculate' Jesus, to reverse the process of emasculation and castration deplored by Nietzsche.

Lady Chatterley's Lover too can be read, at least at one level, as a continuation of the theme of *The Escaped Cock*, although it combines a rewriting of the physical pleasures of the risen Christ with an apocalyptic vision of the re-entry into paradise. The Book of Revelation itself, of course, combines a vision of the 'cataclysmic destruction of the present world' with the coming into being of a new order, 'a new heaven and a new world' (Rev. 21: 1), a recovery of the paradise lost by the first Adam (Urang 1983: 5). Christ, as Virginia Hyde shows, is traditionally depicted as the Risen Adam, as in the central western tympanum of Strasburg Cathedral, where the 'dead Adam (a skeleton), having eaten of the tree of knowledge, lies beneath the cross, which is made from the tree of life' while Christ is depicted first harrowing hell and then ascending to heaven (Hyde 1992: 55). Lawrence, however, gives this traditional typology a Nietzschean twist, combining it with a 'version of the myth of a "fall" into self-consciousness and idealism' in which humanity loses organic relatedness to the universe (Fernihough 1993: 2). The risen Christ of whom Lawrence writes, both in *The Escaped Cock* and in *Lady Chatterley's Lover*, does not ascend into heaven but learns for the first time properly to understand the earth. In *Lady Chatterley's Lover* he can also be seen to harrow the hell of industrial England, bringing about a new earth in which the sacredness of the body will be recognised. This was the gist of Henry Miller's argument in *The World of Lawrence*, which reads the novel as

a posthumous chapter to the life of Christ, what Christ might have realized if he had had the chance to live his life as a man, if he had not castrated himself as Savior and Redeemer of mankind. Christ, if he had been allowed a cock and a pair of balls. (Miller 1985: 178)

Miller, like Lawrence, goes out of his way to shock his readers but he is right, I suggest, about the typological identity of Lady Chatterley's Lover.

This final novel of Lawrence's has an even more complex textual history than its predecessors, going through three main stages, all of which are now in print. *The First Lady Chatterley*, begun late in 1926 and completed the following March, was not published until 1944 in the United States (1972 in Britain). Shorter and less obviously a manifesto than the later versions of the novel, it still makes its religious dimension very clear, Lady Constance seeing her gamekeeper's 'white, firm, divine body' as 'a revelation' (*FLC* 27). After he has made love to her, her own body, like the heavenly chorus in the Book of Revelation, 'cried with a thousand tongues: No! No! He is unique.' He is, in her eyes a 'transfiguration. A man suffused with the brightness of God' (79). The narrative clearly satirises Christian asceticism, Lady Constance being seen to live with her husband 'like a married nun, a sister of Christ' (19) while Sir Clifford urges her to produce an heir if necessary by 'the Holy Ghost' (67). He even wants to paint her as 'a modern Madonna' (246) although she views 'a virgin birth' as 'an obscenity' (248). She continues, however, to see Parkin as a kind of Jesus, likening herself to the woman with the issue of blood in the gospels (85). She badgers her husband with biblical criticism, asking whether he thinks it right for Jesus to tell the woman taken in adultery ' "Go, and sin no more"? After all, he was only a man' (133). But the whole scandal that erupts around Parkin and his wife brings home to her how deep-rooted the 'old Mosaic fear' is, making her aware of 'the horrible power of society and of its commandments' (155). It is a fear she overcomes through meditation upon 'the mystery of the penis' as against the cross, 'the symbol of the murdered phallus' (156–7) and of an ascetic morality which, in Nietzschean terms, castrates masculinity.

Throughout the novel, in language which Lawrence shared with anthropologists of religion such as Frazer, the woods in which Lady Chatterley and her lover meet are described as 'sacred' and 'sensitive . . . filled with pure communication' (54), in contrast with the profane 'world of Wragby . . . the social world where every individual is tense, holding his own or her own against the rest' (141). The binary opposition between body and soul imported into Christianity from Greek metaphysics is also constantly undercut in a manner which anticipates Derrida's more technical deconstruction of Platonism. Sir Clifford, an avid reader not only of Plotinus but of Hegel, one of the other main privilegers of the spirit over the body in the Derridean account of western thought, hankers after the immortality of the soul, introducing much discussion of the two horses in Plato's *Phaedrus*, the white horse of the soul as opposed to the 'poor black horse of her body' (39). He is himself described as 'bodiless' (28) while he and his wife are initially likened to 'two souls free from the body' (35). It is Parkin who recovers for her a sense of the sacredness of the body, returning her to paradise and causing her to announce as she weaves flowers into his body-hair, 'We are Adam and Eve naked in the garden' (174). This apocalyptic theme of the recovery of paradise is more fully developed in the final version of the novel but it is already present in *The First Lady Chatterley*.

The second version of the novel, completed in March 1928 but not published in English until 1972 under the title *John Thomas and Lady Jane*, focuses the biblical themes more centrally upon the resurrection. It is one of the house guests introduced into this version the novel, Tommy Dukes, who first connects the importance of touch, neglected by years of Christian asceticism, with the gospel accounts of the risen Jesus: 'We've had two thousand years of *noli me tangere*. Just imagine *voli me tangere*, for a change' (*JTLJ* 66). This sparks off a long meditation by Lady Constance on the meaning of Jesus' words, which she connects, like Lawrence in his essay on 'The Risen Lord', with the suffering of men like her husband, maimed by the war, who 'had all been crucified' and were now living in 'the strange, dim, grey era of the resurrection . . . before the ascension into new life . . . They lived and walked and spoke, but theirs was still the old, tortured body that could not be touched.' Even Sir Clifford, now that 'the excitement at the rolling back of the gates of the tomb had died down in him', had relapsed into this grey 'descent into hell' (69). Tommy Dukes attacks Sir Clifford's belief in 'the immortality of the spirit' as opposed to 'the resurrection of Man, and the Sons of Man'. For him immortality consists in the ability of men to 'rise up again, with new flesh on their spirits . . . and a new fire to erect their phallus'. So far, he feels, 'we have died, and only got as far as pushing back the stones of the tomb'. His views again provoke Lady Constance to ponder what 'a man with a risen body' might be like (72). She is soon dwelling on the complaint of Swinburne against the 'pale Galilean' and pining for 'the resurrection of the body, not for ever this tomb-stricken spirit creeping about' (90).

This second version of *Lady Chatterley's Lover* was rendered even less publishable than the first by Lawrence's explicit description of Parkin's penis as it appears to Lady Constance 'like some primitive, grotesque god . . . like a mole risen from the depths of the earth. The resurrection of the flesh' (238). Like Marx's mole so celebrated by Bataille in *Visions of Excess*, where it represents the disruptive power of proletarian virility (Bataille 1985: 35), it is important that Parkin's 'mole' is working-class, oppressed for centuries but gradually emerging into freedom. When Constance finds herself in Paris, for example, she contrasts Parkin's genuine sensuality with the 'mental, spiritual lewdness' of the bourgeois males who lack 'his deep defiance' and were willing 'to have the phallus, the phallic man, despised and done to death, crucified in ignominy so that the mental-spiritual man might rise from the corpse' (*JTLJ* 282–3). The profane world, as she encounters it on holiday in Spain with her father and sister, continues to disgust her, as it does the disillusioned musician, Archie Blood, who rails against the cold-blooded modern inhabitants of Sodom and Gomorrah, among whom the Lord cannot find 'ten righteous men, . . . ten warm-blooded, hot-hearted men' (289, 293). So Lady Constance, at the end of the second version of the novel, returns to her sacred woods and her proletarian lover, one of the 'warm-blooded' workers who 'were sons and daughters of god' (294). He may be only *one* of the sons of God, nearer to the gigantic figures of Genesis 6 than the ethereal product of Greek metaphysics, but he has at least avoided emasculation.

The final version of *Lady Chatterley's Lover*, completed in January 1928 and privately published in Florence later that year, although bearing the design of a phoenix rising from the flames, the symbol of resurrection which he 'now decided to use as an emblem on the cover of each copy' (Ellis 1998: 407), places less textual emphasis on the resurrection. Lady Constance still cries out for 'the democracy of touch, the resurrection of the body' (*LCL* 78). She still pleads to be 'born again', expressing her faith in 'the resurrection of the body' (87). She still quotes Swinburne. But Mellors, as the gamekeeper is now rechristened, becomes even less like a risen Christ and more like one of the sons of God from Genesis 6, hankered after by Ursula in *The Rainbow*. When Lady Constance touches him, feeling the beauty of his buttocks and the 'strange weight of the balls', it is these 'sons of god with the daughters of men' she calls to mind (174). Foucault complains that Lawrence's subversion of Christian asceticism is too cerebral, too much in the mind. But the point of the novel, as of Lawrence's defence of it which Foucault quotes, is that such subversion requires not only sexual activity but 'the full conscious realization of sex' (Foucault 1979: 157). Both body and mind, Lawrence claims, need to be involved in this rebellion against centuries of Christian asceticism.

Lawrence certainly redeploys and subverts even more biblical quotations in this final version of the novel. When Constance needs to find a father for her child, for example, she is made to think of Jeremiah's injunction (Jer. 5: 1): 'Run ye to and fro through the streets of Jerusalem, and see now, . . . if ye can find a *man*' (*LCL* 64). Mellors now echoes the angels at Christ's birth, celebrating 'the peace on earth of her soft, quiescent body' (116), and, even more shockingly, coaxes John Thomas to request entry into Lady Jane in the language of Psalm 24: 'Lift up your heads o' ye gates, that the king of glory may come in' (210). His far-from-Pauline letter at the very end of the novel celebrates not 'the peace that passeth understanding' (Phil. 4: 7) but 'the peace that comes from fucking' (*LCL* 301). Mellors also revises the account of the descent of the spirit upon the disciples in Acts. 'The old Pentecost,' he insists, 'isn't quite right. Me and God is a bit uppish, somehow. But the little forked flame between me and you . . . That's what I abide by' (300–1). For Lawrence as for Mellors, the biblical claims are not 'quite right'; their neglect of the body needs correcting. So he literally rewrites them, aggressively reversing what he sees as unnecessarily idealistic. He even has Mellors warn Connie, in the language of Leviticus 18, with its warnings against such 'abominations' as uncovering a woman's nakedness and lying 'carnally' with her, that Sir Clifford will want to 'spew you out as the abominable thing' (302). All these biblical allusions have been seen to 'support a consistent movement in the third version from the divine to the human, from the spiritual to the carnal' (Cowan 1985: 105).

Even the sexual relations in this final version of the novel become more explicitly transgressive, the re-entry into paradise being achieved once more through the back door, through anal intercourse. That the lovers are to be seen as regenerate versions of Adam and Eve is made abundantly clear. Tommy Dukes warns Lady Constance that the real 'fall' was from a state of organic connection with the cosmos into self-consciousness:

while you *live* your life, you are in some way an organic whole with all life. But once you start the mental life, you pluck the apple. You've severed the connexion between the apple and the tree: the organic connexion. And if you've got nothing in your life *but* the mental life, then you yourself are a plucked apple . . . you've fallen off the tree. And then it is a logical necessity to be spiteful, just as it's a natural necessity for a plucked apple to go bad. (*LCL* 37)

This fall from connectedness to the tree of life is blamed upon the modern, industrial world, which Mellors attacks for placing Mammon above feeling, 'making mincemeat of the old Adam and the old Eve' (217), a reference not only to St Paul's attack on sinfulness in Romans 6: 6 but to the slang term for the penis, violently castrated by Christian asceticism (359).

The manuscript of the scene in which the lovers weave flowers round their private parts in this final version of the novel has the two lovers very consciously acting the parts of Adam and Eve, Mellors addressing Constance as Eve and labelling his land 'Paradise'. Lawrence even experimented with a dialect version of his speech before cutting it altogether (360). His intentions are made abundantly clear in 'A Propos of *Lady Chatterley's Lover*', which describes 'the meaning of the sexual act' as a return to the communion symbolised by the rivers in 'Paradise . . . , or the Park of Eden' (325). This long essay begins with an attack on the pirating of the novel, including, ironically, one edition 'bound in black and elongated to look like a bible' (305), perhaps not such a severe distortion of the novel's ambition (to replace the Bible) as it might at first appear. For the connection with *Lady Chatterley's Lover*, not always apparent in the logic of the essay, is clear in its biblical imagery, confirming that the novel, in all of its versions, is indeed about resurrection and renewal.

The essay ends with a renewed attack upon the Word or Logos as inadequate to meet the needs of the harmonious mind and body. Conventional Christian language about being 'saved . . . from sin, whatever that may be', is rejected as no longer relevant while Jesus himself is labelled one of the three most influential 'pessimists as regards life'. And yet both the novel and the essay in its defence remain extraordinarily biblical. There is a particular passage in the manuscript of the final version of the novel, omitted from the first and all subsequent editions, which shares with 'A Propos of *Lady Chatterley's Lover*' a powerful affirmation of Lawrence's continuing faith in the God who 'creates the whole universe anew every day'. While deprecating any sure 'knowledge' of 'a Jewish law-giver' or a 'Chapel-of-today God', it portrays a God remarkably similar to that of the opening chapters of Genesis:

my reason tells me there is a great creative urge, stronger even than death. And my feelings tell me there is God, who dances in the midst of space in delight, and who pauses sometimes in the vast, vast wonder of it all, [and who is sometimes angry, cheated.] And even my reason tells me that the creative urge touches me with renewal. And my feelings tell me that God is like a great laughing naked man in the park of dawn, and he looks even on my shabby appearance kindly, and encourages me, and then vanishes again from me, leaving the sea soft and silky with the early morning. . . (370–1).

Along with the rather endearing personal touches, the interest this God takes in Lawrence and his writing, He also displays many of the characteristics of *Elohim*, including pausing to admire his own work, and of *Yahweh*, including walking in the park and getting angry when cheated. Here, as elsewhere in his writing, Lawrence is not merely negative in his reworking of biblical material.

Lawrence's reworking of the Bible, as we saw in the introduction, appears in other media than writing. When he resurrected his interest in painting in Italy in 1927, for example, he turned to a number of biblical subjects, in particular that of the supposed fall. The introduction to the Mandrake edition of the paintings, reprinted in *Phoenix*, also plays with the theme of the fall, distinguishing between 'the old Adam,' which is 'our primary self', and the secondary 'self-aware-of-itself'. Like Nietzsche, Lawrence blames the Sermon on the Mount, 'a long string of utterances from the self-aware-of-itself', for much of the damage caused by the egoistic spirit, which 'cuts immediately at the wholeness of the pristine consciousness, the old Adam, and wounds it'. The spirit, or self-conscious self, 'that pale Galilean *simulacrum* of a man', attempts to instil principles of self-sacrifice, to discipline 'the Old Adam while the Old Adam is still lusty and kicking: like breaking in a bronco' (*Phoenix* 768–9). The consequences of this whole ascetic tradition, Lawrence warns, are quite literally fatal.

Many of the paintings in the original exhibition and accompanying volume develop this theme, playing variations on the biblical original. One watercolour, 'Throwing Back the Apple', depicts a Blakean God with white beard (and trousers) ducking as Adam hurls an apple at him, a somewhat plump Eve crouching in the centre of the canvas, her gaze directed away from God at Adam. Lawrence added some dialogue to this scene in a letter which describes Adam and Eve 'driving the Lord God out of Paradise' while yelling, 'Get out of here, you righteous old bird!' (*Letters* VI 190). The Adam and Eve of this painting utterly reject the guilt associated with their 'disobedience' in taking the apple and cast back at God the symbol of their supposed 'fall', the condition on which their 'innocence' was based. The fact that God wears trousers is taken by Robert Millett to suggest 'that Western civilization has even forced the concept of God to fit the mentally conceived morality' it has invented (Millett 1983: 77). Perhaps Lawrence himself drew the line at depicting a completely naked God, although Millett finds 'hints of the phallus' in the erect trees on the right and left of the painting (78). An erect penis is certainly to be seen through the rear window of the cottage in 'A Holy Family', a painting described by Catherine Carswell as rendering

the Eternal Triangle of Father, Mother and Child posed in front of their cottage crocks – that cheeky, clever little Jesus, who was going to upset everybody's applecart, that mindless, smiling big-breasted Eve, and that mustachioed Father and Husband who was so clearly the master in his own house. (Carswell 1932: 273)

This is, of course, *a* holy family, not *the* holy family but the phallus in the window presumably represents precisely what is missing from the conventional understanding of *the* holy family, in which Mary remains virginal and altogether immaculate. It should perhaps be seen as one of the stone phalluses celebrated in *Etruscan Places* (Millett 1983: 115).

Other paintings of this period which are based upon the Bible include an oil painting originally called 'Eve Regaining Paradise' before being retitled 'Flight back into Paradise', which depicts a naked woman breaking the fetters of industrial civilisation (black ropes which tie her to the dark Satanic mills in the top left-hand corner of the painting) preparatory to ducking under the flaming sword of the large, bearded, angry cherub who attempts to guard the gates of paradise. Philip Trotter emphasised the pathos of 'the poignant face, struggling form, and huddled figure of the machine-shackled Eve' (Levy 1964: 68). But Lawrence described this painting to Dorothy Brett in terms which leave no doubt that he saw Adam and Eve as successfully escaping a burning industrial world. He proceeded to describe plans for two further paintings on this theme, which would presumably have comprised a sacred triptych:

I should like to do a middle picture – inside paradise, just as she bolts in, God Almighty astonished and indignant, and the new young god, who is just having a chat with the serpent, pleasantly amused. Then the third picture, Adam and Eve under the tree of knowledge, God Almighty disappearing in a dudgeon, and the animals skipping. (*Letters* V 639)

These last two paintings, unfortunately, appear to have remained entirely in his imagination.

The biblical element is less obvious in other paintings of this period. 'North Sea', which was given to Maria Huxley and destroyed in their house fire in 1961 (*Letters* VII 370), depicts a female figure about to be embraced by a Lawrentian man. The link with Genesis is through the title, echoing Heine's poem 'Die Nordsee', which attempts to recapture 'the ancient time' when 'the Gods of heaven came down to the daughters of men and embraced the daughters of men' (Levy 1964: 33, my translation). This painting too, in other words, like *The Rainbow* and *Lady Chatterley's Lover*, celebrates the sexual union which seems so to have angered the God of Genesis 6.

The celebration of the naked body in all these paintings was designed to cause offence. Lawrence explained in a letter to Brewster in 1927 that he included a phallus 'in each one of my pictures somewhere' in order to 'shock people's castrated social spirituality', insisting that 'the phallus is a great sacred image' which 'represents a deep, deep life which has been denied in us' (Levy 1964: 68). He even added 'a black virile business' to what she thought 'a perfectly sensible phallus' in Juliette Huxley's embroidery of Adam and Eve in the same year (*Letters* VI 313). He also wrote to her in March 1927 about his painting 'Le Pisseur', which depicts 'a naked man pissing against a wall, as the Bible says' (VI 344), a reference to several synecdochic descriptions of the uncircumcised enemies of Israel in the Old Testament (cf. 1 Samuel 25: 22). For Lawrence, reacting against centuries of Judaeo-Christian guilt, not only is the male member sacred but its activity 'utterly shame-free' (Ellis 1998: 410). His art, in whatever medium, attempts to shock people into recovering a sense of the sacred and into recognising the scandalous elements to be found in their sacred stories. He recorded with a certain gleeful despair that the Exhibition at the Warren Gallery was 'black with peering parsons' before the police raided it, confiscated some of the paintings and destroyed copies of the catalogue (*Letters* VII 373, 361). Copies of *Lady Chatterley's Lover*, of course, suffered a similar fate. He may have found it easier to shock his contemporaries than to renew their sense of the sacred, a note of desperation entering into his attempts at both. But it is important to recognise the genuinely religious motivation of these late attempts to invest Christianity with a more positive attitude to the body.

CHAPTER 13

'Apocalypse': the conflict of love and power

The 'final proof of insanity', as Lawrence told the Brewsters, is 'to have a theory about the Apocalypse' (Brewster 1934: 307). With its riot of violent images and 'visceral repulsion expressed towards the bodily, the sensual and the sexual', the Book of Revelation has itself been labelled 'a sick text' with a special appeal for the psychotic (Self 1998: xii). Lawrence's *Apocalypse*, written in the last six months of his life and published posthumously, presents his own theories not just on the Book of Revelation, but on the Bible as a whole, how it should and should not be read. It is fragmentary, a number of false starts surviving as appendices to the Cambridge edition, along with a revised introduction to Carter's manuscript 'Dragon of the Apocalypse' and a review of one of the many commentaries on the Book of Revelation which he read. These fragments, however, combine with the text as first published to form a complex, sophisticated and sustained reading of what is perhaps the most difficult book in the Bible. Lawrence anticipates deconstructive modes of reading, disentangling the conflicting strands of love and power to be found in the text. His argument, however, is even more complex than this, for he detects two kinds of love and power within Revelation: a positive Nietzschean celebration (a vestige of earlier pagan layers) and a negative denial (reflecting the need of the early Church to control its growing membership).

The Book of Revelation, of course, as well as being the final book of the Bible, is about the end of the world, the final defeat of Satan and the installation of the New Jerusalem, the 'new heaven and new earth' (Rev. 21: 1). It provides, a model for our whole culture's sense of an ending, an archetypal climax to the history of the world. It has been called 'the one great poem which the first Christian age produced', containing 'a whole world of spiritual imagery to be entered into and possessed' (Farrar 1986: 6). It certainly took possession of Lawrence's imagination, providing phrases and images which have been seen to recur throughout his work. L. D. Clark identifies two particular phases of Lawrence's life when his 'apocalyptic inclinations manifested themselves most strongly': the first during the First World War, when the whole of western civilisation seemed to be coming to an end, and the second, as a result of Carter's influence, in the last seven years of his life, reaching a climax in *Apocalypse* itself (Clark 1970: 141).

Lawrence's wartime letters, as we saw in the introduction, are full of apocalyptic references to the struggle with evil which the Book of Revelation depicted as culminating in the end of the world. It was also during the war, as we saw, that he developed his interest in theosophy, being particularly impressed by James Pryse's account of the Apocalypse as a disguised esoteric initiation manual (*SM* 75). *Apocalypse* itself, however, is more than 'a close adaptation of Pryse and Blavatsky' (Tindall 1972: 156–7). Under Carter's tutelage, Lawrence had also read some of the main commentaries on the Book of Revelation produced in the 1920s, including those by the Presbyterian John Oman, the Anglican R. H. Charles and the Catholic Modernist Alfred Loisy. I will first consider these, attempting to assess both what Lawrence took from them and how his approach differed from conventional biblical critics before proceeding to discuss his debt to the theosophists. His own *Apocalypse* will be found to be as complex in its intertextuality as the book it discusses.

Oman's commentary on *The Book of Revelation* (1923) was the subject of a short review by Lawrence in which he accepted his identification of its main theme as 'the conflict between true and false religion'. This review also reveals what it was in the original text which appealed so strongly to someone of Lawrence's temperament, 'John's passionate and mystic hatred of the civilization of his day' providing 'a feeling of relief, of release into passionate actuality, after the tight pettiness of modern intellect' (*A* 41). Lawrence feels drawn, in other words, to a writer as full of mistrust for his contemporaries as he was himself. Even in this review, however, he suggests another stratum of meaning, a layer preceding that of John, in which the symbols borrowed by the prophets from earlier religions had an astrological sense, contributing to its 'inexhaustibility' of meaning (42). This review contains in outline the whole argument of *Apocalypse*, clarifying what Lawrence found attractive in both pagan and Christian layers of the Book of Revelation. Oman highlights the intertextual elements in the Apocalypse itself, the use made by John of Old Testament material, although he is at pains to insist that the result is not 'a mere mosaic of Scripture passages', since these citations are woven together 'to serve one purpose', to find expression for his own unique vision in terms of 'the accepted literary prophetic form' (Oman 1923: 110). This is an argument Lawrence finds difficult to accept; one of the radical features of his reading of the Apocalypse is his refusal to accept traditional biblical critical insistence on the final unity of the text, riddled as it is with contradictory elements which he attempts to tease out.

The most complete commentary on the Book of Revelation at that time was by R. H. Charles, Archdeacon of Westminster, published in what Lawrence, triumphantly recording its acquisition, called 'two fat volumes' in 1920 (*Letters* VII 519). Charles believed the Apocalypse to have been the product of a Palestinian Jew called John, who 'had so profound a knowledge of the Old Testament that he constantly uses its phraseology not only consciously, but even unconsciously' (Charles 1920: I xxi). The work of this 'great spiritual genius, a man of profound insight and the widest sympathies', had, according to Charles, been left incomplete, to be edited and thrown into 'hopeless mental confusion' by 'a faithful but unintelligent disciple' (xliv–l). Charles confirmed Lawrence's belief that some of the sources upon which John drew were pagan. The account of the miraculous birth and war in heaven in chapter 12, for example, 'could not have been written originally by a Christian' while the description of the scarlet woman and the kings of the earth in chapters 17 and 18, 'though recast by our author to serve his main purpose, preserve incongruous elements and traces of an earlier date' (lxii–iii). A whole section of Charles' lengthy introduction is devoted to 'Books of the Old Testament, of the Pseudepigrapha and of the New Testament Used by Our Author', bringing out the complex intertextual relationships involved (xlv–lxxxvi). As Charles explains, 'Our Seer had many sources at his disposal' but edited and adapted them for their new contexts. Such significant passages as the sealing of the 144,000 and the description of the heavenly Jerusalem may be 'constructed and re-written largely out of pre-existing material, but their meaning is in the main transformed' (cviii). Since Ephesus was 'a hot-bed of every cult and superstition', Charles argues, it is not surprising that John, who had settled there after leaving Palestine, should have incorporated elements not only from Jewish apocalyptic texts but from obscure pagan texts as well (I 48), taking the symbolism of the seven seals from Roman legal practice (I 137) and the heads of the four beasts from Babylonian sources encountered in the captivity (I 121). Charles, however, places more emphasis on the Jewish 'forerunners of our text' than on 'primitive Oriental materials' such as the four horsemen (I 156). Even the goddess crowned with the signs of the zodiac, he argues, 'must have had a Christian meaning for our author', a final meaning which supplanted all others (I 300). This was an argument Lawrence was loath to accept, preferring to emphasise the contradictions between the pagan and Jewish elements in the text.

Charles's attitude towards the body, however, would have pleased Lawrence more. In relating the Tree of Life in Revelation 22: 14 to the Tree of Knowledge in Genesis, for example, Charles comments, 'The ancients did not distinguish sharply, as we do, between the material and spiritual life' (I 268). He complains indignantly about John's unintelligent 'monkish glosser' making all the saved celibate in 14:5 (II 9–11). He points out that the 'doctrine of a bodily resurrection is consistently taught' in Jewish apocalyptic texts such as 1 Enoch (II 195), which seems to have spurred Lawrence into demanding a translation of that pseudepigraphal text from Frederick Carter. 'Some parts are rather nice', he reported, on reading Enoch for himself (*Letters* VII 599). One part of Enoch's reworking of Genesis which found its way into *Apocalypse* was a reference to the impressively sized members of 'the sons of God who came down and knew the daughters of men' (*A* 101). Charles clearly provided Lawrence not only with useful details of Jewish belief but with a general sense of the rabbis' more relaxed attitude towards the body than that of the final redactor of the Book of Revelation.

The third major scholarly commentary on the Book of Revelation which we know Lawrence read was *L'Apocalypse de Jean* by Alfred Loisy, published in Paris in 1923 and sent to him in Bandol in October 1929 (*Letters* VII 539). Loisy sees the Book of Revelation as particularly disconcerting for modern readers, revealing as it does, more faithfully than the gospels and the epistles, the seemingly violent, even fanatic origins of Christianity in Jewish apocalypse (Loisy 1923: 5, 37). Loisy, like Charles, draws on Gunkel's work on the pagan elements which had found their way into the Book of Revelation (18–19), the Chaldean and Babylonian material that surfaces in Ezekiel and Daniel respectively (39). He too discusses the importance of Jewish pseudepigrapha for the Book of Revelation, contributing to the oriental as opposed to the occidental aspects of early Christianity. He distinguishes between the Jewish base of the Book of Revelation as opposed to its Christian reclothing (50). He recognises also the difference between its portrait of Christ and that of the gospels, in particular the Galilean preacher of the synoptics (51). For Loisy, however, the main value of the Book of Revelation is historical, illustrating both the origins of Christianity in Jewish apocalypticism and the spirit of the early Christian communities of Asia Minor at the close of the first century, penetrated as it was with ideas from gnostic and other oriental pagan cults (53).

These scholarly commentaries were of great importance to Lawrence, tempering, modifying and in some respects substantiating some of the views he had inherited from esoteric writers such as Pryse and Carter. His revised introduction to Carter's 'Dragon of the Apocalypse', sent to his agent Curtis Brown in January 1930 and published as a separate essay in the *London Mercury* that July, is characteristically dismissive of the conventional reading of the Book of Revelation of the 'orthodox commentators', dismissing 'the final intentional meaning of the work', so beloved of Charles, as 'a bore', a 'stale bun . . . invented for the Aunties of this world'. But, like Derrida, he needs first to spell out this 'superficial meaning' before subjecting it to deconstruction. He accordingly provides a summary of the 'orthodox interpretation' of the book as

a prophetic vision of the martyrdom of the Christian Church, the Second Advent, the destruction of worldly power, particularly the power of the great Roman Empire, and then the institution of the Millennium, the rule of the risen Martyrs of Christendom for the space of one thousand years: after which, the end of everything, the Last Judgment, and souls in heaven; all earth, moon and sun being wiped out, all stars and all space. The New Jerusalem, and Finis! (*A* 47)

This, however, by no means exhausts its meanings, since 'the Apocalypse is a compound work', the product of 'different men, of different generations and even different centuries'. We should not therefore restrict it to 'one meaning' but acknowledge its plurality of 'meanings. Not meaning *within* meaning; but rather meaning against meaning'. The 'ultimate intentional, Christian meaning of the book', he argues, is 'only plastered over . . . like the magnificent Greek pillars plastered into the Christian Church in Sicily' (48).

Again, it is important to recognise the extent to which Lawrence's archeological metaphors, as well as reflecting the tendency of higher criticism to disintegrate biblical texts into separate layers, anticipate more recent literary critical emphasis on the fragmentary nature of all texts, their intertextual genealogy and their consequent tendency to contain contradictory elements. All this, Lawrence insists, adds to the symbolic resonance of the book, which has a much deeper meaning than the final redactor intended because it goes so far back in human experience, in this case to the Chaldeans and their 'great imaginative experience' of the universe, of God and the stars, the sun and the moon, a connection with the cosmos long since lost (53).

Lawrence is quite clear in his 'Introduction to *The Dragon of the Apocalypse*' that he no longer accepts Carter's view of the Book of Revelation as a 'disguised star-myth' but he does see grounds for finding within it 'a sort of submerged star-meaning', a vestigial trace of earlier cosmic awareness. He proceeds to acknowledge how much he owes to the biblical scholars he has been reading for helping him to escape from the 'all-too-moral chapel meaning of the book' to this 'older, more magnificent meaning'. One of 'the real joys of middle age', he claims, is 'coming back to the Bible, reading a new translation', such as James Moffatt's *New Testament* of 1913, along with 'modern research and modern criticism', from which one acquires

a whole new conception of the Scriptures altogether. Modern research has been able to put the Bible back into its living connexions, and it is splendid: no longer the Jewish-moral book and a stick to beat an immoral dog, but a fascinating account of the adventure of the Jewish – or Hebrew or Israelite nation, among the great old civilized nations of the past . . . (55)

Charles, Oman and Loisy, in other words, with their constant intertextual references, had awakened Lawrence to the complex layers of meaning embedded in the Book of Revelation. It was to them as much as to Carter that he was indebted for the ability to discover in the Apocalypse 'the ruins of an old temple incorporated in a Christian chapel' (56).

Lawrence's response to this fragmented text was itself fragmentary. He appears to have made three different attempts at starting *Apocalypse* in November 1929. The first, 'Fragment 1', begins by once more celebrating the liberating defamiliarisation brought by a new translation of the New Testament, which had enabled him to escape some of the unfortunate effects of the Authorized Version, forever associated with 'the parson's voice, and to rediscover the freshness and humanity of the original' (153). This fragment also celebrates the rich intertextuality of the Bible, of which he had only recently been made aware, claiming that the 'Bible is full of all the gods' because the Jews were in contact with so many peoples (157). Only by separating the Bible from surroundings, in fact cutting it off from 'the contact with history', had it been possible to read it as the narrow history of a chosen people rather than 'a strange and fascinating Odyssey of a whole race wandering among strange races that attracted them intensely' (158). He introduces what is perhaps the central argument of the whole book that there were two basic strands in early Christianity, 'two distinct sets of feeling, one focusing in Jesus and in the command: Love one another! – the other focusing, not in Paul or Peter or John the Beloved, but in the Apocalypse'. This 'second sort of Christianity' involved a narrow 'doctrine of the chosen people, of the elect', based upon 'everlasting hatred of worldly power', longing for 'the end of the world, and the destruction of everybody except the *Saved*'. This second, negative form of Christianity, he claims, had become dominant by the time the Book of Revelation reached its final form (154–5). Jesus, whom Lawrence labels a 'pure idealist', had underestimated the need for power in the Christian community, but others in the early church saw the new movement as 'the *new* great Power', transforming the image of Jesus himself from a teacher of tenderness to a symbol of power. The Apocalypse is seen to provide some of the strongest evidence of this later strand of Christianity, being 'a book of power-lust', paradoxically written by 'a prisoner, denied all power' (164).

Suspicions that Nietzsche lies behind Lawrence's argument at this point are confirmed by a reference to the German philosopher as having recognised love and power as 'the two divine things in life' (165). Jesus had focused solely on the former, failing to see that

Power is a definite and positive thing, an enrichening which comes to us from Rule, from a Ruler, an Almighty, a Lord of Hosts. Try to get away from it as we may, ultimately we must come back to the ancient fact that the universe, the cosmos, is swayed by a great Ruler, an Almighty. (166)

To refuse the Kosmokrator, the 'great and terrible Ruler of the cosmos, who gives forth life' and is the 'source of our strength and power and our glory', is for Lawrence to refuse life itself (166).

Religion, he appreciates, must involve both power and love, but the power in early Christianity had become perverted, turned against the glory of the cosmos. The Book of Revelation thus displays both kinds of power, the positive power of its pagan sources, with their celebration of the cosmos as 'the great Power that Is', and the negative, distorted power, evident in its 'vengeful chapters', full of resentment of the powerful and glorious (170–1).

Lawrence presents a far from flattering portrait of 'John of Patmos', a very different figure from the author of the Fourth Gospel, 'perhaps the greatest of Christian documents' written by 'one of the great religious spirits of all time'. He accepts the linguistic evidence presented by Charles that the author of the Book of Revelation '*thought* in Hebrew' but rejects the notion that he was 'a rustic old Rabbinical Jew who emigrated late from Galilee', insisting that the Apocalypse was 'a sophisticated work if ever there was one' (173). Its opening 'messages' to the seven churches in Asia, a set of promised rewards which culminate in the promise 'to him that overcometh' to share the very throne of God (Rev. 3: 21) seem to Lawrence more pagan than Christian, reflecting the mysteries of communion mediator-gods such as Isis, with whom an initiate might expect to sit down, rather than Judaeo-Christian awe before Almighty God. 'Fragment 1' accepts that it is impossible fully to recover or reconstruct the pagan elements hidden in the text, partly because the manuscript had been 'tampered with' and 'messed about' and partly because John of Patmos had encoded its secret meanings too cleverly, had 'tied the knots too tight'. Lawrence expresses confidence, however, about two things: the gulf between the Jesus of Revelation and the Jesus of the Gospels and the need to regain contact with the cosmos. 'The way of Jesus is good, but we want a greater way, a more ample contact' (*A* 175–6). This fragment breaks off at the point where it begins to elaborate on the differences between the Jesus of Revelation and the Jesus of the Gospels. But it is clear that Lawrence's main aim is to rescue the positive side, the pagan traces, of the worship of power to be found in the Apocalypse while continuing to deplore its negative, distorted, life-denying power exercised by the early Church.

'Fragment 2' begins by attempting to define what was new in Christianity, the 'tenderness of Paul in some of the Epistles' exempli-fying 'a new human relationship' it had brought into the world, 'a new sort of love' without desire (177). Lawrence presents Christianity as having broken with paganism first (on the positive side) in 'the intense feeling of community' which it inspired in the early churches but also (less fortunately) in loosening the connection celebrated by earlier religions between man and the cosmos (178). He draws a rather Renanian picture of Jesus in Galilee, mixing freely and happily with Greeks and other pagans before his encounter with the dangerously fanatical Jews in Jerusalem. The Galilean Jesus, according to Lawrence, would have been familiar with pagan religion, appreciating the 'charm' of its temples, 'sensitively aware' of its rites and culture. He would therefore, the argument goes, have imbibed at least some of the spirit of 'the ancient star-lore, and the ancient symbols' of the Babylonians and Chaldeans whose beliefs still lingered in 'the Jewish consciousness', even if the stars had been turned into archangels (179–80). Lawrence here brings the scholarly intertextuality to be found in Charles and the other commentaries to imaginative life, arguing that the ancient connection with the cosmos had not been entirely lost but was imprinted or inscribed in the consciousness of Christ himself.

This fragment of *Apocalypse* also reworks the theosophical narratives Lawrence had found in Blavatsky, Pryse and Carter about a 'fall into knowledge, or self-awareness' and out of cosmic connection, finding vestiges of the ancient wisdom in Hebrew prophets such as Ezekiel and other Jewish 'dreamers' bold enough to venture beyond the Mosaic law (among whom he numbers Jesus). St Paul and the Apostle John, he argues, were also open to these mysteries, but the early fathers responsible for the formation of the canon and the development of orthodox Christian theology, who were 'good suppressors', had attempted to rid Christianity of all these alien, pagan elements: its star-lore, its blood-rites, its power-cults, its visions and symbols. It is particularly ironic, therefore, that 'having cast out the old pagan and starry devil bit by bit, they let him in whole again at the very last minute, and there he is, the old demon, sitting at the very end of the Bible, in the Apocalypse' (183–4).

This second frament again challenges Charles' view that the author of the Book of Revelation was a Galilean Jew, 'rustic and unlettered, arriving from the country in the city of Greeks when he was already old'. John of Patmos, for Lawrence, was 'a city Jew who had spent most of his years in reading "religion" and discussing it', developing a deep interest in pagan cults, 'the mysteries and the symbolic ritual' and even 'the many forms of sorcery extant in the pagan world of Ephesus' (184–5). He displays little of the new Christian spirit of love, his cosmic Lamb combining Jewish expectations of the Messiah, 'that strange semi-magical figure of the Jewish imagination,' with esoteric mystery religions. Whereas John's Gospel had presented a Jesus who abjures secrecy, speaking 'openly to the world . . . in the synagogue, and in the temple' (John 18: 20), the Book of Revelation, in spite of the bowdlerising work of its Christian editors, remained 'an esoteric work', advocating 'a secret "plan" of regeneration' and describing 'the processes of initiation into a higher form of life', culminating in 'the "re-birth" of the spirit through fusion with the Saviour' (185–6). Lawrence specifically rejects Charles's hypothesis of an unknown editor causing the textual confusion at the beginning and end of the text, but displays a fairly sophisticated awareness of the complex processes by which the final form of New Testament texts was reached.

'Fragment 2', like its predecessor, rejects the reading of the Book of Revelation favoured by 'orthodox critics' as 'historical-prophecy' of the kind to be found in earlier apocalyptic such as the Book of Daniel (187). For Lawrence, as for Pryse, the seven seals represent a symbolic description of the seven levels of being of 'the natural man' progressively conquered by the 'higher consciousness or spirit' while the 'new Jerusalem, esoterically, is the new body of a re-born man' as well as 'the new body of the community, the Church of Christ' (188–9). Lawrence links the esoteric teaching to be found within the Book of Revelation with ancient Greek philosophy, proceeding to contrast 'two ways of knowing the universe: religious and scientific'. The former he calls synthetic, 'a process of association . . . referring back towards a centre and a wholeness', the latter analytic, distancing itself from its object in order more clearly to apply 'logical reason' upon it. He cites two passages from the Bible as examples of synthetic or religious consciousness, the opening verse of Psalm 90, 'Lord, thou hast been our dwelling place in all generations', and the description in Psalm 19 of the sun as 'a bridegroom coming out of his chamber' (19: 5). To compare the sun rising to a bridegroom coming forth from his chamber may not make sense scientifically, according to our present knowledge of the movement of the planets, but it has an emotional truth, corresponding to our feelings about both events. There are thus 'two forms of truth', two ways of consciousness, both of which should be acknowledged. This fragment is probably trying to do too many things at once: to provide a reading of the Book of Revelation *and* to develop a general argument about the kind of religion, submerged in that text, which Lawrence would like the modern world to rediscover. His failure to clarify his own aims may well have contributed to his inability to complete these early fragments, but his wrestling with Revelation remains full of interest not least for the manner in which it reveals him attempting to forge a fruitful way in which to continue to read the Bible.

'Apocalypsis II', the third of the fragments of *Apocalypse* dating from November 1929, begins at the point where 'Fragment II' left off, with the difficulties currently experienced in reading the Bible:

The Psalms are really antipathetic to the modern mind, because the modern mind is so abstracted and logical, it cannot bear the non-logical imagery of the Hebrew hymns, the sort of confusion, the never going straight ahead. But there *was* no straight ahead to the ancient mind. An image, an emotional conception completed itself, then gave place to another, and sometimes even the emotional sequence is puzzling, because the images started different trains of feeling then, from those they start now. (195)

The connection, in other words, is emotional and poetic rather than logical or scientific. Lawrence gives a lengthy account, derived from Burnet's *Early Greek Philosophy*, of the growth of logic among the ancient Greeks and their consequent loss of 'immediate connection with the cosmos' (196). The abstract notion of God as 'Supreme Mind' or 'Logos' brought a triumph of spirit over matter represented symbolically by Jesus (198). This triumph presents itself as progress but had merely substituted a theological 'conception' of God for a 'real' sense of the cosmos, leaving 'poor modern man, with his worship of his own god, which is his own mind glorified, . . . permanently out of touch' (200). The link with the later fiction, in particular *The Escaped Cock* and *Lady Chatterley's Lover*, is evident here. Lawrence sees the theological conception of Christ provided by the Book of Revelation as replacing the 'real' Jesus of tenderness and connectedness to the cosmos. John of Patmos becomes for Lawrence 'a death-bringer and a true enemy of man', not only attempting to dominate the Cosmos by Mind but to bring about the end of the whole material world (200).

The final version of *Apocalypse*, typed at the turn of the year, begins where the previous fragment had ended, deploring the inability of the 'modern mind' to read the Bible. 'On the whole,' Lawrence claims, 'the modern mind dislikes mystification, and of all the books in the Bible, it finds Revelation perhaps the least attractive' (59). Since so many of its own products are, in fact, exhausted in one reading, the modern mind tends to think every book is the same, 'finished in one reading' (59–60). Lawrence confesses himself to disliking some of the 'splendiferous' and unnatural imagery of the Book of Revelation, much of which is 'utterly unpoetic and arbitrary, some of it really ugly, like all the wadings in blood', while 'such phrases as "the wrath of the Lamb" are on the face of them ridiculous'. Such language, and the emotions it embodied, were for him redolent of gas-lit chapel evenings, the product of 'popular' as opposed to 'thoughtful religion', appealing to the desire of the 'uneducated' to bring down the rich and powerful of this world (61–3).

This final version of *Apocalypse* also develops the distinction made in its earlier fragments between 'the Christianity of tenderness' preached by Jesus and 'the Christianity of self-glorification' embodied in the Book of Revelation. Lawrence notes the Nietzschean paradox that the 'religion of the strong taught renunciation and love' while 'the religion of the weak' focused on power and glory. The Apocalypse, he claims, provides the 'grand biblical authority' for this cry of the 'weak and pseudo-humble' who want 'to wipe all worldly power, glory and riches off the face of the earth'. Again, Nietzsche is the clear model for Lawrence's complaint about the superseding of Christ's original teaching by that of his supposed followers, with their hatred for 'all strong, free life' (65). The Apocalypse, he complains, embodies a Christianity 'which has none of the real Christ, none of the real Gospel, none of the *creative* breath of Christianity', appealing to 'second-rate minds in every country and every century' (66). Nietzsche too is evident in Lawrence's claim that the Book of Revelation 'is the revelation of the undying will-to-power in man'. Again, as in the fragmentary versions of *Apocalypse*, the power-spirit, the 'grand enemy' of the religion preached by Jesus, is seen to have enthroned itself in the final book of the Bible (67).

In order to make its Nietzschean point about power being the 'real' subject of the Book of Revelation, *Apocalypse* produces parodies of the gospels, rewriting Christ's promise of Matthew 18: 20, 'As soon as two or three men come together, . . . then power comes into being' (68) and claiming that the Book of Revelation gave 'the death-kiss to the Gospels' as effectively as Judas himself (69). The problem with the kind of power too often preached in the Apocalypse, Lawrence again argues, is that it is a distorted, negative kind, 'a grim determination to destroy all mastery, all lordship, and all human splendour out of the world, leaving only the community of saints as the final negation of power, and the final power' (70). The Christianity of the Church (as opposed to that of its founder) continued to wield this negative 'power of mediocrity', attempting to control all spontaneity and desire with negative commandments, its 'perpetual mean thou-shalt-not' (72). The Book of Revelation displays too much of this distorted, negative, life-denying power, 'the dangerous snarl of the *frustrated, suppressed*, collective self' as it tries to control 'the true and positive Power-spirit' (73).

The final text of *Apocalypse* repeats the complaint that there are two Jesuses portrayed in the New Testament. The opening vision of the Book of Revelation, 'with the sword of the Logos issuing from his mouth and the seven stars in his hand', is clearly different from the Jesus of Mark 14: 34, 'sad even unto death' in the garden of Gethsemane. The Jesus of the Apocalypse 'is the great Splendid One, almost identical with the Almighty in the visions of Ezekiel and Daniel . . . the source of life itself, the dazzler, before whom we fall as if dead' (74). This Jesus knows neither humility nor suffering, embodying 'man's *other* conception of God' (75). 'It' (even beyond gender) remains for Lawrence as a vestige of an earlier pagan consciousness of the power of the cosmos, going back to 'the centuries before Ezekiel and John' when 'the sun was still a magnificent reality' from which men drew 'strength and splendour' (76). By the time of John of Patmos, however, 'men, especially educated men, had already almost lost the cosmos', treating the world as a prison from which Christians attempted to escape 'by denying the body altogether' (78). The Apocalypse nevertheless gives us 'flashes' of such cosmic consciousness, buried as they are beneath the more orthodox Christian hatred of the world (79).

The final version of *Apocalypse* also contains a variation on the archeological metaphor used to describe the different layers within the text of the Book of Revelation:

It is one book, in several layers: like layers of civilisation as you dig deeper and deeper to excavate an old city. Down at the bottom is a pagan substratum, probably one of the ancient books of the Aegean civilisation: some sort of a book of a pagan Mystery. This has been written over by

Jewish apocalyptists, then extended, and then finally written over by the Jewish–Christian apocalyptist John: and then, after his day, expurgated and corrected and pruned down and added to by Christian editors who wanted to make of it a Christian work. (81)

John of Patmos, like his text, is also described as a strange inter-textual construct, 'full of the Hebrew books of the Old Testament, but also full of all kinds of pagan knowledge', 'pagan vestiges' that fascinate Lawrence (81–2). He repeats his general argument that to recognise these traces of other cultures is to read the Bible more broadly as 'a book of the human race, instead of a corked up bottle of "inspiration"' (82–3). Christian critics who are frightened that once they 'start admitting that *anything* in the Bible is of pagan origin and meaning . . . God escapes out of the bottle once and for all' (84–5), produce only 'pettifogging work', attempting to 'cover up the pagan traces' (86).

Lawrence proceeds to celebrate the genuinely if differently reli-gious basis of the civilisations that preceded the period when the Bible was written, arguing as in 'Apocalypsis II' that the Psalms provided examples of the thinking in images and sensual awareness characteristic of those earlier cultures (91). He derives from Burnet and Murray a sense of the divinity of matter still evident in the pre-Socratic Greeks but lost in the dualistic division of matter from spirit (95–6). He finds evidence of a similar 'fall' from symbolic to allegorical thought, from the free 'flitting from image to image' characteristic of the Psalms to the carefully constructed patterns of the Apocalypse, within the Bible itself. Nevertheless, because it retained some of the ancient pagan symbols, even the Book of Revelation 'had difficulty getting into the Bible at all' without being mutilated, having the noses and hands knocked off its mythical beasts 'in Cromwellian fashion' (96–7). Hence the anomaly of John's Lamb, related to the somewhat grander creatures who were the subject of Mithraic sacrifice, such as lions and bulls, but scaled down in accordance with tamer Christian allegory, being expected to display curiously unlamblike 'wrath' (99, 105).

Among the 'obviously pagan' symbols Lawrence celebrates are the four horses and their riders whose meaning could not be precisely fixed, as in the more boring forms of allegory, but meant something different to everybody:

Far back, far back in our dark soul the horse prances. He is a dominant symbol; he gives us lordship: he links us, the first palpable and throbbing link with the ruddy-glowing Almighty of potency: he is the beginning even of our godhead in the flesh. (101)

The seven seals are again seen to represent the seven centres of the body, the seven spheres of consciousness to be conquered by the initiate in ancient esoteric lore, which Lawrence tries to imagine, reconstructing a ceremony with 'the pagan initiate, perhaps in a temple of Cybele, suddenly brought forth from the under-dark of the temple into the grand blaze of light in front of the pillars', with flutes, dancing women, hymns and a breathless crowd (106–7). This part of *Apocalypse*, bringing esoteric theories to imaginative life, echoes the ceremonies described in *The Plumed Serpent*, although critics could argue that it is equally fictitious.

The symbols in the second half of the Book of Revelation, seven angels with seven trumpets and so on, interest Lawrence less than the vestiges of pagan ritual he claims to have identified. He becomes quite flippant about various apocalyptists adding their own details, 'brimstone horses' and different coloured breastplates after their own 'gay fancy', tacking on serpent tails to the horses and letting them gallop. He is unimpressed too by the lakes of fire, the stock-in-trade of all 'Patmossers' who 'could not be happy in heaven unless they *knew* their enemies were unhappy in hell' (112). His excitement resumes, however, when he comes to the symbolism of chapter twelve, 'the pivot of the apocalypse' (119). The goddess there described, 'this wonder-woman clothed in the sun and standing upon the crescent of the moon' is, for Lawrence, 'splendidly suggestive of the great goddess of the east, the great Mother, the Magna Mater', who looms 'far back in history in the eastern Mediterranean', although how she came 'to tower as the central figure in a Jewish Apocalypse' continues to baffle him, since the Jews generally and the late apocalyptists in particular were 'more at their ease cursing her and calling her a harlot', as they do in chapter 17. Nevertheless, Lawrence acknowledges the fact that she has 'brought into the Bible what it lacked before', an element of splendour and beauty, 'a great queen and queen-mother' before whom to worship (120).

Chapter twelve provides evidence for Lawrence of the ancient 'pagan bed-rock' upon which Jewish and Christian apocalyptists had built, changing the worship to condemnation, cursing 'the harlot . . . with her golden cup of the wine of sensual pleasure in her hand', resenting her splendour while all the time longing to drink from her cup (121). The Dragon too, as celebrated by Carter, 'is one of the oldest symbols of the human consciousness', representing the 'fluid, rapid, startling movement of life . . . which runs through us like a serpent', producing sudden depths of feeling, of desire, of anger, even the kind of 'violent hunger' which 'made Esau sell his birthright', uncontrollable, beyond the limits of our normal selves (123). Like Carter, Pryse and Blavatsky, Lawrence separates the good dragon, symbolically represented by the brazen serpent lifted by Moses in the wilderness, from the bad dragon, the serpent of the Garden of Eden. In his 'good aspect, the dragon is the great vivifier', the source of life, the redeemer, as when Christ too 'was "lifted up" for the redemption of men' (125). For Lawrence it is the Logos which is now the evil snake, threatening to destroy the primal energies waiting coiled like a serpent to be released (125–6). He gives yet another version of the theosophical version of the 'fall' into self-consciousness, the loss of primal innocence, when men and women lived 'in naked contact with the cosmos', when the 'flesh of man' was not separated from his spirit, before 'he ate of the Tree of Knowledge instead of the Tree of Life, and knew himself *apart* and separate' (131). He also finds in Genesis and Ezekiel, with its 'four great creatures amid the wheels of the revolving heavens', later taken as symbolic of the four evangelists, symbols from an ancient wisdom still not entirely forgotten by the time of the Book of Revelation. Some of the number symbolism of the Apocalypse is also presented as a survival from earlier occult wisdom.

Most of this ancient wisdom, however, Lawrence laments, has been edited out of the second half of the Book of Revelation, leaving only the 'moral angels and moral devils' by whom 'we are acutely bored', the orthodox concepts of sin and salvation, and only 'a hint of the old cosmic wonder'. The 'poor dragon henceforth cuts a sorry figure', disappearing with all the other positive things in life into the burning lake. Even in the account of the final downfall of Rome 'the best poetry is all the time lifted from Jeremiah or Ezekiel or Isaiah' (143). He has little time for the saints in their 'new white garments', all 'white and clean' (Rev. 19: 14). Their 'priggish rule' represents the final triumph of the 'middling masses'. 'How beastly their new Jerusalem', he laments, 'How terribly bourgeois to have unfading flowers' (*A* 144). This final part of the Book of Revelation, for Lawrence, displays an entirely negative spirit, a hostility to life and to the cosmos, frantically destroying the beauty of the world and all people who are not 'sealed'. Lawrence, by contrast, ends his own *Apocalypse* with a vision of what life should be, celebrating 'the marvel of being alive in the flesh . . . and part of the living, incarnate cosmos' (149).

Apocalypse remains a fragmentary and incomplete text, like the biblical original upon which it is such an astonishing commentary. As with the Book of Revelation, the sources upon which he draws are at times all-too evident. This part, we can say, comes from Carter, this from Pryse, this from Charles. And yet it is a deeply personal work, drawing upon Lawrence's own religious development from the chapel evenings of his childhood through the reading of his later years. As with John of Patmos, it can be claimed that Lawrence wove his disparate sources into a sometimes esoteric but often powerful reading of what all critics have recognised to be a complex, many-layered text. *Apocalypse* demonstrates, perhaps more than any other of Lawrence's works, the complexity of the intertextual process too simply described as reading and writing. He brings to an already difficult text a range of mediating theories, disentangling its conflicting strands of love and power. In the process he not only argues but demonstrates that to read the Bible fully requires not the one-dimensional passivity thrust upon him in childhood, but a critical engagement involving all the knowledge and imaginative insight it had taken a lifetime to acquire.

'Last Poems': final thoughts

Lawrence's last years at Bandol from November 1928 onwards saw a regeneration of his interest in poetry which was to result in four volumes of verse: *Pansies* (1929), *Nettles* (1930), *More Pansies* and *Last Poems*, the last two edited from his notebooks by Richard Aldington in 1932. The word 'pansies', as Lawrence explains in his introduction to the volume, derives (in Derridean fashion) from a conflation of the French for to think (*penser*) and to soothe (*panser*) (*CP* 417). Sandra Gilbert, acknowledging their spontaneous, deliberately rough and fragmentary quality, calls them 'inspired graffiti' (Gilbert 1990: 259). *Nettles* are particularly slight, provocative little stings at bourgeois convention, while *More Pansies* bridge the gap between 'the slangy doggerel of *Pansies* and the more serious music of *Last Poems*' (266). It is undoubtedly on this last volume that the strongest claims for Lawrence as a serious religious poet rest. James Wood, who labels Lawrence 'one of the century's greatest religious writers', clearly has this volume in mind when he discusses poems 'about flowers or animals or people . . . about the need to die into a new life', in all of which Lawrence is 'a mystic literalist . . . always a poet and always a preacher at the same time' (Wood 1999: 122). *Last Poems* in many ways rounds off Lawrence's revisionary reworking of the Bible, continuing 'the process of revising, reinterpreting, and revaluing Scripture' (Lockwood 1987: 172). After briefly noting some of the biblical echoes to be found in the earlier volumes, I will focus on some of these *Last Poems*, which represent Lawrence's final thoughts about life as he faced imminent death. I will then offer some final thoughts of my own, a few tentative conclusions about Lawrence's reworking of the Bible throughout his career.

Pansies continues Lawrence's battle with the Bible, the introduction playfully (if not very subtly) experimenting with the substitution of the word 'arse' for the word 'Word' at the beginning of John's Gospel

(*CP* 418). This is not the dominant tone of the volume, however. Lawrence remains open to the divine, he insists in 'Give us Gods', 'But not gods grey-bearded and dictatorial, / nor yet that pale young man afraid of fatherhood . . . Thou shalt have other gods before these' (437). He is still, the first version of this poem assures us, 'a religious soul'; he believes that 'the Father of all things swims in the vast dusk of all the atoms' (950). But he resolves, in an image from *Apocalypse* combined with a version of Christ's warning not to put 'new wine into old bottles' (Matt. 9: 17), 'to drink life direct / from the source, not out of bottles and bottled personal vessels'. He wants 'What the old people call immediate contact with God' (*CP* 481). In spite of once more abjuring Jesus, claiming 'We have worn out the gods', especially 'That pale one, filled with renunciation and pain' (439), Lawrence perpetually quotes or echoes him. 'Let the dead go bury their dead', he insists (440, cf. Matt. 8: 22), also quoting, 'Give, and it shall be given unto you' (449, cf. Luke 6: 38). 'The Risen Lord' celebrates a resurrection not confined to the spirit but clamouring 'forth from the flesh' (461). 'What was lost is found', he asserts after the manner of the father of the prodigal son (461, cf. Luke 15: 24). 'If he is not with me but against me', he warns (468, cf. Matt. 12: 30) he is indeed 'My Enemy'. He entitles another poem 'Noli Me Tangere' while 'The Root of All Evil' imagines Jesus taking a different line from that recorded in the gospels, not 'Get thou behind me, Satan!' (cf. Matt. 16: 23) but 'Come, Satan, don't go dodging behind my back any longer.' Jesus, according to Lawrence, was 'frightened to look round', scared of seeing what was in the world (*CP* 483). If, as Lawrence claims in 'Dies Irae', 'our word is dead,' it is also true that 'we know not how to live wordless' (510). *Pansies* provides yet more evidence of Lawrence attempting to go beyond Christianity by means of its own scriptures, which are cited in new contexts in ways which generate new meanings.

More Pansies continues to employ the throw-away manner of *Pansies*. In 'Moral Clothing', stripping himself of all pretence, Lawrence even plays with the words of God to Moses: 'I am that I am' (608, cf. Exod. 3: 14). He continues his reform of the Church, advocating for priests not only marriage but magenta (609). His attempt to 'put forth new roots / into the unknown' (610) involves a 'resurrection into touch' (611), rejecting the concept of salvation (613), pronouncing sin 'obsolete' (618), redefining the Holy Ghost as 'the deepest part of our own consciousness' (621) and calling the gods 'nameless and imageless' (650). The 'truth of yesterday,' he insists, 'becomes a lie tomorrow' (661). Nevertheless, he is soon driven back to dialogue with the Bible and with Jesus in particular. 'Dark Satanic Mills' again (via Blake) questions Christ's injunction 'Retro me, Satanas!', which simply allowed evil to take place 'behind your back'. 'What is man,' asks Lawrence after the psalmist, 'that thou art no longer mindful of him? / and the son of man, that thou pitiest him not?' (629, cf. Psalm 8: 4). He disputes St Paul on the significance of the cross, upholding the division of human beings into male and female, 'slave and freeman' (636, cf. 1 Cor. 12: 13). Jesus's words provide the titles of three poems: 'But I say unto you: love one another', 'Love They Neighbour' and 'As Thyself' (644–5). Another, a two-line proverb in the manner of Blake ('And whover forces himself to love anybody / begets a murderer in his own body') is called 'Retort to Jesus'. 'Commandments' argues that the imperative to love produces only 'faked love' (653–4). Lawrence continues to 'lift up mine eyes unto the hills' (660, cf. Psalm 121: 1) and begins another poem with the poetically unpromising line from Hebrews 9: 22, 'Without shedding of blood there is no remission of sin' (678). 'Let There be Light' returns to Genesis, while the final poem in the collection is a prayer which draws its images from the Book of Revelation: 'Give me the moon at my feet / Put my feet upon the crescent, like a Lord!' (684, cf. Rev. 12: 1). The constant resort to Scripture, the compulsion to continue the argument with Jesus and Paul, as in some of his less convincing prose, appears at times a habitual reflex. Lawrence seems to be turning to the Bible quite literally for inspiration, almost for a prompt, a trigger to set his own imagination in motion.

In *Last Poems*, however, the engagement with the Bible is integrated into a more sustained meditation on what Christian tradition labels the 'four last things': death, judgment, heaven and hell. Lawrence, of course, does not understand these terms conventionally but, faced with his own imminent death, attempts to clarify what he still believes. Janik argues that the volume should be read 'as if it were a single long poem' dealing with the key issues of God, the nature of evil, death and what follows death (Janik 1974–5: 739–40). One of the first poems, 'Demiurge', insists that 'Religion knows better than philosophy', which always privileges the spirit above the body, believing 'pure being' to be 'bodiless'. Religion, in contrast, stresses the importance of (the) incarnation:

> Religion knows that Jesus was never Jesus
> till he was born from a womb, and ate soup and bread
> and grew up, and became, in the wonder of creation, Jesus,
> with a body and with needs, and a lovely spirit.   (*CP* 689)

Lawrence, as we saw in the introduction, dwells on the physical side of 'The Work of Creation', calling God 'a great urge, wonderful, mysterious, magnificent', which necessarily 'takes shape in the flesh' (690). He cannot imagine 'the Most High' having a clear idea of what he wanted to produce, thinking 'in the abstract . . . "Now there shall be tum-tiddly-um" '; instead he pictures 'God sighing and yearning with tremendous creative yearning' before suddenly a thing of beauty such as a red geranium appeared (690–1). 'The Body of God' also dramatises the way God 'urges towards incarnation':

> There is no god
> apart from poppies and the flying fish,
> men singing songs, and women brushing their hair in the sun.
> The lovely things are god that has come to pass, like Jesus came.
>
> (691)

Lawrence continues to mock Greek metaphysical theology, as in 'The Man of Tyre' who 'went down to the sea / pondering, for he was Greek, that God is one and all alone and ever more shall be so' (692). His own God is not to be captured in creeds or concepts but to be found in his creation, in whales for example, though 'he is also love, but without words' (695).

Phrases from the Scriptures crop up throughout this final volume, sometimes in titles such as 'The Breath of Life' (Gen. 2: 7) and 'The Hands of God', which opens with a verse from Hebrews (10: 31): 'It is a fearful thing to fall into the hands of the living God' before countering that 'it is a much more fearful thing to fall out of them' and pleading never to fall 'into the ungodly knowledge / of myself as I am without God' (*CP* 699). Fragments of the psalms also find their way into many of these poems, for example 'Silence', which breaks into Psalm 24: 7: 'Lift up your heads, O ye gates!', and 'Pax', which demands not to be a doorkeeper but 'a creature in the house of the God of Life' (700, cf. Psalm 84: 10). 'Lord's Prayer' has been called 'Lawrence's ultimate piece of biblical rewriting' (Lockwood 1987: 174), reworking Jesus' words to leave God 'nameless' and to claim for his creatures some of his power and glory (*CP* 704). The poems also play less seriously with the sacred text, as in 'The Four' whom 'we have always with us' (cf. Matt. 26: 11). A number of poems rewrite the time 'When Satan Fell' (710) while 'The Ship of Death', perhaps the most powerful poem in the whole volume, provides a final reworking of the fall of man.

'The Ship of Death' is set in autumn with apples falling and its persona too seeking to 'find an exit / from the fallen self'. The smell of death is quite literally in the air as he contemplates both their decay and that of his own 'bruised body' and 'frightened soul' (716–17). He combines the traditional Christian image of 'the ark of faith' with more pagan burial practices (possibly Etruscan) involving a 'little ark' furnished with food, cakes and wine 'for the dark flight down oblivion'. He can assert no confident belief in heaven:

> There is no port, there is nowhere to go
> only the deepening black darkening still
> blacker. . . utterly dark.   (718–9)

All that remains of the pillar of fire which guided the Israelites through the desert is 'a horizontal thread / that fumes a little with pallor upon the dark' and the onset of dawn, which brings 'a flush of rose'. And yet, in the final section of the poem, the body emerges from its immersion in water 'strange and lovely' while 'the frail soul steps out, into her house again / filling the heart with peace' (719–20). It would be wrong to read too firm a belief in rebirth or reincarnation into these images. But they do suggest at least some faith in the continuing cycle of existence, a faith which necessarily finds expression in the familiar symbols of the Judaeo-Christian tradition.

The final poems in this volume continue to seek some kind of new 'beginning' in his 'end' (724). In 'Forget' he enters 'the sleep of God', believing that

> To be able to forget is to be able to yield
> to God who dwells in deep oblivion.
> Only in sheer oblivion are we with God.
> For when we know in full, we have left off knowing. (725)

Paul's words to the Corinthians (1 Cor. 13: 12) here combine with an apophatic or negative theology, a theology fully aware of the severe limits of its own knowledge. In 'Shadows' he waits to be 'dipped again in God, and new-created', for it is in death, he believes, that

> I am in the hands [of] the unknown God,
> he is breaking me down to his own oblivion
> to send me forth on a new morning, a new man. (*CP* 727)

God remains 'unknown', his ways mysterious and unfathomable, but there is still some faith and hope in a future life, not in individual immortality so much as the continuation of life in general, reflected in the final poem, 'Phoenix'.

These are perhaps his most powerful, certainly his most religious poems, displaying a confident faith which is still not orthodox, still refuses to take the products of Greek metaphysics that seriously, but which demonstrates the extent to which the texts (and even some of the beliefs) instilled into him as a boy remained with him until the end of his life. Lawrence continues to grapple with the Bible, to wrestle with this material, never content simply and uncritically to accept it. Properly to read the Bible, as he illustrates, is to engage with it at the deepest level, entering into it imaginatively and reproducing its living meaning in the current context, the time of reading. Here, at the point of death, Lawrence turns once more to the Bible and finds that it continues to provide comfort, to soothe as well as to make him think, to give meaning both to his life and to his death.

It is difficult, after following the long, labyrinthine trail of Lawrence's constant reworking of Scripture, to come to clear, unambiguous conclusions about its overall significance. His own feelings about the Bible, from the time of his rejection of Congrega-tional orthodoxy until his death, remained ambivalent, a complex mixture of love and hatred, acceptance and rejection. Many of his readers, I suggest, retain a similar mixture, wherever precisely they locate themselves in the broad spectrum from committed belief to outright denial. Few of them, at the end of the twentieth century, possess such a profound and detailed knowledge of the Bible, and perhaps it is the loss of knowledge of the Bible along with a decline in the kind of religious intensity characteristic of Lawrence that lies at least in part behind the apparent decline in his standing over the last few decades. He continues, of course, to be read and to be studied widely. But he is not accorded quite the same reverence as he was in the 1960s. Bishops no longer queue to praise his recognition of the sanctity of sexual relations while a new generation of students, differently 'liberated' from the constraints of earlier generations, find it hard to understand what the 'fuss' was all about, why his books were ever banned or his publishers prosecuted.

It is nevertheless an education in itself to engage in reading Lawrence's struggle both with the Bible and with the whole critical tradition that surrounds it, from the higher criticism which was the subject of my third chapter through a range of intermediate writers such as Renan and Nietzsche, Frazer and Blavatsky, whose contribution to Lawrence's reading and rewriting of the Bible I have attempted to trace. His work, I would argue, remains a monument not only to the particular biblical tradition in which he was brought up, but also to the philosophical and literary traditions in which he educated himself. Nor is it simply a 'dead' monument, of merely historical interest, a record of how people used to think about the Bible in the years of modernist rebellion against tradition. I have repeatedly remarked throughout Lawrence's work a number of ways in which he anticipates our own belated postmodern condition, more distantly and detachedly but still significantly related to the Judaeo-Christian tradition. Lawrence, I have suggested, sometimes anticipates the deconstructive reading of biblical texts usually associated with later thinkers such as Derrida, with whom he shares a peculiarly ambivalent relation to the Judaeo-Christian tradition, a complex position both within and beyond it, retaining a 'faith' (necessarily bounded by scare quotes, maintained only under erasure) which is more provisional and tentative than orthodoxy but nonetheless recognisably related to it.

In Lawrence's work, I want to claim, the Bible continues to live, to generate meaning and to stimulate thought on the 'big' questions of religion which it addresses, questions of life and death, ethics in its broadest sense, ways of relating to the 'other' in nature, in other people and even beyond the natural, in areas which we call sacred, which are never fully grasped by the limited economies of explanation characteristic of modernity. Occasionally, as we have seen, Lawrence appears to present his work as a 'counter-Bible', a supplanting rather than a mere supplement or commentary upon the original. It is often deeply critical of elements within the Bible, especially its logocentrism, its white mythology, its importing from Greek metaphysics a spirituality which threatens to overwhelm the body. Throughout his work, however, Lawrence engages in creative dialogue with the Bible in a manner which recognises both its power and its importance, its continuing capacity to give life meaning and purpose. The Bible can legitimately be called the genesis of his fiction, its most significant precursor text; it not only generates a great deal of his own writing but provides the most important context for its understanding.

References

Abrams, M. H. (1971) *Natural Supernaturalism*, New York: Norton.
Abrams, M. H. ed. (1988) *A Glossary of Literary Terms*, 5th ed., New York: Rinehart and Winston.
Aldington, Richard (1950) *Portrait of a Genius, But ...*, London: Heinemann.
Alldritt, Keith (1971) *The Visual Imagination of D. H. Lawrence*, London: Edward Arnold.
Alter, Robert and Kermode, Frank, eds. (1987) *The Literary Guide to the Bible*, London: Collins.
Armin, Arnold (1963) *D. H. Lawrence and German Literature*, Montreal: Heinemann.
Atkins, A. R. (1992) 'Textual Influences on D. H. Lawrence's "The Saga of Siegmund"', *D. H. Lawrence Review* 24: 7–26.
Baker, Paul G. (1983) *A Reassessment of D. H. Lawrence's "Aaron's Rod"*, Ann Arbor, Michigan: UMI Research Press.
Bakhtin, Mikhail M. (1981) *The Dialogic Imagination: Four Essays*, ed. Michael Holquist, trans. Caryl Emerson and Michael Holquist. Austin: University of Texas Press.
  (1984) *Problems of Dostoevsky's Poetics*, ed. and trans. Caryl Emerson, Manchester University Press.
  (1986) *Speech Genres and Other Late Essays*, trans. Vern W. McGee. Austin: University of Texas Press.
Balbert, Peter, and Marcus, Phillip L., ed. (1985) *D. H. Lawrence: A Centenary Consideration*, Ithaca: Cornell University Press.
Baldanza, Frank (1961) 'D. H. Lawrence's Song of Songs', *Modern Fiction Studies* 7: 106–14.
Barthes, Roland (1977) *Image-Music-Text*, trans. Stephen Heath, Glasgow: Fontana.
Bataille, Georges (1985) *Visions of Excess: Selected Writings, 1927–1939*, trans. Allan Stoekl, Minneapolis: University of Minnesota Press.
Bell, Michael (1991) *D. H. Lawrence: Language and Being*, Cambridge University Press.
  (1997) *Literature, Modernism and Myth: Belief and Responsibility in the Twentieth Century*, Cambridge University Press.

Besant, Annie (1898) *Esoteric Christianity*, London: Theosophical Publishing Society.

Black, Michael (1986) *D. H. Lawrence: The Early Fiction*, Cambridge University Press.

(1991) *D. H. Lawrence: The Early Philosophical Works*, Basingstoke: Macmillan.

Blake, William (1971) *The Complete Poems*, ed. W. H. Stevenson, London: Longman.

Blatchford, Robert (1904) *God and My Neighbour*, London: Clarion Press.

Blavatsky, Helena P. (with the following abbreviations)

IU: *Isis Unveiled: A Master-Key to the Mysteries of Ancient and Modern Science and Theology*, 2 vols., Pasadena, California: Theosophical University Press, 1970 [1877].

SD: *The Secret Doctrine: The Synthesis of Science, Religion and Philosophy*, 2 vols., Pasadena, California: Theosophical University Press, 1970 [1888].

Bloom, Harold (1961) 'Lawrence, Blackmur, Eliot, and the Tortoise', in Moore 1961: 359–68.

(1973) *The Anxiety of Influence*, Oxford University Press.

(1975) *Kabbalah and Criticism*, New York: Seabury Press.

(1994) *The Western Canon*, New York: Harcourt Bruce.

Bonds, Diane S. (1987) *Language and the Self in D. H. Lawrence*, Ann Arbor, Michigan: UMI Research Press.

Boyarin, Daniel (1990) *Intertextuality and the Reading of Midrash*. Bloomington and Indianapolis: Indiana University Press.

Brewster, Earl and Achsah (1934) *D. H. Lawrence: Reminiscences and Correspondence*, London: Martin Secker.

Bridgwater, Patrick (1972) *Nietzsche in Anglosaxony: A Study of Nietzsche's Impact on English and American Literature*, Leicester University Press.

Brown, Keith, ed. (1990) *Rethinking Lawrence*, Milton Keynes: Open University Press.

Brunsdale, Mitzi M. (1978) *The German Effect on D. H. Lawrence and His Works*, Berne: Peter Lang.

(1983) 'D. H. Lawrence's *David*: Drama as a Vehicle for Religious Prophecy', *Themes in Drama* 5: 123–37.

Burwell, Rose Marie (1970) 'A Catalogue of D. H. Lawrence's Reading from Early Childhood', *D. H. Lawrence Review* 3: iii–330, reproduced as 'A Checklist of Lawrence's Reading' in Sagar 1982: 59–110.

Byrne, Janet (1995) *A Genius for Living: A Biography of Frieda Lawrence*, London: Bloomsbury.

Carey, John (1973) 'D. H. Lawrence's Doctrine' in *D. H. Lawrence: Novelist, Poet, Prophet*, ed. Stephen Spender, London: Weidenfeld and Nicolson.

Carlyle, Thomas (1908) *Sartor Resartus and On Heroes and Hero-Worship*, London: Dent.

Campbell, R. J. (1907) *The New Theology*, London: Chapman and Hall.

Carswell, Catherine (1932) *The Savage Pilgrimage: A Narrative of D. H. Lawrence*, London: Chatto and Windus.

Carter, Frederick (1926) *The Dragon of the Alchemists*, London: Elkin Matthews.
(1931) *The Dragon of Revelation*, London: Desmond Harmsworth.
(1932) *D. H. Lawrence and the Body Mystical*, London: Denis Archer.
Cavitch, David (1969) *D. H. Lawrence and the New World*, Oxford University Press.
Chadwick, Owen (1970) *The Victorian Church*, 2 vols., London: Adam and Charles Black.
Chambers, J. D. (1972) 'Memories of D. H. Lawrence', *Renaissance and Modern Studies* 16: 5–24.
Chambers, Jessie (1980) *D. H. Lawrence: A Personal Record by E.T.*, Cambridge University Press.
Charles, R. H. (1920) *A Critical and Exegetical Commentary on the Revelation of St John*, 2 vols., T. and T. Clark, Edinburgh.
Charlesworth, James H., ed. (1983) *The Old Testament Pseudepigrapha*, 2 vols., Garden City, New York: Doubleday.
Clark, Katerina, and Holquist, Michael (1984) *Mikhail Bakhtin*, Cambridge, Mass.: Harvard University Press.
Clark, L. D. (1964) *Dark Night of the Body: D. H. Lawrence's 'The Plumed Serpent'*, Austin: University of Texas Press.
(1970) 'The Apocalypse of Lorenzo', *D. H. Lawrence Review* 3: 141–59.
Clarke, Colin (1969) *River of Dissolution: D. H. Lawrence and English Romanticism*, London: Routledge.
Clements, R. E. (1983) *A Century of Old Testament Study*, Guildford: Lutterworth Press.
Cobau, William W. (1976) 'A View from Eastwood: Conversations with Mrs. O. L. Hopkin', *D. H. Lawrence Review* 9: 126–36.
Corke, Helen (1933) *Lawrence and Apocalypse*, London: Heinemann.
(1975) *In Our Infancy: An Autobiography*, Cambridge University Press.
Cowan, James C. (1970) *D. H. Lawrence's American Journey: A Study in Literature and Myth*, Cleveland, Ohio: The Press of Case Western Reserve University.
(1980) 'D. H. Lawrence and the Resurrection of the Body', in Partlow 1980: 94–104.
(1988) 'Allusions and Symbols in D. H. Lawrence's *The Escaped Cock*', in Jackson 1988: 174–88.
(1990) *D. H. Lawrence and the Trembling Balance*, University Park: Pennsylvania State University Press.
ed. (1982, 1985) *D. H. Lawrence: An Annotated Bibliography of Writings About Him*, 2 vols., Dekalb: Northern Illinois University Press.
Cruden, Alexander (1954) *Cruden's Complete Concordance to the Old and New Testaments*, Guildford: Lutterworth Press.
Crumpton, P. I. (1985) 'D. H. Lawrence and the Sources of *Movements in European History*', *Renascence and Modern Studies* 29: 50–65.
Cushman, Keith (1992) 'The Brewsters at Borghi and Co.', *D. H. Lawrence Review* 24 66–7.

Daleski, H. M. (1965) *The Forked Flame: A Study of D. H. Lawrence*, London: Faber.

(1985) *Unities: Studies in the English Novel*, Athens: University of Georgia Press.

Davie, Donald (1978) *A Gathered Church: The Literature of the Dissenting Interest, 1700–1930*, London: Routledge.

Delany, Paul (1979) *D. H. Lawrence's Nightmare: The Writer and His Circle in the Years of the Great War*, Hassocks, Sussex: Harvester.

Delavenay, Emile (1971) *D. H. Lawrence and Edward Carpenter*, London: Heinemann.

(1972) *D. H. Lawrence: The Man and His Work*, London: Heinemann.

Deleuze, Gilles, and Guattari, Felix (1988) *A Thousand Plateaus*, trans. Brian Massumi, London: Athlone Press.

Dentith, Simon (1995) *Bakhtinian Thought: An Introductory Reader.* London: Routledge.

Derrida, Jacques (1976) *Of Grammatology*, trans. Gayatri Spivak, Baltimore and London: Johns Hopkins University Press.

(1979) 'Living On / Border Lines' in *Deconstruction and Criticism*, ed. Harold Bloom *et al.* New York: Continuum.

(1981) *Dissemination*, trans. Barbara Johnson, Chicago: University of Chicago Press.

(1982) *Margins of Philosophy*, trans. Alan Bass, University of Chicago Press.

(1986) *Glas*, trans. J. P. Leavey, Jr., and Richard Rand. Lincoln: University of Nebraska Press, 1986.

(1988) *Limited Inc*, ed. Gerald Graff, Evanston, Illinois: Northwestern University Press.

(1993) 'Circumfession' in Geoffrey Bennington and Jacques Derrida, *Jacques Derrida*, Chicago University Press, 1993.

(1994) *Specters of Marx*, trans. Peggy Kamuf, London: Routledge.

(1995) *The Gift of Death*, trans. David Wills, University of Chicago Press.

Docherty, Thomas, ed. (1993) *Postmodernism: A Reader*, New York: Harvester Wheatsheaf.

Doherty, Gerald (1982) 'The Salvator Mundi Touch: Messianic Typology in D. H. Lawrence's *Women in Love*', *Ariel* 13: 53–71.

(1987) 'White Mythologies: D. H. Lawrence and the Deconstructive Turn', *Criticism* 29: 477–96.

(1991) 'One Vast Hermeneutic Sentence: The Total Lawrentian Text', *PMLA* 106: 1134–45.

Doughty, Charles (1908) *Adam Cast Forth*, London: Duckworth.

Eagleton, Terry (1973) 'Lawrence', in Ian Gregor and Walter Stein, eds., *The Prose for God: Religious and Anti-Religious Aspects of Imaginative Literature*, London: Sheed and Ward.

Ebbatson, Roger (1987) 'A Spark beneath the Wheel: Lawrence and Evolutionary Thought', in *D. H. Lawrence: New Studies*, ed. Christopher Heywood, London: Macmillan.

Eggert, Paul (1986) 'Edward Garnett's *Sons and Lovers*', *Critical Quarterly* 28: 51–61.

(1988) 'D. H. Lawrence and Literary Collaboration', *Etudes Lawrenciennes* 3: 153–62.

Eliot, T. S. (1934) *After Strange Gods: A Primer of Modern Heresy*, London: Faber.

Ellis, David (1998) *D. H. Lawrence: Dying Game 1922–1930*, Cambridge University Press.

Ellis, David, and Mills, Howard (1988) *D. H. Lawrence's Non-Fiction: Art, Thought and Genre*, Cambridge University Press.

Emerson, Ralph Waldo (1994) 'The Divinity School Address', in the *Norton Anthology of American Literature*, 4th edn., 2 vols., New York: Norton, vol. I, pp. 1033–45.

Farrer, Austin (1986) *A Rebirth of Images*, Albany: State University of New York Press [1949].

Fernihough, Anne (1993) *D. H. Lawrence: Aesthetics and Ideology*, Oxford: Clarendon Press.

Fewell, Danna, ed. (1992) *Reading Between Texts: Intertextuality and the Hebrew Bible*. Louisville, Kentucky: Westminster / John Knox Press.

Fisch, Harold (1988) 'Bakhtin's Misreadings of the Bible', *Hebrew University Studies in Literature and the Arts* 16: 130–49.

Fitz, L.T. (1974) '"The Rocking-Horse Winner" and *The Golden Bough*', *Studies in Short Fiction* 11: 199–200.

Fleishman, Avrom (1985) 'He Do the Polis in Different Voices: Lawrence's Later Style', in Balbert and Marcus 1985: 162–79.

(1988) 'The Fictions of Autobiographical Fiction [*Sons and Lovers*]' in Jackson 1988: 68–71.

(1990) 'Lawrence and Bakhtin: Where Pluralism Ends and Dialogism Begins', in Brown 1990: 109–19.

Ford, George H. (1965) *Double Measure: A Study of the Novels and Stories of D. H. Lawrence*, New York: Holt, Rinehart and Winston.

Foucault, Michel (1979) *The History of Sexuality*, vol.1, London: Allen Lane.

Fraser, Robert, ed. (1990) *Sir James Frazer and the Literary Imagination*, London: Macmillan.

Frazer, James George (1994) *The Golden Bough: A Study in Magic and Religion*, ed. Robert Fraser, Oxford University Press.

Frye, Northrop (1982) *The Great Code: The Bible and Literature*, London: Routledge.

Gamache, Lawrence (1982) 'Lawrence's *David:* Its Religious Impulse and Its Theatricality', *D. H. Lawrence Review* 15: 235–48.

ed. (1996) *D. H. Lawrence: The Cosmic Adventure*, Nepean, Ont.: Borealis Press.

Garnett, Richard, ed. (1899) *International Library of Famous Literature*, 20 vols., London: Standard.

Gibbon, Edward (1910) *The Decline and Fall of the Roman Empire*, 6 vols., London: J. M. Dent.

Gilbert, Sandra M. (1990) *Acts of Attention: The Poems of D. H. Lawrence*, 2nd edn, Ithaca: Cornell University Press.

Glazer, Myra (1982) 'Why the Sons of God Want the Daughters of Men: On William Blake and D. H. Lawrence', in Robert J. Bertholf and Annette S. Levitt, eds., *William Blake and the Moderns*, Albany: State University of New York Press.

Goodheart, Eugene (1963) *The Utopian Vision of D. H. Lawrence*, University of Chicago Press.

Green, Eleanor H. (1975) 'Schopenhauer and D. H. Lawrence on Sex and Love', *D. H. Lawrence Review* 8: 329–45.

Green, Martin (1974) *The von Richthofen Sisters: The Triumphant and the Tragic Modes of Love*, London: Weidenfeld and Nicolson.

Gutierrez, Donald (1977) 'A New Heaven and an Old Earth: D. H. Lawrence's *Apocalypse* and the *Book of Revelation*', *Review of Existential Psychology and Psychiatry* 14: 61–85.

Habel, Norman C. (1971) *Literary Criticism of the Old Testament*, Philadelphia: Fortress Press.

Haeckel, Ernst (1929) *The Riddle of the Universe*, trans. Joseph McCabe, London: Watts.

Handelman, Susan A. (1982) *The Slayers of Moses: The Emergence of Rabbinic Interpretation in Modern Literary Theory*, Albany: State University of New York Press.

Harper (1985): *Harper's Bible Dictionary*, ed. Paul J. Achtemeier *et al.*, San Francisco: Harper and Row.

Harrison, Jane (1927) *Ancient Art and Ritual*, London: Thornton Butterworth [1913].

Hartman, Geoffrey H., and Budick, Sanford, ed. (1986) *Midrash and Literature*, New Haven and London: Yale University Press.

H.D. (1984) *Bid Me to Live*, London: Virago.

Hesse, Hermann (1995) *Demian*, trans. W. J. Strachan, London: Macmillan.

Hinz, Eveleyn J. (1979) '*Ancient Art and Ritual* and *The Rainbow*', *Dalhousie Review* 58: 617–37.

Hinz, Evelyn J. and Teunissen, John J. (1976) 'Savior and Cock: Allusion and Icon in Lawrence's *The Man Who Died*', *D. H. Lawrence Review* 5: 279–96.

Holderness, Graham (1982) *D. H. Lawrence: History, Ideology and Fiction*, Dublin: Gill and Macmillan.

Hough, Graham (1956) *The Dark Sun: A Study of D. H. Lawrence*, London: Duckworth.

Humma, John B. (1974) 'D. H. Lawrence as Friedrich Nietzsche', *Philological Quarterly* 53: 110–20.

 (1990) *Metaphor and Meaning in D. H. Lawrence's Later Novels*, Columbia: University of Missouri Press.

Huxley, Aldous, ed. (1932) *The Letters of D. H. Lawrence*, London: Heinemann.

 (1933) *Point Counter Point*, London: Chatto and Windus.

Hyde, G. M. (1991) *D. H. Lawrence*, New York: St Martin's Press.

Hyde, Virginia (1992) *The Risen Adam: D. H. Lawrence's Revisionist Typology*, University Park: Pennsylvania State University Press.

Iida, Takeo (1991) 'Lawrence's Pagan Gods and Christianity', *D. H. Lawrence Review* 23: 179–90.

Jackson, Dennis, and Jackson, Flea Brown, eds. (1988) *Critical Essays on D. H. Lawrence*, Boston: G. K. Hall.

Jackson, Rosie (1994) *Frieda Lawrence*, London: Pandora.

Janaway, Christopher (1994) *Schopenhauer*, Oxford University Press.

Janik, Del Ivan (1974–5) 'D. H. Lawrence's "Future Religion": The Unity of *Last Poems*', *Texas Studies in Literature and Language* 16: 739–54.

Jansohn, Christa (1990) *Zitat und Anspielung in Fruhwerk von D. H. Lawrence*, Münster: Lit Verlag.

Jeffrey, David Lyle (1992) *A Dictionary of Biblical Tradition in English Literature*, Grand Rapids, Michigan: Eerdmans.

Jenner, Katharine Lee (1910) *Christian Symbolism*, London: Methuen.

Kalnins, Mara (1985) 'Lawrence's Travel Writings', *Renascence and Modern Studies* 29: 66–77.

    ed. (1986) *D. H. Lawrence: Centenary Essays*, Bristol Classical Press.

Kaufmann, Walter (1968) *Nietzsche*, 3rd. edn., Princeton University Press.

Kennedy, Andrew (1982) 'After Not So Strange Gods in *The Rainbow*', *English Studies* 63: 220–30.

Kent, John (1977) 'A Late Nineteenth-Century Nonconformist Renaissance', *Studies in Church History* 14: 351–80.

Kermode, Frank (1962) 'Spenser and the Allegorists', *Proceedings of the British Academy* 48: 261–79.

    (1968) 'Lawrence and the Apocalyptic Types', *Critical Quarterly* 10: 14–38.

    (1973) *Lawrence*, Glasgow: Fontana.

Kinkead-Weekes, Mark (1968) 'The Marble and the Statue: The Exploratory Imagination of D. H. Lawrence', in *Imagined Worlds: Essays on Some English Novels and Novelists in Honour of John Butt*, ed. Maynard Mack and Ian Gregor, London: Methuen, pp. 371–418.

    (1993) 'Re-Dating the Overtone', *D. H. Lawrence Review* 25: 75–80.

    (1996) *D. H. Lawrence: Triumph to Exile, 1912–1922*, Cambridge University Press.

Laird, Holly (1988) 'Heroic Theater in *David*' in Jackson and Jackson eds. 1988: 203–9.

Lawrence, Frieda (1935) *Not I, But the Wind . . .*, London: Heinemann.

Leavis, F. R. (1964) *D. H. Lawrence, Novelist*, London: Penguin.

    (1976) *Thought, Words and Creativity: Art and Thought in Lawrence*, Oxford University Press.

LeDoux, Larry (1972) 'Christ and Isis: The Function of the Dying and Reviving God in *The Man Who Died*', *D. H. Lawrence Review* 5: 132–48.

Leitch, Vincent B. (1983) *Deconstructive Criticism: An Advanced Introduction*, London: Hutchinson.

Levy, Mervyn, ed. (1964) *The Paintings of D. H. Lawrence*, New York: Viking.

Lockwood, M. J. (1987) *A Study of the Poems of D. H. Lawrence*, London: Macmillan.

Loisy, Alfred (1923) *L'Apocalypse de Jean*, Paris: Alfred Firmin.

Lodge, David (1990) *After Bakhtin: Essays on Fiction and Criticism*, London: Routledge.

Luhan, Mabel Dodge (1932) *Lorenzo in Taos*, New York: Knopf.

McGuffie, Duncan (1985) 'Lawrence and Nonconformity', in Andrew Cooper, ed., *D. H. Lawrence 1885–1930: A Celebration*, Nottingham: D. H. Lawrence Society.

Maddox, Brenda (1994) *The Married Man: A Life of D. H. Lawrence*, London: Sinclair-Stevenson.

Magnus, Bernd and Higgins, Kathleen M., eds. (1996) *The Cambridge Companion to Nietzsche*, Cambridge University Press.

Manicom, David (1985) 'An Approach to the Imagery: A Study of Selected Biblical Analogues in D. H. Lawrence's *The Rainbow*', *English Studies in Canada* 11: 474–83.

Masson, Margaret (1988) 'The Influence of Congregationalism on the First Four Novels of D. H. Lawrence', Durham University doctoral dissertation.

(1990) 'D. H. Lawrence's Congregational Inheritance', *D. H. Lawrence Review* 22: 53–68.

Meyers, Jeffrey, ed. (1985) *D. H. Lawrence and Tradition*, Amherst: University of Massachusetts Press.

(1990) *D. H. Lawrence: A Biography*, Basingstoke: Macmillan.

Miller, Henry (1985) *The World of D. H. Lawrence: A Passionate Appreciation*, London: John Calder.

Millett, Robert W. (1983) *The Vultures and the Phoenix: A Study of the Mandrake Press Edition of the Paintings of D. H. Lawrence*, Philadelphia: Art Alliance Press.

Milton, Colin (1987) *Lawrence and Nietzsche*, Aberdeen University Press.

Montgomery, Robert E. (1994) *The Visionary Lawrence: Beyond Philosophy and Art*, Cambridge University Press.

Moore, Harry T., ed. (1961) *A D. H. Lawrence Miscellany*, Kingswood: Windmill Press [1959].

Moynahan, Julian, (1963) *The Deed of Life: The Novels and Tales of D. H. Lawrence*, Princeton University Press.

Murfin, Ross C. (1983) *The Poetry of D. H. Lawrence: Texts and Contexts*, Lincoln: University of Nebraska Press.

Murray, Gilbert (1925) *Five Stages of Greek Religion*, Oxford: Clarendon Press.

Murry, John Middleton (1931) *Son of Woman: The Story of D. H. Lawrence*, London: Jonathan Cape.

Nehls, Edward, ed. (1957, 1958, 1959) *D. H. Lawrence: A Composite Biography*, 3 vols.: University of Wisconsin Press.

Neville, George (1981) *A Memoir of D. H. Lawrence (The Betrayal)*, ed. Carl Baron, Cambridge University Press.

Newman, Judie (1995) *The Ballistic Bard*, London: Edward Arnold.

Nietzsche, Friedrich (with the following abbreviations)

BGE: Beyond Good and Evil, trans. R. J. Hollingdale, Harmondsworth: Penguin, 1973.

BT: The Birth of Tragedy, trans. Shaun Whiteside, Harmondsworth: Penguin, 1993.

D: Daybreak, trans. R. J. Hollingdale, Cambridge University Press, 1997.

GS: The Gay Science, trans. Walter Kaufmann, New York: Random House, 1974.

HA: Human, All Too Human, trans. Marion Faber and Stephen Lehmann, Harmondsworth: Penguin, 1994.

NR: A Nietzsche Reader, ed. R. J. Hollingdale, Harmondsworth: Penguin, 1977.

OGM: On the Genealogy of Morals, trans. Douglas Smith, Oxford University Press, 1996.

TI: Twilight of the Idols / The Anti-Christ, trans. R. J. Hollingdale, Harmondsworth: Penguin, 1968.

TSZ: Thus Spoke Zarathustra, trans. R. J. Hollingdale, Harmondsworth: Penguin, 1961.

WP: The Will to Power, trans. Walter Kaufmann and R. J. Hollingdale, Harmondsworth: Penguin, 1968.

Nin, Anais (1964) *D. H. Lawrence: An Unprofessional Study*, Chicago: Swallow Press.

Niven, Alastair (1978) *D. H. Lawrence*, Cambridge University Press.

Oman, John (1923) *The Book of Revelation*, Cambridge University Press.

Pagels, Elaine (1979) *The Gnostic Gospels*, New York: Random House.

Panichas, George A. (1964) *Adventure in Consciousness: The Meaning of D. H. Lawrence's Religious Quest*, The Hague: Mouton.

    ed. (1967) *Mansions of the Spirit: Essays in Literature and Religion*, New York: Hawthorn Books.

Partlow, Robert B., and Moore, Harry T., ed. (1980) *D. H. Lawrence: The Man Who Lived*, Carbondale: Southern Illinois University Press.

Paulin, Tom (1989) '"Hibiscus and Salvia Flowers": The Puritan Imagination', in Preston 1989: 180–92.

Peters, Joan Douglas (1996) 'Modernist Dialogics of Form in *The Rainbow*', in Gamache 1996: 205–221.

Pinkney, Tony (1990) *D. H. Lawrence and Modernism*, University of Iowa Press.

Pinto, Vivian de Sola (1967) 'The Burning Bush: D. H. Lawrence as Religious Poet', in Panichas 1967: 213–38.

Pollnitz, Christopher (1986) '"Raptus Virginis": The Dark God in the Poetry of D. H. Lawrence', in Kalnins 1986: 111–38.

Poplawski, Paul (1993) *Promptings of Desire: Creativity and the Religious Impulse in the Works of D. H. Lawrence*, Westport, Conn.: Greenwood Press.

Poston, Murray (1968) *Biblical Drama in England: From the Middle Ages to the Present Day*, Evanston, Illinois: Northwestern University Press.

Preston, Peter, and Hoare, Peter, ed. (1989) *D. H. Lawrence in the Modern World*, Cambridge University Press.

Price, A. Whigham (1956) 'D. H. Lawrence and Congregationalism', *Congregational Quarterly* 34: 242–52 and 322–33.

Pryse, James M. (1910) *The Apocalypse Unsealed*, London: John M.Watkins.

Qualls, Barry (1982) *The Secular Pilgrims of Victorian Fiction*, Cambridge University Press.

Raleigh, John Henry (1996) 'The Edward Garnett Editing of the *Sons and Lovers* Ms.', in Gamache 1996: 250–63.

Renan, Ernest (1927) *The Life of Jesus*, London: Dent.

Rice, Thomas Jackson (1983) *D. H. Lawrence: A Guide to Research*, New York: Garland.

Roberts, Warren (1982) *A Bibliography of D. H. Lawrence*, 2nd edn, Cambridge University Press.

Ross, Charles, and Jackson, Dennis, ed. (1995) *Editing D. H. Lawrence: New Versions of a Modern Author*, Ann Arbor: University of Michigan Press.

Rossman, Charles (1970) 'The Gospel According to D. H. Lawrence: Religion in *Sons and Lovers*', *D. H. Lawrence Review* 3: 31–41.

Sagar, Keith (1966) *The Art of D. H. Lawrence*, Cambridge University Press.

    ed. (1982) *A D. H. Lawrence Handbook*, Manchester: Manchester University Press.

Salaquarda, Jorg (1996) 'Nietzsche and the Judaeo-Christian Tradition', in Magnus and Higgins eds., 1996: 90–118.

Salgado, Gamini and Das, G. K., ed. (1988) *The Spirit of D. H. Lawrence: Centenary Studies*, Basingstoke: Macmillan.

Schneidau, Herbert (1983) 'The Antinomian Strain: The Bible and American Poetry', in *The Bible and American Arts and Letters*, ed. Giles Gunn, Philadelphia, Pennsylvania: Fortress Press.

Schneider, Daniel J. (1986) *The Consciousness of D. H. Lawrence: An Intellectual Biography*, Lawrence: University Press of Kansas.

Schopenhauer, Arthur (1883–6) *The World as Will and Idea*, trans. R. B. Haldane and J. Kemp, 3 vols., London: Kegan Paul, Trench, Trubner and Co.

    (1974) *Parerga and Paralipomena*, trans. E. F. J. Payne, 2 vols., Oxford: Clarendon Press.

Schorer, Mark, ed. (1977) *Sons and Lovers: A Facsimile of the Manuscript*, Berkeley: University of California Press.

Self, Will (1998) 'Introduction' to *Revelation*, Edinburgh: Canongate Books.

Sheerin, Daniel J. (1978) 'John Thomas and the King of Glory: Two Analogues to D. H. Lawrence's Use of Psalm 24: 7 in Chapter XIV of *Lady Chatterley's Lover*', *D. H. Lawrence Review* 11: 297–300.

Shestov, Leo (1920) *All Things Are Possible*, trans S. S. Kotel)iansky with a foreword by D. H. Lawrence, London: Martin Secker.

Skinner, M.L. (1972) *The Fifth Sparrow: An Autobiography*, Sydney University Press.

Sklar, Sylvia (1975) *The Plays of D. H. Lawrence*, London: Vision Press.

Smith, Frank Glover (1971) *D. H. Lawrence: 'The Rainbow'*, London: Edward Arnold.

Sparks, H. F. D., ed. (1984) *The Apocryphal Old Testament*, Oxford University Press.

Spencer, Herbert (1911) *First Principles*, 2 vols., London: Williams and Norgate.

Spilka, Mark, (1955) *The Love Ethic of D. H. Lawrence*, Bloomington: Indiana University Press.

  (1992) *Renewing the Normative D. H. Lawrence*, Columbia: University of Missouri Press.

Squires, Michael, and Jackson, Dennis, ed. (1985) *D. H. Lawrence's 'Lady': A New Look at 'Lady Chatterley's Lover'*, Athens: University of Georgia Press.

Steinberg, Leo (1996) *The Sexuality of Christ in Modern Art*, Chicago University Press.

Still, Judith, and Worton, Michael, ed. (1990) *Intertextuality: Theories and Practice*, Manchester University Press.

Terry, C. J. (1974) 'Aspects of D. H. Lawrence's Struggle with Christianity', *Dalhousie Review* 54: 112–29.

Thatcher, David S. (1970) *Nietzsche in England 1890–1914: The Growth of a Reputation*, University of Toronto Press.

Thomas, David (1986) 'D. H. Lawrence's "Snake": The Edenic Myth Inverted', *College Literature* 13: 199–206.

Thompson, Leslie M. (1971) 'D. H. Lawrence and Judas', *D. H. Lawrence Review* 4: 1–19.

  (1975) 'The Christ Who Didn't Die: Analogues to D. H. Lawrence's *The Man Who Died*', *D. H. Lawrence Review* 8: 19–30.

Tindall, William (1972) *D. H. Lawrence and Susan His Cow*, New York: Cooper Square Publishers, [1939].

Urang, Sarah (1983) *Kindled in the Flame: The Apocalyptic Scene in D. H. Lawrence*, Ann Arbor: UMI Research Press.

Vickery, John, ed. (1965) *Myth and Literature: Contemporary Theory and Practice*, Lincoln: University of Nebraska Press.

  (1973) *The Literary Impact of 'The Golden Bough'*, Princeton University Press.

Vivian, Philip (1906) *The Churches and Modern Thought*, London: Watts.

Walker, Grady J. (1972) 'The Influence of the Bible on D. H. Lawrence as Seen in His Novels', University of Tulsa Ph.D.

Washington, Peter (1993) *Madame Blavatsky's Baboon: A History of the Mystics, Mediums, and Misfits Who Brought Spiritualism to America*, New York: Schocken Books.

Whelan, P. T. (1988) *D. H. Lawrence: Myth and Metaphysic in 'The Rainbow' and 'Women in Love'*, Ann Arbor: UMI Research Press.

Widdowson, Peter, ed. (1992) *D. H. Lawrence*, London: Longman.

Widmer, Kingsley (1962) *The Art of Perversity: D. H. Lawrence's Shorter Fiction*, Seattle: University of Washington Press.

Williams, Linda (1997) *D. H. Lawrence*, Plymouth: Northcote House.

Wood, James (1999) *The Broken Estate: Essays on Literature and Belief*, London: Jonathan Cape.

Woodman, Leonora (1986) ' "The Big Old Pagan Vision": The Letters of D. H. Lawrence to Frederick Carter', *Library Chronicle of the University of Texas* 34: 39–51.

(1989) 'D. H. Lawrence and the Hermetic Tradition', *Cauda Pavonis* 8: 1–6.

Worthen, John (1981) 'Introduction' to the *The Rainbow*, Harmondsworth: Penguin, pp. 11–33.

(1991) *D. H. Lawrence: The Early Years, 1885–1912*, Cambridge University Press.

Wright, Terry R. (1999) 'Lawrence and Bataille: Recovering the Sacred, Re-membering Jesus', *Literature and Theology* 13: 46–75.

Zoll, Allan R. (1978) 'Vitalism and the Metaphysics of Love: D. H. Lawrence and Schopenhauer', *D. H. Lawrence Review* 11: 1–20.

Zytaruk, George J., ed. (1970) *The Quest for Rananim: D. H. Lawrence's Letters to S. S. Kotelianski 1914 to 1930*, Montreal: McGill-Queen's University Press.

(1971) *D. H. Lawrence's Response to Russian Literature*, The Hague: Mouton.

(1987) 'D. H. Lawrence's *The Rainbow* and Leo Tolstoy's *Anna Karenina*: An Instance of Literary "Clinamen"', *Germano-Slavica* 5: 197–209.

Index

Index of biblical references

271